grace notes

grace notes

The Waking of a Woman's Voice

Heidi Hart

The University of Utah Press

Salt Lake City

The Defiance House Man colophon is a registered trademark of
The University of Utah Press. It is based upon a four-foot-tall
Ancient Puebloan pictograph (late PIII) near Glen Canyon, Utah.

Printed on acid-free paper

08 07 06 05 04
5 4 3 2 1

Library of Congress Cataloging-in-Publication Data

Hart, Heidi, 1971–
   Grace notes : the waking of a woman's voice / Heidi Hart.
      p.   cm.
   ISBN 0-87480-787-5 (pbk. : alk. paper)
   1. Hart, Heidi, 1971–   2. Mormons—Biography.   I. Title.
BX8695.H35 A3 2004
289.3'092—dc22

                              2003020070

For my parents

and for Kent and Kate,
who keep the way open.

Peace begins here, I think, when we
commit acts of music — crazy and human . . .
— Joan Oliver Goldsmith

contents

one

diary

June 11. Landed at JFK at 6 a.m. Or maybe I've landed in someone's gothic novel. I'm driving to Hartford with licorice and pretzels to keep me awake, on the hunt for a long-dead voice locked up in the Connecticut State Library. Here goes the spunky young woman in search of the cobwebbed diary written by her ancestor, the book that may unlock her own dark secrets . . . except I've never thought of myself as spunky, and the nineteenth-century diarist in question isn't exactly my ancestor. Catharine Seely never had children. She was a cousin of my great-great-great-great-grandfather. I've flown three thousand miles to find her because, yes, we have some things in common. We both lived on the Connecticut coast, she all her life, I for the

1

two years that changed my life. Like me, she became a Quaker as a young woman. And, like me, she lived for years without a voice.

Warm bottled water. Merritt Parkway backed up for miles. How I don't miss the morning rush here. How I miss the shade. Without the signs—Greenwich, Long Ridge Road, High Ridge Road, New Canaan, Darien, Norwalk—I could wander all day in this illusion of forest, oak and beech and staghorn sumac crowding the guardrails. But I have somewhere to go. I keep my eyes on the road. Fresh asphalt. Stone bridge. Saugatuck River.

As I drive I fix these words in my head, the closest thing to a diary I have right now. Daybook, journal, journey . . . Years ago my Mormon Sunday-school teacher scooted forward on her folding chair, the blue chain swinging from her bifocals, and whispered, "Boys and girls, the prophet has told us angels will quote from your journals one day." I squirmed in my chair. I didn't want anybody, in this life or the next, poring over the words I spilled into the yellow legal pads I sneaked from my father's drawer. No wonder my mother said, "I don't write anything in my journal that I wouldn't want the public to know." I pictured a committee of white-suited angels examining her cursive and nodding their approval—or not.

Details of a day. As I drive I note the morning radio talk: the usual delays on the George Washington Bridge, accident on the Van Wyck Expressway, which I drove with ease an hour and a half ago. To think I've been mispronouncing it all this time. Now it's the folk music hour. Irish fiddling, a jig in twelve-eight time. I hum along. The pavement hums under me, this road that once took me to the babysitter's in Greenwich, to choir practices in New Canaan, to my friend Kate's house in backcountry Stamford, where I sang as rain dripped from the rhododendrons. The place where my voice began to wake up.

The road broadens after New Haven. A vista, at last: steeple, smokestack, bridge, forest for miles. I glance at my directions. For an instant I watch my body as though suspended outside the car windows, as though I am myself ten years ago, the young married woman whose muscles locked into a panic if she had to drive into a neighborhood she didn't know. Or talk to a stranger on the phone. Or sing. She stares at me, her mouth open, and reels away into traffic. The signs lead me under a bridge, through a construction zone, and into Hartford's government center. I find a parking meter, take a swig of water and a long breath, and get out of the car. The humid air sticks fast to my skin. I cross the street and climb the steps into the supreme court building, which also houses the library.

A security guard directs me to the basement. There, behind a desk stacked with a check-in notebook and official forms, is the woman who's been answering my e-mail inquiries for three weeks. Her voice is soft and efficient: "We pull books twice a day. We can access yours at ten-thirty, but it sometimes takes longer. You can come back at eleven. That'll give you time to process your I.D. in the security office. Have you read our regulations?"

I nod, remembering the pages of tiny print she sent me, and sit down to fill out forms. Name, address, purpose for research. What do I say, "Bonding with another silent woman"? I write, "Writing." I know that whatever I find, I'll have to explore it with language of my own, to connect with the nineteenth-century invalid who's been pecking at my brain for weeks. It's only nine a.m. If only I'd had the sense to photocopy Catharine's diary four years ago, when I found it in the Stamford public library's genealogy room. I don't know why it's been moved to safer quarters. But ever since the thought entered my head as I sat in Quaker meeting last month, I've told myself I'll do whatever it takes to read Catharine's words again.

She was born in 1799 in Darien, not far from the part of Stamford where I lived with my husband and sons during graduate school. In her time, the shady neighborhoods and crowded parking lots in the area had names like Short Rocks, Hardy's Hole, Slason's Wolf Pit, Rump Swamp, Jagger's Den, and Elbow Plain. The Long Island Sound beaches, now crowded with Rollerbladers and toxic-shellfish signs, were mostly marshland. People grazed their cattle near the water and caught malaria from swarming mosquitoes. The dominant culture was Puritan. Catharine became a Quaker at nineteen, in a state once so hostile to the Society of Friends that a seventeenth-century policy threatened its members with hot irons on the tongue. Even in the early nineteenth century, Connecticut Quakers affiliated with meetings in other states—in Catharine's case, New

York. Besides this, all I know about her is that she lived with a debilitating illness that cost her her voice, that she eventually hosted Friends meetings in her sickroom, and that she died at thirty-seven. When I first skimmed her diary, shifting my weight from one foot to the other between the stacks in the Stamford library, I didn't want to hear her private spiritual musings peppered with lists of excruciating symptoms. I didn't want to hear the words this woman couldn't say aloud. Now I do.

Two weeks before I moved to Connecticut for graduate school, my mother phoned to say, "Did you know we have ancestors who lived in Stamford three hundred years ago?" Weeds. Scofields. And Seelys, Catharine's family. One of these ancestors, Catharine's cousin and contemporary, joined the infant Mormon Church, moved west, and became an apostle in his later years. His granddaughter spawned the black sheep in our family, my great-grandfather who left his wife and kids in Hiawatha, Utah, and took to the road. My grandmother was nine at the time. All I know about this rascal forefather I've heard through my mother's voice. I can still hear the words she's spoken, usually over the phone, about the yodeling cowboy who couldn't keep a wife or a job. "He had red hair, like you when you were born, like your boys when they were born. I felt such dismay when I first saw you. I didn't want you to look like him. . . . He used to sing on the radio. . . . He married six more times after he divorced my grandma. . . . When I was in high school, people said they saw him standing at the back of the auditorium when I sang. . . . Our fear of abandonment goes back to him, we feel it in our bodies, it's made us sick." When she poured these last words through the phone as I paced the living room, I pictured a green miasma floating just under my skin, in my mother's skin, and her mother's, and her mother's. The inherited body toxic. Maybe I have more connection to invalid Catharine than I realized.

I follow the librarian's directions to the security office and wait while a uniformed man frowns at my driver's license, makes a crack about my native Utah, and disappears into a back room. Soon he returns with a laminated I.D. card I'll never need again after today. It's only nine-thirty. I walk outside and sit on the steps, taking in the soft hot air I remember. A maple blankets me in shade. Red-eye-flight exhaustion hasn't hit me yet. In my mind I see my mother back in Utah, as she wakes in her Queen Anne bed and steps downstairs. She fills a glass with lukewarm springwater. Her throat tightens as she swallows fat herbal capsules, one after another. I see Grandma in her double-wide mobile home in the San Fernando Valley, her body so racked with arthritis since she was thirty-five that she never leaves her room before noon. Pillboxes and a jug of distilled water stand ready on her nightstand. I see Great-Grandma propped on pillows in a stale room in Los Angeles, the last time I saw her before her death, her body still in pain from a spider bite during the earthquake in 1971. The year of my birth. I used to have nightmares about that brown recluse spider, legs clicking out of a chasm in the street, as people hauled water from cracked swimming pools to fill their toilets. In reality the spider fell from the ceiling shortly after the earthquake and bit my great-grandmother on the forehead. Several weeks later, she came to care for my mother and me just after I was born. "She got dizzy and started hallucinating," my mother remembers. "Finally I thought to take her to a doctor, and he diagnosed the brown recluse bite. The pain got worse and worse, and the skin on her forehead turned black. She was almost unconscious for months."

Nine-forty-five. Ten o'clock. Another half hour and someone inside the court building will pull Catharine's diary from its shelf. Though I'm not as sure about life after death as I used to be, I wonder what she'd think if she were hovering here in the shade. I remember hovering over my mother's journal, which she kept on the nightstand next to her paperback *Persuasion,* the novel she read once a year. I never opened her journal, though it tempted me. I used my eyes and ears instead. My mother in her flannel nightgown, smelling of cold cream, reading Jane Austen in bed. Or reading Deuteronomy as she sat on the heat vent in the bathroom. Her knuckles pressed white as she knelt by the bed and prayed for twenty minutes at a time. My parents' whispered voices at the top of the stairs, their chains of sibilants, *colitis, arthritis, she, she.*

Ten-thirty. I shake the damp air from my head and start back inside. "You may need to wait another half hour," the librarian says when she sees me. Then she adds helpfully, "We have a snack bar down the hall."

Back into the basement corridor. I phone my husband, Kent, at home in Salt Lake City. He's about to leave for work, and the boys are at their cousins' house, not even thinking about us the last time he checked. Tomorrow he'll board a plane and meet me in Manhattan. "I miss Connecticut," he says. I tell him I do, too.

Eleven o'clock. This time the librarian stands up when I walk in. "You'll have to put your things in a locker before you enter the restricted area," she says. "You can bring paper and one pencil with you." Once I've stowed my bag, she leads me not into the barred cell I expect but five feet away to the other side of the room, where she hands me more forms to fill out. I suppose by now I've more than earned the privilege of reading someone else's journal. At last. I take the book from her hand.

It's not cobwebbed, not even dusty. It's the same hardback I opened in Stamford four years ago. I carry it to the end of a long wooden table and sit down. At the other end, a man lifts christening records with the tips of his finger and thumb. I pull out my pencil and paper. I open the book, not ready to start at the beginning. After flying three thousand miles, driving three hours, and waiting two more, I want to savor this meeting. The pages flap from my thumb. Phrases surface. *My own hourly danger of being taken from this life. The secret of the heart. Not listening to the inward voice which is continually calling. Had not freedom to express my feelings to anyone. More care would be taken if I were writing for the perusal of others. Permit none to remain drowsy, stupid, deaf, or blind. Fear of being too hasty and of professing more than I possessed. The cloud of silence. Alone as to outward company. Not able to speak above a whisper.*

nine openings

I grew up surrounded by sound. Breath blew through our house, through horn and recorder and human body.

A house full of vowels. Downstairs in my mother's studio dangling with ferns and spider plants, *Aaaaah*. A girl—Brenda, Pam,

Michelle, I lost track—had opened our gate and tramped down the path to the basement door, hair swinging, music in hand. From the top of the stairs, I could hear her singing up and down the scale. My mother stopped her and placed her hands, I knew without looking, on the girl's sweatered belly. My mother's voice: "Let your breath fall into my hands." I closed my eyes and saw feathers and snowflakes pillowing down. I imagined myself in that girl's cable-knit sweater, being touched, being that breath. A creak as my mother sat on the green-cushioned Wurlitzer bench and played a chord. She moved up the scale, half step, half step, *Aaaaah*. After fifteen minutes came the songs. "My Mother Bids Me Bind My Hair." "When I Bring to You Colored Toys." *"Care selve." "L'heure exquise."* From the top of the stairs, I mouthed the words, diphthong, nasal, open *Ah*.

All summer I heard voices, as I arranged my stuffed animals on the stairs and directed them in chorus, as I sailed a ship from my perch on the back porch, as I foraged for berries in the backyard that was my jungle island, as my friend and I sent messages to our Mother Ship one galaxy over, and as I followed a quiet Greek neighbor around her garden, making up stories out loud. My mother left the door to our walk-out basement open. Inside or out, I heard voices trying on Italian phrases or singing the words of Emily Dickinson. One afternoon, a young woman with silver-blonde hair sang a melody that twined around and around: *The Moon was but a Chin of Gold / A night or two ago. . . .* I overheard my mother's words, explaining that the composer had set Dickinson's words to a *vocalise* that *he'd* overheard in a studio down the hall from his office. Years later, a music teacher would point out a Liszt quotation buried in the song's piano accompaniment. For now, at eight years old, I heard only a circular melody that sang of the moon as a woman's face. I hummed along as my friend and I hunkered down on the porch, pencils pressed to paper, writing the latest chapter of our stuffed animals' adventures in the Arabian desert. The sun baked our hair and our bare legs. I closed my eyes and imagined the desert at night. I'd read somewhere that it was cold. Hot sand, cold air. The moon a chin of gold. My heroine, a lopsided sheep named Miss Lamb, watched the moon from her swaying caravan. I imagined her writing a poem. From inside the house, the familiar voice sang Dickinson: *Her Forehead is of Amplest Blonde— / Her Cheek—a Beryl hewn*. . . .

I heard voices the minute I walked in the door after school. One day, over milk and Oreos, I recognized the silver-blonde woman's voice at the bottom of the stairs: *When I am laid, am laid in earth* . . . I stopped mid-milk-dip. I'd never heard of the composer Henry Purcell or his descending chromatic scale, the "step of sorrow" that wrenched something in my rib cage, but I didn't want the music to end. Soon the woman who sang it was engaged to my uncle. Sometimes they'd come to my mother's studio and sing together, her mezzo-soprano and his baritone rising like steam from the basement.

From the top of the stairs, I often heard my mother practicing. Air rose through her and spilled out, gold. Her "Hello, Young Lovers" made me think she really had loved and lost. From where I sat, cheek pressed to the curving banister post, I pictured her on-stage in her hoopskirt, cradling a locket in her palm. I pictured her in the yellow ball gown that I hook-and-eyed her into, every night in her dressing room. I pictured her dancing with the king, a young man I thought too handsome to be real, who had shaved his head just like Yul Brynner. I could hear the orchestra pulsing "Shall We Dance" as dancers in glitter-crusted costumes stretched out around me in the wings, where I sat on a folding chair each night, watching. The dancers draped their arms around each other; they chatted and laughed in undertones. But here at home, as my mother's voice floated up to the kitchen, no one broke into my silence. I could worship in peace.

Human bodies weren't the only instruments in our house. From the top of the stairs, late at night, I heard my father playing the French horn, sometimes alone, sometimes with his partner from the community orchestra. One night I crept downstairs and pressed my ear to the wall. Two horns blared in the parquet-floored studio. One stopped, and then I heard a clicking sound: someone shaking out spittle. "I need the mute," said my father's voice. Here came a slow, sad song. "Let's do *Carmen*," said the other voice. Who was Carmen? My father's breath sang into the horn. The music sang in my bones.

Once or twice a year, I heard my father's recorder. He kept it in a narrow box lined with felt. He called it a "blockflute" because he'd brought it home from his Mormon mission in Germany, years before I was born. I knew, listening, that he played with no music in front of him. A melody blew out of the holes in the wood and up the stairs. It moved up and down the scale, almost a voice. I thought my father must be homesick for something. I didn't know that in thirteenth-century Persia, the poet Rumi had compared the human body, with its nine openings, to a reed flute torn from the reedbed; it sings out its longing for home. What my father longed for he never said, though I could guess. Most nights after dinner, he disappeared down the stairs and shut the door to his study. Sometimes, if the door happened to be open, I could see him pacing the floor in his green corduroy jacket with holes in the elbows, whispering to himself. I knew he'd wanted to be a college professor. He owned hundreds of books on history, philosophy, and theology, shelved in tidy, dustless rows. His study was his intellectual temple. My mother told me he'd rebelled against his father's plan for him to attend medical school—but not enough to chase his dream. He'd chosen law school instead; now, after a long day in court, he would don his academic's coat in the privacy of his study. When I sneaked in there during the day, I found his pencils lined up on the desk in perfect symmetry, and his thoughts arranged on yellow legal pads. Each column was titled and subtitled in his neat, rounded handwriting: "Aristotle." "Plato." "The Nature of the Soul." As far as I know, he never kept a diary. This was as personal as he got.

One summer night, my father brought his blockflute to our cabin. We were sleeping over, so he lit a fire, crumpling old newsprint and tossing in coal from the garage. He wore his leather work gloves and looked as sure of himself as the old Scoutmaster in the painting over the fireplace. The flames split and folded. I sat as close as my father would let me, tracing patterns in the braided rug. Here I was safe from the towering cottonwoods outside, the blue spruce full of spiderwebs, and the stars so thick they seemed to press down on the roof. My father settled into the leather armchair. He examined his recorder in the firelight. My mother sat on a stool and opened *The Hobbit*. She read aloud for a while, and I felt like a hobbit, happy to spend my days safe in these walls, in this threesome. I didn't need to wander out in the wide world. My mother put down the book. My father lifted the blockflute to his mouth. As he made up a melody, eyes focused on the fire, my mother took both my hands, and we danced. Around and around the braided rug, we reeled until the log walls blurred. I gripped her cold hands, hard. This was nothing like our dancing in the dark basement at home, my mother wild and untouchable as I moved beside her, watching.

Every night when my mother wasn't in a church meeting or in rehearsal for a community theater production, we danced. I loved the stereo with its webby speakers built into the cabinet, and the needle I learned to let fall without a skip. First, a crackling sound. Then the memory of a live performance, bow scraping string, flute piping, drums shuddering, all of it played back into our basement. "Sometimes I pretend I'm dancing with a handsome prince," my mother told me. I thought of the men who kissed her onstage, and shivered. When we danced, I pretended I was onstage, not in any-one's arms but gleaming in costume, flying across the masking-taped boards on my sure feet. The music blew through me. One night, as *Fiddler on the Roof* sawed through the room, I could hear my mother humming as she danced, arms flung in the air. I watched as she danced in place, air singing through her reed-thin frame, her elbows and shoulders loosening. In that moment, she seemed as much at ease in her body as she did onstage. More at ease, in fact. No one was telling her how to move or what to say. She could let her body invent its own wild choreography. Like Nora dancing her tarantella, swirling off the crust of patriarchy in Ibsen's *Doll's House,* my mother flung off the expectations of male church leaders and theater directors, of my father and his father, when she danced. It almost hurt to watch her.

When I was nine, my parents bought a new stereo, with a glass top and sleek black speakers. My father set it up in his study, where no one could dirty it with fingerprints or jostle the needle while pre-tending to stag-leap across the floor. When the stereo was set up and dusted and plugged in, he invited my mother and me into the study. He slid a record out of its black jacket and white sleeve. He set it gently in place, careful to touch only the edges with the palms of his hands. He laid down the needle and adjusted the volume. No crackling sound. Just the sound of a harp and a simple oboe melody in a minor key. Then, for the first time, I heard Pavarotti's voice. I shut my eyes. I pictured not a human body but a tree, bark split open with sadness, and fire at its heart.

A year later, I crouched in the corner of our duplex in Germany, listening to the same record. The Mormon Church had called my father to work as an attorney in its Frankfurt office, and the new stereo had followed us across the Atlantic in a shipping crate. Whenever my parents left me home alone, I slipped a record out of its sleeve. Outside I could hear the other children on our all-Mormon cul-de-sac, racing each other down the hill on their bikes or playing kick-the-can under the strange, top-heavy pine trees. I never joined them. I felt foreign in this place, and foreign to myself. At ten I had started to menstruate, my body opening not for music but for sheets and knots of blood. I stopped it up the best I could with paper towels. I said nothing to my mother, who lay in her room with a chronic sinus infection, a hot washcloth over her face. At night when my father came home from the office, he seemed troubled. I didn't want to bother him. I closed my eyes in the corner and listened to Mozart, Donizetti, or Puccini. I rocked myself to the rhythm of the music as the children chased and shouted outside. Voices leaped from the speakers, these more-than-human, invisible beings who spoke to me and touched me in a way no one else did.

When we returned to Salt Lake City a year later, I stopped speaking and started humming. My body, homesick for its childhood, carried every melody I heard. I hummed as I paced the floor to opera in the basement. I hummed in the halls at school and at my desk. I hummed in my parents' car, on the bus, or alone in my room. Vibration filled my body's hollow places, my closed mouth. Rumi's reed-flute cries out for its watery home; I did not dare cry aloud.

chant

A sign hangs on the chapel door: SILENCE IN CHURCH PLEASE. THE LORD IS PRESENT. My friend Kate whispers in my ear, "They really believe he is." I shut the door behind us. We slide into a wooden pew facing the choir stalls. I've been visiting this monastery in Huntsville, Utah, across the highway and down a farm road from my family's cabin, since early childhood. I came here after my dog died. I sat in the loft, numb with hurt, after my first romantic breakup. The Mormon chapel I entered for meetings, though white and high-windowed like this one, was not a refuge. During the week it was locked. On Sundays it filled with voices greeting and scheduling, babies, laughter, the organ's hum note. A place for doing, not being. Kate remembers; we grew up in the same Salt Lake City neighborhood and attended the same church, thirty-five years apart. I want her to know this place, too, the ovoid monastery chapel that has served me like the onyx worry rock my father once gave me. A smooth hollow to hold my troubles.

As we sit in silence, I remember the Mormon chapel in Connecticut where Kate and I met. Sunday after Sunday, I watched her meet the eyes of every person she encountered, as she laughed her rich laugh or passed on an article she thought would be of interest; she combined vigorous intellect with passion for people in a way I'd never seen. I remember the soft-curtained meeting room where women stood up and bore testimony of the "only true church on the earth"; in this room Kate and I found each other's eyes and understood, somehow, that we both had our doubts about this. Now that we're both living back in Salt Lake City, in the heart of the culture that raised us, we've had to face those doubts. Sometimes we talk for hours about questions of faith and human suffering; we find comfort in our shared "I don't know."

This afternoon we stopped at my family's cabin, where Kate examined a photograph of my great-great-great-grandfather baptizing a shivering Shoshone in a river, dozens more waiting their turn. "This picture has always made me sad," I told her. "I wonder what they were thinking, standing there." Later we walked up the street to the Old Home, the family's pioneer homestead. During my childhood, my paternal grandmother had led tours of this house every Saturday in the summer. A Mormon prophet, my great-grandmother's brother, had grown up in that house. Kate and I looked up into the hundred-foot cottonwoods and peered in the windows. As we pressed our faces to the glass, I pointed out the antique cradle and spinning wheel, and the piano that had been hauled across the plains in a covered wagon. There was the marble bust of the prophet, who had died before I was born, still smiling benignly in front of the fireplace. "I heard him speak once," Kate said. "I remember his stunning white hair." I told her about the night my cousins and I huddled in a sleeping porch on an upper floor of this house, making up a ghost story, and my grandmother scolded us: "There are no ghosts in this house. Only nice people lived here." These were the people whose "family name" my grandparents advised me, often, to live up to. Bishop. Patriarch. Prophet. Nobody talked about the real ghosts in our family—my grandfather's lost sense of humor, his sons' buried longings to study and teach and climb mountains, his wife's lost dreams of being an actress (yes, this was the same woman who stopped our ghost stories), his granddaughters' newlywed misery.

As Kate and I circled the Old Home this afternoon, ducking under lilac bushes to peek in the back windows, I spoke of these ghosts aloud: a sad-eyed uncle so quiet that I'd never known who he was; my grandmother's costume trunks, banished to the basement; the unhappiness my girl cousins and I could not voice in the first years of our marriages. The house stood silent in the shade. We stopped to take in the scent of white lilacs, the flowers my family had always placed on our ancestors' graves. Kate's ghost stories intertwined with mine. No one was there to scold us for telling them.

Five-twenty. Vespers will begin in ten minutes. What attracts me to this place, where women aren't allowed past the outer chapel? It's not the Catholic Church, I know. Rules and rituals have tied me in a knot I'm still trying to untangle. Is it the influence of my father, who dreams of retreating to a monastery? Possibly. It could be the architecture that draws me, this egg shape, these curved windows, and the red-and-blue stained-glass Madonna behind the altar, an image of the mother goddess I longed for years to see in place of God the Father. I know I love the silence here. But this afternoon, for once, I find it hard to sit still. Crusty bread and portabella mushrooms wait for us in the cabin kitchen, piles of postcards on the sofa. We're catching up after Kate's return from two weeks in Italy. We've saved up more stories to tell, poems and articles to read, worries to confide. I want this familiar quiet, but I want what will come after, too. What Kate calls "woman talk."

Five-thirty: a bell clangs, and one by one, eighteen brown-and-white-robed monks enter, genuflect, and take their places in the choir stalls. Three men in jeans, guests at the monastery, enter from a side door and sit near us in the pews. We're the only women in this light, womb-shaped space, except for the stained-glass Madonna. We can see through her to the blackbirds flying in and out of the cottonwoods outside.

One of the oldest monks begins the vespers office. Though Trappists no longer obey a strict rule of silence, I'm often startled when the first note sounds. The monk's voice slides up and down in narrow intervals, like a wheel in a well-used track. I recognize some of the faces in the choir stalls: there's Father Patrick, who used to sell whole wheat bread in the gift shop. The monk in the skullcap who began the service is often here between choral offices, sitting alone in his stall, so still I regret having entered and stirred the air.

Every pitch in a chant becomes a radical act of attention, maybe even more for visitors like us, who don't hear these simple melodies daily. The monks sing in unison now; the chant rests on one pitch, and then moves up and down only slightly on the scale. This musical phrase returns, sometimes with different words, throughout the service. Today when I hear this melody, worn in the voice the way a monk's body wears its literal habit, day after day, I think of a different kind of chant, composed by a woman in the twelfth century.

Hildegard von Bingen was born in 1098, the same year eight French monks founded an austere, experimental community that would become known as the Cistercian order. Hildegard grew up to become a Benedictine abbess and visionary; the Cistercian order evolved into Trappist communities like this one.

For much of her life, Hildegard did not feel free to use her intellectual and creative gifts. In her forties, she experienced what she later called a "fiery light of exceeding brilliance that permeated my whole brain" and inspired her to give voice, at last, to her vivid spiritual life. She started to write words and music for the women in her abbey. Her poetry linked sensual experience with religious awakening. Like Rumi, she compared the body to a musical instrument, "open like a wooden frame in which the strings have been fastened for strumming," or a "poor earthly vessel . . . sounding a little like the small sound of a trumpet."

In the hymns and sequences she composed, Hildegard broke the boundaries of twelfth-century plainchant. Church reform had set strict rules for liturgical music, based on existing modal formulas. Musicologist Richard Hoppin notes that Cistercian monks took literally the Psalmist's words, "upon a psaltery and an instrument of ten strings will I sing praises unto thee" (Ps. 144:9), and determined that a chant should move in close steps within a ten-note range. Hildegard's sophisticated compositions, in which female voices swirl loosely around a center pitch, were different. More like "woman talk," as two voices circle from story to story and back again, or a dance, as bodies meet and separate and embrace.

The melodic line in Hildegard's hymn *Ave generosa* moves by leaps of fourths and fifths. The music reaches its highest pitch when Hildegard writes, addressing Mary, *For your womb held joy, when all the heavenly symphony rang out from you*. The chant's melodic line spans an octave and a sixth. In her song *O viridissima virga,* Hildegard allows a repeated melody to change slightly each time it is sung, and lets the words stretch out over more than one pitch. When I hear a recording of this piece, as the women's voices overlap and extend, I can't help but picture a time-lapse film of a tulip or an orchid blooming, the kind of imagery Hildegard uses to address the Virgin Mary. In some antiphons, in which groups of voices respond alternately to each other, the women's voices rise on pure vowels, a conversation beyond words.

As far as I can tell, the monks at Our Lady of the Holy Trinity rarely move more than a fourth up or down the scale. Today, listening with Kate, I remember the simple melodies my child self learned by rote, the songs my sons and her granddaughters sing on Sundays: "Father, I Will Reverent Be," "This Is God's House," "I Am a Child of God." These tunes once circumscribed my world, not only by their small range in pitch but also by the cosmos their words defined. Father. Christ. Holy Ghost. In the Mormon Church, it would be unthinkable to sing songs to the Virgin Mary or any other female figure. I once asked my mother about a rumor I'd heard from a friend, that there really was a Mother in Heaven. "Maybe there is," my mother said, "but we don't know anything about her." I got the idea that I shouldn't ask too many questions about this invisible woman in the sky. Sometimes I had the urge to pray to her, to talk, to ask her about Heaven, but I never dared, any more than I dared tell a ghost story in my grandmother's presence. I carried this longing for years into adulthood, as I became more and more uneasy in a church that withholds its priesthood from women. I projected my sense of lack onto the God I wanted to believe in.

Kate and I sit as still as we can. The monks on the right side of the chapel sing words of despair; across the white aisle the others, one a monotone, answer in the voice of God the Father. After the antiphon, a long silence. No Madonna descends to relieve the human pain in the words we have just heard. Only this: two women on a hard pew, breathing in counterpoint, our words stored up and ready to spill.

passaggio

Some voice teachers call it a "transition." Others, to make it sound like something natural and beautiful, use the word *color point*. Some say it occurs every four pitches on the scale. Some call it the result of faulty technique. One famed teacher in Los Angeles has made a career out of aiding singers troubled by theirs: "People call me from Tokyo for this," he told my mother once. I didn't know what the word meant until I discovered my own *passaggio*. It came on like a sudden illness.

I was eleven years old, alone in the house. I'd sneaked my mother's music from its shelf, the song she'd been working on since our return from Germany. "Connais-tu le pays?" from the opera *Mignon*. "Do You Know the Land?" A song about homesickness, sung by an orphan who remembers very little about her native country, except that there were orange trees and gentle breezes. I could understand. My own homeland looked very different from the one I'd left a year before. My best friend seemed to speak a foreign language (Rubik's Cube? Knickers?). Even in my own house, I felt like a stranger to my parents and kept to my basement room. I wanted more than anything to learn this song, to sing the longing I couldn't express in my own words.

I set the music on the piano and played the introduction the best I could. I started to sing. The French words came easily, after years of listening to my mother and her students, after the lessons I'd copied in secret from my mother's college textbook, and after our many trips to Paris, the only place where my mother had seemed healthy and happy during our year in Germany. But when I opened my mouth for the second phrase, which arched higher than the first, my sound cracked in half. I tried again. Same thing. I panicked and tried the phrase over and over, pushing the air through my vocal cords until they hurt. I didn't sound like myself anymore. Not only had my childhood ruptured; so had my voice.

"It's just your *passaggio*," my mother said when she noticed it during my weekly voice lesson. "It's the place where you move from one register to another." A passage from low voice to high voice. My mother explained that I had a *primo passaggio* near middle C, and a *secondo passaggio* where my voice changed from middle to upper middle range. She quoted a book on vocal technique that called the *passaggio* a "pivot point." I pictured a door opening on its hinge. No. That didn't help. I pictured a literal passageway, a windowless corridor. Or "passage" meaning movement, a train bearing down on the tracks, or a ship cutting into the ocean. What about the sun's rising and setting . . . ? None of the images in my mind changed what happened when I opened my mouth. Whenever I approached the pitch an octave above middle C, I did exactly what my mother had told me not to, and clenched my tongue at the root. I never knew what would come out. A squeak? A breathy waver? Sometimes both.

Even in high school, when I was starting to make friends, when my family had grown to include an adopted baby girl, when I was learning to drive, my voice seemed stuck in an endless puberty. One night, singing for a competition, I could hardly feel the ground under my feet. I could think of nothing but the C that loomed in the first phrase of my song. My mother stood at the back of the class-room behind the judges, clutching her purse. Something clutched in my throat. She'd prepared me for this, hadn't she? Hours at the piano in the basement, and all those instructions: "Breathe into your lower abdomen." "Release your jaw." "Lift your soft palate." "Don't let your chest collapse." "Keep the tip of your tongue against your bottom teeth." Already the girl at the piano had started playing the rocking-cradle pattern in the Fauré song I'd learned by heart. My feet still couldn't feel the floor. The faces in front of me blurred. My mouth opened and made French sounds, a poem about ships leaving the harbor—how I'd wanted it to ebb and flow, and now I could only gasp for breath. In the wrong place. My voice cracked. The floor seemed to buckle under my high heels.

I finished the song and followed my mother out of the class-room, my face burning. I didn't hear what she said to me. I heard in my head what she'd said again and again from the piano bench, whenever my voice split open: "It's just your *passaggio*." Just. It felt like grinding the gears in driver's ed. What was wrong with me? I knew girls my age who could trip up and down the scale like Snow White. I hated Snow White. My mother hoped I'd get over that. "You're a coloratura," she'd tell me, as though she were handing me a precious heirloom. "I used to have high notes like yours, until you were born. It took a long time to get my voice back after that."

Because of me, or maybe just hormones, my mother could no longer sing "The Maids of Cadix." Sometimes I felt guilty, as she practiced the approach to a high F over and over, trying to lighten or sweeten it, anything to make her own most dominant *passaggio* less noticeable. Still, her golden voice made people cry. I couldn't even sing a hymn in church without squawking.

When my mother sat on the piano bench, listening to every note in the scales I sang, her forehead tightened. She tried to think of en-couraging things to say. I wished she didn't have to try. Often I left the room in tears. I knew she worried about my speaking voice. "I think you might be speaking too low," she told me once. "You're a

grace notes

high soprano. You need to place your speaking voice higher." She offered to take me to a speech pathologist. She gave me her old
Deanna Durbin book full of runs and trills. When we stayed up late
watching Jeannette MacDonald movies, all fluttering eyelashes and
fluttering vibrato, we laughed together, but in secret I wanted to
throw up. The music I loved wasn't even written for soprano. It was
lower, darker, and richer, like Mignon's song about the orange trees
she misses back home, or trouser-role arias, like Cherubino's attempt
to seduce the countess in *The Marriage of Figaro,* or Orpheus's
lament for his dead wife. Another aria I longed to sing was "When I
Am Laid in Earth" from Purcell's *Dido and Aeneas,* the song with
the haunting passacaglia that I'd once heard my aunt-to-be sing in
my mother's studio. But there I was with a breathy space where my
lower voice should have been, a light, clear top, and a train wreck in
between.

I knew my anatomy, thanks to my mother's thickly labeled illus-
trations of the human head. I'd even sat in an ear-nose-and-throat
specialist's office, watching my vocal cords on a video screen while
the doctor dangled a camera down my nostril and into my throat. I
knew that the vocal cords look thick and short when you sing lower
pitches, and that in the middle range, these muscles make smooth,
wavelike vibrations. I knew that as you move up the scale, muscles
called cricothyroids start to lengthen the cords, and that as the edges
of the vocal folds become thinner, tension increases, and vibrations
quicken. And yes, I knew that if you reach for a high note without
allowing the cords to lengthen smoothly and gradually, the voice
may "crack." My mother had shared many a pedagogical insight with
me, from Pavarotti's notion of the vocal range shaped like an hour-
glass, with the *passaggio* as the skinny part you have to squeeze
through, narrowing the vowel, to one teacher's insistence that every
note is a *passaggio.* The goal, I understood without questioning, was
never to let it show. But how? I was doing all the right things, lifting
this and releasing that, even sticking a cork between my teeth to
make more room for my vowels.

Had I—or my mother—known what we both know now, we
would have realized that our training focused too much on pretty

high notes to address the voice as a whole. Had I been more media savvy, I would have seen that episode on *The Brady Bunch* when Peter's voice cracks in public and he ends up accepting the fact with perfect sitcom aplomb. I wish some all-knowing person had explained to me that girls' voices change, too. That even after puberty, some pitches trouble every singer if she hasn't warmed up, or when a song is new to the voice. That every *passaggio* is simply a signpost (CHEST VOICE. HEAD VOICE. CAUTION: LEAVING THE RANGE OF SPEECH. GLASS-BREAKING NOTES AHEAD.). But an all-knowing person would have told me things I wasn't ready to hear. That I was so disconnected from my body, I'd be stuck in my pubescent voice for years. That my voice would change again. That maybe I had more than one.

conversation

My husband squeezed my hand. I watched him vanish into the men's dressing room. I breathed deeply and walked through the women's door. A temple worker in a long white dress smiled at me and pointed toward the lockers. I was twenty, newly married, and uneasy in this softly carpeted House of the Lord. Since childhood I'd heard speeches from the pulpit encouraging members of the church "in good standing" to attend the temple at least once a month, to perform rituals in proxy for the dead. These rituals, according to Latter-day Saint doctrine, give righteous Mormons the keys to the highest level of Heaven. Now that I was eligible to go, I watched the calendar with dismay as the end of each month approached. I knew my husband would say, over dinner or on the way home from the university, "We should try to get to the temple this month." I would nod and check my calendar. I would hide the frustration that clutched my heart.

Another white-clad temple worker smiled at me and pointed me toward my individual dressing stall. I locked the metal door and leaned my face against it. Cold comfort. In nearby stalls, women rustled out of their street clothes and into long white temple dresses. One by one, they banged their lockers shut and shuffled away in soft slippers. They were going upstairs to the endowment rooms, where the main temple rites are performed. I just stood in silence, my cheek against the door. What was Kent thinking as he undressed on the other side of the building? Was he disappointed in me? He knew, though I tried to hide it, that I felt ill at ease in the church. Sometimes, after watching the churchwide General Conference broadcast on TV, I couldn't help but blurt out my anger at male authority figures' speeches on womanhood: "They tell us we have this divine nature, but they sound so patronizing!" Kent would remind me that they were "inspired men" and that even if most of them were over seventy and showed the bias of their generation, "they're very sincere." I shut my mouth. In my mind, there was nothing I could do. I'd bound myself to this church, body and soul, in my temple initiation shortly before our marriage. I'd made covenants so serious that being struck by lightning would be the least of my worries if I ever broke them.

The night before the initiation ceremony, a week before our wedding, Kent and I had sat down to read Mormon Scriptures about eternal marriage. This union begins with the temple "sealing" of husband and wife, hands joined across a lace-covered altar, for this life and beyond. As the book lay open across our knees, Kent read aloud a revelation church founder Joseph Smith dictated in 1843, commanding his wife to accept the law of marriage "restored" from Old Testament times: "And let mine handmaid, Emma Smith, receive all those that have been given unto my servant Joseph, and who are virtuous and pure. . . . But if she will not abide this commandment she shall be destroyed." God had given Abraham more than one wife, the revelation said, and David his many wives and concubines. This was the "new and everlasting covenant." My mother had told me Emma Smith once burned a copy of this revelation in front of her husband. I didn't blame her one bit. Kent kept reading. Tears burned in my eyes. Would I have to share my husband, too—if not in this life, then in the next? Would I have to be an eternal procreator of spirit bodies, the glorious role women were supposed to look forward to after death? And if I didn't agree to this, would I be destroyed? Kent finished reading the section and looked at me. "Nobody talks about polygamy," I burst out. "Nobody talks about

Joseph Smith's dozens of wives. Did you know that some of them were barely teenagers, and some were already married to other men? The General Authorities want that part of our history to go away. But our own Scriptures say it's still an eternal law." Kent nodded and looked a little frightened. This was the first time he'd heard me talk like this. He advised that I humble myself and take some things on faith.

Now, several months after our own temple sealing, Kent saw the books stacked on our nightstand: Virginia Woolf's *Room of One's Own,* Adrienne Rich's poetry and prose, Marina Warner's feminist treatise on the Virgin Mary. He knew I was questioning the gender hierarchy we'd taken for granted all our lives. I didn't discuss with him what I read, but he was suspicious enough to caution me about "intellectual pride." He didn't know what deep waves of relief I felt, reading on paper the thoughts I'd never dared voice, even in my journal. The rhythm of Adrienne Rich's 1975 essay "Women and Honor: Some Notes on Lying" rose and fell in my head: "We have been rewarded for lying. . . . Lying is done with words, and also with silence. . . . There is a danger run by all powerless people: that we forget we are lying. . . . The liar is afraid. . . . She is afraid, not so much of prison guards and bosses, but of something unnamed within her."

I had been lying for years. I had missed the women's movement, and so had my mother. When my new husband sulked because I wasn't making his lunches every day, I snapped to and made them—just as my mother had done for my father, for as long as I could remember. I burned with resentment. I did not complain. When Kent dropped me off at my secretarial job at the university, morning after morning, I shut the car door behind me and let the tears go. *Why isn't he speaking to me?* I whispered as I walked to the Student Services Building, my face to the ground. *What have I done this time?* I didn't yet know that Kent's sulking came not only from his upbringing in our culture of male achievers and female caretakers, but also from the chemical depression that runs in his family. We had our sunny days; we joked and played; but more often than not I felt as helpless as my mother had in my father's cloud of silence. All I could do, I thought, was tiptoe around Kent's emotional low-pressure zone and cry in secret. I had come from a family in which hurt feelings were rarely discussed.

No wonder reading feminist writers stung and exhilarated me. Now, at last, I could do my own painful consciousness raising—though in my secrecy I was still a liar. I read in bed as Kent watched baseball or studied for law school exams in the living room. I never even considered telling him what was happening to me. The fault line in me went so deep, I feared that even to speak of it would rip my life apart. Now, when I sat in church and heard soothing messages, usually spoken by men, about the "divine role of women in the home," I heard something else in my head: Virginia Woolf's words about "the Angel in the House" who must be killed if a woman is to speak in her own voice. When I sat in the temple, watching a film of white-robed male gods striding among transparent pillars, I wondered where the women were. In the film, Eve posed behind a bush, gazing vacuously at Adam, ready to make his lunches the minute they got kicked out of Eden. I watched and said nothing. The unnamed thing within me rumbled.

It was still rumbling as I leaned against the metal door in the women's dressing room. On this temple visit, Kent and I were not going upstairs to the endowment room to watch the Adam and Eve film and perform the ritual gestures, handclasps, and donning of ceremonial robes. This time he'd suggested we do the initiatory rite, a preparatory washing and anointing, on behalf of people who had died. I shivered as I shed all my clothes in the stall and put on the heavy polyester-blend "shield" worn in the initiatory. I had not done this since my first time in the temple. The memory shook me: I'd felt ashamed of my nakedness under the shield. The shoulder-to-knee undergarments slipped onto me by a smiling temple worker, her eyes averted, had been far too big for me. Once upstairs in the endowment room, I'd cried in front of my extended family and future in-laws—not because I was moved by the spirit, but because no one had told me I'd have to memorize an elaborate system of codes and signs to get into Heaven. And because a disembodied male voice was informing us that yes, the wife must answer to the husband. And because my initiation seemed so irrevocable. I was being asked to give my whole life to the church. It felt like a death. I was making covenants with God that would keep me in these sacred undergarments, this gender role, this prescription for salvation, for eternity. From now on, I thought, my body would not be my own. It belonged to the church. I traced the stitches on the symbolic fig-leaf apron my aunt had sewn for me as an early wedding gift. It must have taken her hours. She'd told me once that on her first temple visit, she wanted to run screaming out the door. My mother had said the same thing about her own initiation. I wanted them both to explain everything, why this fig-leaf gift, why the assumption that I'd do exactly as they had. My mother sat near me in her white veil, her lips pressed tight. I could not call out to her; she did not come to my rescue; no one had come to hers.

Today, despite my unease, I knew what to expect in the temple. I found my way to the curtained enclosures where the washing and anointing ritual is performed. A temple worker smiled at me and opened a fold in the heavy cotton draperies. Inside, another woman took my hand and sat me on a stool. Water dribbled into a basin at my left. The woman whispered a blessing. Others pulled back new openings in the enclosure and guided me through the ceremony; they touched me with water and oil. Without speaking, I stepped in and out of initiatory garments, once for every deceased person's name pinned to my shield. Did it matter to the dead that their proxy had serious doubts about this church? I imagined each spirit, most of them with heavily consonanted Dutch names, floating above the white draperies, arms stretched out in gratitude. No, that was the image I'd been brought up to see. Maybe they were floating somewhere else. Maybe they were nowhere.

Over and over, a temple worker's hands pressed down on my head. This was the one place I'd seen Mormon women lay their hands on someone's head and pronounce blessings, a priesthood privilege usually reserved for men. I liked their touch, the sound of female voices in my hair, the way they spoke blessings on the head, the spine, the loins. These women did not know how much I needed them—not because of their blessings, too sacred to be repeated outside the temple, but simply because of their presence. That comfort I could take with me as I reentered my daily life. When Kent scolded me for failing to wipe the bathroom faucets to a satin shine, when we sat in silence in the car, when I shed my tears on the way to work, knowing I couldn't even tell my mother about my hurt, I could remember this anonymous gentleness.

One of the initiatory workers spoke with an Italian accent. During a brief pause in the ceremony, I took a risk and whispered a question to her: "Are you from Italy?" The sound of my own breath startled me, but the woman brightened and whispered back that yes, she and her family had moved to Salt Lake City from Rome after their conversion. For the next hour, in every silent moment as I was passed from enclosure to enclosure, between the scripted prayers and dialogue the women recited, Maria and I spoke Italian. It was the first time I'd opened my mouth to speak my own words during a temple ceremony. I doubt I could have done it in English. Even as a student in Italy, I'd found strange courage as my mouth formed pure vowels and rolling *r*s, enough courage to argue with my landlady. Now, with the familiar taste of Italy in my mouth, my nerve came back. I told Maria I'd studied in Siena. She told me about her family's tailoring business, a block away from the temple. If the other temple workers could hear us, they didn't say. We whispered and smiled. Our talk strengthened me.

This conversation, which had nothing to do with the ceremony being performed, was my one whole-souled experience in the temple. It reminded me of the day I'd seen Giotto's enormous *Ognissanti Madonna* in the Uffizi museum in Florence. I stood in front of that nearly eleven-foot-tall altar panel, unable to move. This was not a shimmering metallic angel painted into an S curve, like most fourteenth-century Madonnas; this was no ideal goddess but a plain-faced woman who took up space on her throne. Gravity pulled on the folds of her robe, from her shoulders to her massive knees. I looked into her calm almond eyes. I wanted to touch her fingers, so round they looked real. The unnamed within me rose into my throat.

My Sunday-school teachers had sometimes spoken of a Mother in Heaven. When asked why we never heard anything about her, they said, "She's too sacred to talk about" or, in the case of a former Mr. Universe who tried to impress our class of sixteen year olds, "Maybe Heavenly Father has so many wives, there are a thousand Mothers in Heaven." I'd read that in the Gnostic Gospels, female divinity is personified as Sophia, or wisdom, and that in Jewish tradition, the divine presence called Shechinah is sometimes referred to as a woman, the exiled one who visits on the Sabbath. But as Maria touched my hair with oil, I no longer wanted to believe in the divine absence in Mormon doctrine, a female mask for a theological idea, or a romanticized mother goddess. I wanted to believe in the women of this world. I wanted to take their hands and tell them everything.

silence

Quakers might call what happened to me "a Leading." It did not come out of nowhere. It was a moment of illumination I was ready, after years of struggle, to welcome.

Kent and I had been married for eleven years. I'd become more uncomfortable than ever in the Mormon Church, since our return to Salt Lake City from Connecticut. In our congregation in Stamford, I'd felt somewhat free of the Mormon-majority culture and duty-bound family that had stifled me, growing up in Utah. But now we were back in the heart of it, and I did not belong. I had even gone so far as to pray about leaving the church; I'd known in my heart for a year that it was time. Two of my close friends had left: one felt for the first time that Sunday was actually a day of rest; the other found her spiritual high running up and down a canyon on Sunday mornings. I'd seen Jewish friends find joy in their liberal, reconstructionist congregation. Kate and I had enjoyed a weekend retreat at a Benedictine convent. I told myself there must be a way to have a rich spiritual life without being fed all the answers and told exactly how to live. But something in me held back, afraid.

One Sunday night, after coming home from a church meeting with my usual frustration, I sat in bed reading—what, I can't remember. A phrase seemed to loosen from the page: "the Quaker concept of the Inward Light in each person." How beautifully simple. I read the phrase over and over. A week later, as I sat on the same heap of pillows reading a collection of short stories by Andrea Barrett, I encountered a Quaker heroine, a Canadian woman who organizes relief efforts for the Irish potato famine and keeps her jewelry in a locked case, unworn, unneeded. I put the book down in my lap. I'd almost forgotten skimming the diary of my Quaker relative in the Stamford library three years before. I got up and rummaged through my files until I found some notes I'd taken from a book at the Stamford Historical Society. The notes were scribbled on the back of a genealogy sheet: "Friends Meeting—Darien 1828 at Wyx Seely's house in sick room of C. Seely (same room where grandmother Catharine Selleck, 'first member in this place, sat down in the same way, herself alone')." How did Catharine choose the Quakers? Was it because of her grandmother, or because of a "Leading" of her own? I didn't remember any mention of her grandmother in the diary. And what exactly was the Inward Light?

On my next trip to the public library with my sons, I pulled them, one on each hand, into the religion section. I wanted to read something on the language of Isaiah. At least, this is what I told myself. But there on the same aisle that housed the Jewish feminist books I loved to read were three titles with the word *Quaker*. I chose one that looked like a broad historical overview, and Margaret Hope Bacon's *Mothers of Feminism: The Story of Quaker Women in America*. I tucked both books in our bag. "*Now* can we go up to the children's section?" my youngest asked for the third time. Up the escalator we went.

The Quaker books sat on the green sofa we call the Story Couch, lost in a pile of Dr. Seuss, for about a week. I was afraid to touch them. Then, one night when Kent was away teaching the local Mormon Scout troop about the Constitution, I dared myself, and carried the books to bed. Too excited to read the pages slowly, I devoured them.

I read about silent meetings held in dining rooms, in which early Quakers "waited on the Lord" and spoke only if they felt moved to. I read about their efforts to become "tender" to spiritual experience without ritual or creed. I read about Quakers in seventeenth-century

England who refused to take off their hats to nobility because they believed that, in the eyes of God, no one is superior to anyone else. I read about women ministers who were jailed or even hanged for speaking in public, some who traveled in pairs across the Atlantic, leaving their husbands to keep house, and those who refused to send their sons into the Civil War. I read about Lucretia Mott and Susan B. Anthony, Quakers who worked tirelessly for women's rights and the abolition of slavery. I read about some Quaker women, raised in egalitarian homes, who couldn't understand all the fuss over Second Wave feminism. I read about Alice Paul, the originator of the Equal Rights Amendment, which my Salt Lake City neighbors had spoken of in frightened whispers when it came up for ratification in the late 1970s. I read about unprogrammed Quaker communities that function without minister or hierarchy, a system based not on authority but on relationship. I read about the process of reaching consensus, and the emphasis on listening, in Friends meetings for business. I read about the splits and offshoots in Quakerism, a tradition that remains open to change. I read about Quakers' belief that all religions have value. I read about the Inward Light, "that of God in everyone."

When Kent came home, he couldn't wait, as usual, to shed his brown Scoutmaster shirt. As he undressed in our room I thought out the words I wanted to say. *What would you think if I . . . I've been doing some reading . . . You know I've struggled with the church for a long time . . .*

"How was your meeting?" I asked. He told me, and we went to bed.

I couldn't sleep. *Why couldn't I open my mouth?* I demanded of myself again and again as I stared into the darkness. I knew Kent wasn't the same man I'd married, so controlling, so easily threatened by any expression of doubt about the "only true church on the earth." He had seen, early in our marriage, the atrophy of my soul as I gave up my passions to play Angel in the House. Six years into our life together, he had left his job, followed me across the country, and stayed home with our sons during my first year of graduate school. He had stopped trying to get me to put my whole heart into my church assignments. In his work as a criminal defense attorney, he'd found more capacity for compassion than he'd known he had. And now, after a decade of ignorance on both our parts, he was taking the antidepressant he'd needed all along. For the first time, he could see an emotional downturn coming and choose not to follow it. If I worked late at the computer or came home elated from a poetry reading, he no longer met me with punishing silence. Why was I so afraid?

I stared at the ceiling most of the night. The next morning we woke up and got Anders ready for school. I still said nothing. Kent went to work. I poured milk on Evan's Mini-Wheats. As he munched his breakfast, I opened the phone book. Just out of curiosity. I found the Society of Friends in the white pages, just above the Sock Man. There. Now I could call, or not call. I'd never meant to go this far anyway. For years I'd wanted to find a way out of the church I was in, not search out a new one. Besides, I'd always suspected I was a pagan at heart. I could call or not call. Did I dare speak to a stranger, a Friend, even though I'd never met any that I knew of, and even though I hadn't dared bring this up with my husband?

Yes. Something in me was about to break.

I dialed the number, and no real live Friend picked up. A recording of a woman's voice gave me the time for the Sunday, or in Quaker-ese, First Day, meeting. The message said, "Our meetings are unprogrammed," a relief to me after thirty years in the heavily structured Mormon beehive. That night when Kent and I sat on the Story Couch after the boys were in bed, I clutched my hands together in my lap. My heart hammered. "What would you think if I went to a Quaker meeting?"

Silence. He opened and shut his mouth.

"I just want to see what it's about. I've been doing some reading."

He swallowed. When he spoke, I could hardly hear him. "For eleven years I've been afraid this day would come." More silence. "You know I'll support you. What else can I do? I just ask that you support me, too. I can't imagine taking the boys to church by myself. . . ." His voice trembled and trailed off. I reached for his hand.

The next Sunday, I found a substitute for my usual church assignments and drove to the Ladies' Literary Club in brilliant

February sun. "How very Quaker!" a friend had exclaimed when I told her where the local congregation met. As I parked and walked up the steps to the porch, I remembered trailing along with my mother up these stairs and into this building designed as an Arts and Crafts–style mansion. She'd come to sing a program of show tunes for an audience of women in floral dresses.

Today the building was quiet. A bearded man greeted me at the door, handed me a folded paper, and told me I'd picked a good day to visit: a Quaker wedding. I walked into what looked like a ball-room. Light fell in through windows stained in a Frank Lloyd Wright–like design. Wooden folding chairs had been arranged in a square in the middle of the room, the way shape-note singers face each other to pound their feet and thunder out their hymns.

Nobody thundered in here. One by one, pair by pair, Friends and guests wandered into the room and found a place to sit. Some wore jackets and skirts; some wore jeans. I didn't see anyone I knew. We all sat in silence. I tried to "think about Jesus," as I'd been told to do during the sacrament when I was small, but my body was too busy feeling out its new surroundings. Here and there a chair creaked as someone shifted weight. Some people sat with their eyes closed. Others looked at the floor, or into the air. I heard my stomach growl and settle. I watched the groom in his sweater and the bride in her purple satin skirt, hands joined, eyes closed. At last they stood and spoke their vows to each other. They must have been married civilly beforehand, since no authority figure hovered over them, proffering the usual words. I'd read that this was customary for Quaker weddings. No veil, no priest, no organ, only two voices speaking in the still air. Man and woman glowed at each other. He bent toward her yellow hair like a nervous adolescent. I could hardly hear her voice as she spoke.

Afterward, collective stillness. Somewhere a furnace chugged and then clicked off. Birdcall outside. A creak in the floor. Breath in the body next to me. My stomach contracted into a painful knot. I pictured Kent and the boys in our Mormon sacrament meeting, Cheerios and crayons strewn on the padded bench, the organ thrumming, or someone at the pulpit, speaking on an assigned topic.

Tithing, food storage, temple work. Lists of things to do. Or maybe the kind of talk I enjoyed, the story of a death or a miracle or a plan gone wrong. If I were sitting there, I'd listen. I'd see the bishop who had once told me the church needed people like me; I'd see my friend who lived across the street, women in my book club, a composer friend I'd known for years, and my sons' favorite babysitter; I'd see the woman assigned to visit me once a month, who loved to talk about unusual insects and her most gruesome injuries. My neighbors, all of them dear to me. But today, in this quiet, I knew that bench was no longer my home. It had never been my home. By showing up here today, I'd finally owned up to this.

My stomach ached for Kent. I slid down in my chair and tried to release my knotted muscles. It had been so much easier to go to church for my husband's sake. My new freedom frightened me. From now on, my marriage would no longer depend on the Mormon Church to bind it together. I no longer stood in the wedding dress I'd chosen eleven years before, laced so tight I could hardly breathe. Now Kent and I were free to choose each other, to join hands across our differences, or not. I imagined the two of us standing in silence like this bride and groom. I imagined us speaking the truth to each other. I breathed deeply. My stomach calmed. I couldn't wait to tell Kent about this meeting.

A woman stood up to speak. I didn't catch all her words for the newlyweds, but I noticed the brightness of her voice, and her hesitation as words came into her mind. She sat down. Minutes of silence went by. I remembered sitting in Mormon testimony meetings as a child, all nerves when twenty seconds passed and no one spoke. The silence had embarrassed me. Not so this quiet, which held our square of wooden chairs in an invisible cat's cradle. A man rose and spoke about the day he'd heard the groom play the piano, music his spirit had needed that day. Stillness. I wanted to learn to still myself. To let my old words, the niceties I had not meant, the doctrine I had preached without belief, the hymn rhythms I'd sung without thinking, fall out of me. Not to be silenced but to give myself to silence. To begin again.

two

diary

June 30. I won't call this a journal but a "writer's notebook." It has a collage on the front—watercolor poppies and two fragments of scroll covered with Chinese characters. I bought it because of those fragments. They remind me that whatever I write, it will only be part of the story.

Right now I'm not writing but copying bits of information from the Internet. *Scrofula*. My search engine turns up someone's cast of evil characters, virtual or real, I'm not sure, including the gun-toting Count Scrofula. Not what I had in mind. Five references to Samuel Johnson? Now, here's something. A page from *Webster's Revised Unabridged Dictionary*, 1913. I don't want to print the whole thing, so I start scribbling: "A constitutional disease, generally hereditary, especially manifested by chronic enlargement and cheesy degeneration of the lymphatic glands, particularly those of the neck. . . . Scrofula is now generally held to be tuberculous in character."

Well, I knew this much, except for the part about "cheesy degeneration." (My more current dictionary calls the disease "tuberculosis of the lymph nodes and throat.") Because I love odd sentences taken out of context, I copy down the 1913 usage example for the word *scrofulous:* "Scrofulous persons can never be duly nourished." I wonder if this is true. I drift from Web site to Web site and scratch more notes in my Chinese fragment book: "Samuel Johnson suffered effects of scrofula throughout his life." "Disease also known as 'the king's evil.'" "*History of Human Tuberculosis* notes that scrofula 'progresses slowly with abscesses, and pistulas develop' and calls it 'a young person's disease.'" "OBGYN.NET: article 5/5/01 says the disease no longer appears in its classic form even among the poor in India."

I close the notebook and open the manila folder full of photocopied pages, as many as the Connecticut State Library would allow me, of Catharine's diary. On the first page, I find the words of the relative who compiled Catharine's writings after her death: "As a tendency to scrofula was early manifested, her constitution was extremely delicate." Catharine puts it more grimly: "Many times I thought my life would be very short, and my illness served . . . to show me that I stood on a dangerous precipice from which I might be instantly plunged into the fathomless pit." Scrofula not only kept Catharine in bed for much of her life; it also cost her her voice.

In 1824, after teaching children in New Canaan, Connecticut, and taking charge of a school in Westchester County, New York, Catharine became too ill to continue her profession. Years later she wrote,

> I spent eight or ten hours a day at the school house, and mostly in school; for while I kept it, I resolved to discharge my duty as fully as possible, though the latter part of the time I could not bear the light to one eye, and was obliged to omit reading with the classes, in con-

sequence of the weakness of my lungs. The severity of the pain in my back and side occasionally disabled me from rising out of my chair for some hours at a time; and as I frequently raised a little fresh blood in the morning, I felt such a sinking at my lungs that for hours after it was a great hardship to speak.

Two of Catharine's cousins took her home, where "a blister was applied" but gave her no relief from the pain in her head, eyes, and throat. From 1824 until her death in 1838, Catharine stayed in her room in her father's house in Darien. The curtains were shut to keep out the light. Relatives and doctors came and went. She wrote, "At the time it was very difficult for me to raise my voice, and so humiliating to speak to them in a whisper, that I strained my lungs by the exertion, and for nearly seven years after could not make any noise at all with my voice."

I let the papers fall into my lap. These words wear me out. They remind me of the days in my childhood when I found my mother in bed, a humidifier steaming on the floor. Sometimes she'd swallow with effort and say, "My throat is raw hamburger." Sometimes she could only whisper, "I'll be fine." She looked so pale without makeup, I hardly recognized her. I could see through her skin as she lay reading Jane Austen or daydreaming with her eyes closed. I knew she wouldn't be able to read to me that night, *Heidi* or *A Wrinkle in Time* or *The Chronicles of Narnia*, or make up the "mouth stories" I loved. When I was old enough to read myself, she kept a pen and a stack of index cards by her sickbed, so she could write notes to me. "How was school?" she wrote in blue ink, or "Would you mind phoning my students to cancel their lessons tomorrow?" I did mind, phone-phobic that I was, but I never said so. I took a deep breath and dialed. I would have done anything for my mother. I sensed, in my childish, vaguely anxious way, that she was emotionally absent from me; I did whatever I could to earn her love.

The season she was supposed to appear as Marian the librarian in *The Music Man*, my mother developed raw-hamburger throat. The mostly Mormon cast decided to hold a special fast for her recovery, which meant no meals and heavy praying for twenty-four hours.

Because I was in the chorus, my father drove me downtown to the theater that night. I'd skipped three meals. Before rehearsal I folded my arms and prayed with the dancers, the chorus, Widow Paroo and Winthrop and the Grecian-urn ladies. I sat on a folding chair in the basement rehearsal room, too hungry to run around with the other chorus kids. I waited for "The Wells Fargo Wagon" scene, as other chorus members walked past me, whispering, "How's your mother?" The same thing happened at church that Sunday. I already knew what to say to the concerned ladies who came up to me in the chapel. After several years of explaining my mother's bouts with laryngitis and colitis, "She'll be fine" had become my standard answer. Luckily for my mother, who had no understudy, she mended quickly. Two weeks later she appeared onstage in her high-necked blouse and cummerbund, chin in the air as she slapped down a stack of library books, Harold Hill breathing down her neck. Her golden voice poured into her body mike and out into the crowded, darkened house.

"I believe stillness affords more relief than any medicine," wrote Catharine's closest friend, Deborah Roberts, as she nursed the invalid in October 1824. I believe my mother needed stillness, more than even she knew. Her life was consumed by performance, in her studio, in church meetings, or on the stage. I don't think it was coincidence that she often lost her voice before a singing engagement. When I entered her sickroom, when I brought her Tang with cayenne pepper or a get-well card I'd made in school, a hush surrounded me. I'd entered a protected space. I know that this is only part of the story; my mother thrived on performance and panicked at the first trickle of drainage in her throat. But when I picture her unmade bed, the glowing lamp and gurgling humidifier, I see the only place—besides her secret dance hall in the basement—that she could call "a room of her own." She carved out a sanctuary the only way she knew how. She must have learned this from her own mother, who, practically homebound with arthritis for more than forty years, stays cloistered in her room until noon every day. When my mother spoke with her recently about her need for inner quiet, my grandmother whispered, "I have that."

Catharine loved to be alone in her room. She found "true happiness," she wrote, "in the cool sequestered shades of silence and mental retirement." I leaf through my photocopies, looking for other phrases I remember from my hurried reading in Hartford. Here. In one of the early high-toned entries, April (or as she called it in Quaker-ese, "4th Month") 1818, she wrote, "Oh, sweet retirement!—thou art my joyful companion." December 27: "Alone as to outward company—I have often remarked that I was never less lonely than when entirely separated from all earthly companions." March 16, 1823: "When shall I cease to be sad and lonely in the midst of company? And when shall I be privileged with the opportunity of indulging in solitude?" A year later she got her wish. In July 1832 she wrote to her friend Eliza, "At times, when in the extremity of pain by noise and light, I am ready to covet the silence and seclusion of the prisoner's dark and lonely cell. Not that seclusion would have been my choice in health."

Or would it? Was that choice socially acceptable for an educated, unmarried young woman in nineteenth-century New England? I don't think so. That Emily Dickinson insisted on it didn't make it any less strange to those around her—or even to many of her modern readers. Her courage astonishes me. In her 1975 essay "Vesuvius at Home," Adrienne Rich writes, "Emily Dickinson—viewed by her bemused contemporary Thomas Higginson as 'partially cracked,' by the twentieth century as fey or pathological—has increasingly struck me as a practical woman, exercising her gift as she had to, making choices." In "Writing and the Threshold Life," poet Jane Hirshfield celebrates this genius who "retired from the public world, changed her clothing to white in a private ritual of status-leaving, and ordained herself into the wholehearted practice of the word." But Dickinson was unusual. Catharine needed permission to enter a "room of one's own." She found it in the confinement of illness and the loss of her voice. In her quiet, darkened room, she was free to think about God and death and human nature, to listen to the voice inside her, and to write the diary I'm reading now. It saddens me to think that my mother, living more than a century later, needed the same permission for privacy.

After my family's return from Germany, I loved my sickroom,

too. I wonder if I wrote about it. I set down my notebook and run down to the basement, into the "Voodoo Room" we named for the staring wooden mask and purple porcelain head we discovered there the day we moved in. The head is still there, under a film of dust. It rests on a bookcase full of red and green binders, my journals from ninth grade through college. And here's one of the novels I tried to write in junior high. I carry a stack of binders upstairs and open my ninth- and tenth-grade journals on the Story Couch. There are the regurgitations, word for word, of my father's political opinions. The Scriptures I copied in green ink, to make them stand out. References to the boy I adored and my secret woman crush. Catalogs of my mother's symptoms. And this note on the day my parents picked up my baby sister from the adoption agency: "So much for being an only child." I wince. (What would Catharine think of her diary were she to read it now?) Scanning the blackboard-perfect cursive, I start to notice the same words again and again, referring not to my mother but to me: "sinus infection," "sore throat," "lost my voice," "chest pain," "virus," "migraine," "flu," and the ubiquitous "cramps." Every few pages, I find the phrase "stayed home from school." I close my eyes and see my adolescent sickroom in our walk-out basement: the rust-colored drapes I pulled shut in daylight, and the door that shut out the noise of my mother's students. There are the novels on the nightstand: *Jane Eyre, Wuthering Heights, The Tenant of Wildfell Hall.* With my own humidifier gurgling on the floor and a jar of Mentholatum next to the bed, I lost myself in moor or ballroom or drafty farmhouse.

My sickroom was a haven for my creative soul. Propped on pillows in the lamplight, I tried to write novels of my own. After my English teacher scolded me for bringing my creative work to class, I did it when I was home sick—or kind of sick. Alone in my room, I filled dozens of notebooks with the fiction that consumed me, a story about an opera singer based on a real woman my mother knew, or a moody saga about a woman named Charlie who lived during the First World War. Hours went by. The sun rose and set behind my closed curtains. I was safe. I could write anything I wanted to. But this, too, is only part of the story.

In the dim light of my sickroom, I read every Brontë novel I could find in the house. I loved spirited Jane, wildcat Catherine, and resolute Helen, who managed to flee an abusive marriage. But as I wrote my own prose, I talked myself more and more into the very social norms I longed to escape. By the time I was thirteen, my writing mirrored the powerlessness I felt as a pubescent girl in upper-middle-class Mormon culture. The opera singer, after struggling to regain her lost voice, got married and became an Angel in the House. In the last scene I wrote for her, she pulled a vacuum cleaner out of the closet. She was doing "the right thing" by choosing domestic hearth over recital hall. Part of me believed this. Almost every week in my young women's class at church, I heard about "the divine role of women," meaning wife- and motherhood. One of my teachers was writer Terry Tempest Williams, then at the beginning of her career, but travel kept her away for weeks at a time, and her example did not stick. I internalized my mother's example—not as the respected singer and voice teacher most people saw, but as the servant wife so anxious to please her husband that she remained, as she puts it now, "a paralyzed child."

I invented the woman named Charlie when I was fourteen. Today I open the blue binder that holds her story. This is the last version I wrote, 317 typed pages with changes scribbled in the margins. Charlie enters her narrative already wounded. Her real name is Simone; her almost-incestuous brother has nicknamed her "after a flying-machine." She is French, and Catholic. In her first scene, she appears in a Protestant church in small-town America, my Currier-and-Ives idea of New England. The words that introduce her are as awkward as she: "a tall figure with narrow stooping shoulders, whose hands played around the edges of the hymnal they held, and whose eyes darted sharply from one end of the chapel to the other." Charlie is the widow of an expatriate American who grew up in this town. She's left her heart in Paris. She can remember dancing with tipsy intellectuals in the Latin Quarter. She's fled the horrors of war. As I thumb through the manuscript, I find the moment when she learns that her brother, Jerome, a pilot taken prisoner by the Germans, is still alive. He joins her in her small-town exile. I find him so shell-shocked he's confined to bed, where he hallucinates and repeats the phrase "It takes so long to die" until it weighs down all the pages I wrote.

Like me after my return from Germany, Charlie feels like an outsider. Speaking of the picturesque town she's escaped to, she says, "Now I see it is only really beautiful to the people who have not gone away." Like my mother in her midthirties, Charlie remains an emotional child. Tom, her unfulfilled love interest in the book, notes this often. On page 177 he remarks to himself, "Sometimes I see the grown woman inside her—and then she goes right back where she was before. And as long as she has her brother, I doubt she'll ever grow up at all." By the end of the book, Charlie is still a tight-mouthed, woman-sized child. The book ends with her brother's ubiquitous whisper: "Why does it take so long to die?"

The binder is heavy in my lap. I'm holding my adolescent burdens all over again. Charlie's story, as I read it now, reflects my ambivalence toward growing up. Her eternal childhood paralyzes her, as my mother's did; at the same time, she and her brother mirror the slow death of the exuberant, androgynous child self I was before my family moved to Germany. Charlie and I even share a name. At three I named myself "Charlie Monkey," baffling the mothers in the neighborhood whose kids I invited to my birthday party. "Does Charlie Monkey live here?" one of them asked my mother on the phone. Just as my family eventually shortened my nickname to "Monk" (because I spent so much time alone in my room?), my fictional Charlie finds herself shrunken and stooped. Monklike herself, she keeps to her small house, all that's left of her late husband's fortune. She is stuck. She cannot outgrow the dead and deranged men in her life. As I fought my own growing up, whatever remained of the daring pilot Jerome in me became a bedridden, hallucinating invalid. I'd been a kind of prisoner in Germany, too. And like Jerome, I did not recover. For me, childhood had meant sailing a ship from my perch on the back porch, or leading expeditions through the neighborhood after school; growing up meant waiting, helpless and mute, for the boy who sat in front of me in English class to turn around and smile. The adventurer in me was replaced, slowly and painfully, by real males who had the power to rescue or dominate. I saw no possibility of equal partnership. I would play victim, invalid, and doll, as convincingly as my mother did.

As I wrote my sad stories at thirteen and fourteen, I pictured my own death-by-adulthood in the language of daydream. I no longer imagined myself as astronaut or chemist or archaeologist, the way I had as a young child. I no longer posed the question I had in my journal at ten: "Should I be an author and an opera singer, or an author and a regular singer?" Now, in the half-sleeping fantasies I nursed in my sickroom, a handsome orchestra conductor rescued a soprano in distress. The scene played over and over in my mind. Though too beautiful to be me, the woman worked as my double. I did not imagine her singing on a stage. I pictured her collapsed on the steps of the Paris Opera, whether from illness or injury I can't remember. Either way, she seemed as helpless as I felt in my matted, unwashed sheets. I saw her lift her face, pale and tear-stained, from the richly carpeted steps. I saw her swaddled in a wedding dress. End of story. In the darkness of my sickroom, I sentenced this woman, and myself, to infantile silence.

I was no Brontë. My juvenilia found no sisterly encouragement. My heroines did not break free of their softly furnished prisons. I stayed ensconced in mine. When I was thirteen, I didn't know that Sandra Gilbert and Susan Gubar had recently published *The Madwoman in the Attic,* their landmark study of the nineteenth-century women writers I loved. It wasn't until my early thirties that I read these words about the Victorian cult of female illness, which sounds eerily like my own bedridden state in the early 1980s: "Any young girl, but especially a lively or imaginative one, is likely to experience her education in docility, submissiveness, self-lessness as in some sense sickening. To be trained in renunciation is almost necessarily to be trained in ill health." No wonder I took to my room. No wonder I daydreamed about a sick or wounded woman. No wonder my mother read *Persuasion* again and again in her sickbed, the story of what Gilbert and Gubar call "an angelically quiet heroine who has given up her search for a story and has thereby effectively killed herself off." My mother could understand this. She had banished her wild dancing to the basement; her upstairs self tried minute by minute to please husband, in-laws, bishop, or director. Our culture accepted her music career because it made her a showpiece for her husband; as an individual woman, she had almost no voice. She learned to mirror other people's opinions, instead of speaking her own. "Oh, isn't that true," she would say. Irrepressibly verbal as a child, she learned as an adult not to talk too much at dinner parties. She nodded and smiled. She dabbed the corners of her mouth with her napkin. She told people whatever they wanted to hear. When she wasn't onstage, she might as well have been mute.

In my sickroom, I lived suspended between my need for creative solitude and the passive silence I had learned from my mother. Still, something in me did long to speak, and not just in my notebooks. When I wasn't silent, I talked to myself. I had done this since I was a child. I'd learned the habit from my father, who would pace his study at night, whispering—from what I could overhear—about God and man, spirit and matter. Sometimes he spoke of these things to me. Most often he spoke to the air. Now, as I paced the floor of my own room, whispering, I imagined a confidante sitting near me under the window. She had no name; she didn't resemble anyone I knew. I could almost see her laughing eyes. She leaned close to hear me. I could almost hear her voice as she answered with a low "Mmmmm." I told her everything.

April 5, 1835. Catharine rests under a white quilt. Sunlight cuts between the closed curtains, touches the faces of two women sitting on a divan, and lays a ragged line across the bed. The women, Catharine's cousins, speak in whispers. One dimples into a smile. The other covers her laughter with one hand. Catharine has been watching them for more than an hour. They don't see her reach for her pencil, her only writing instrument since she became too ill to use pen and ink. She starts to write, and stops. She knows they think her too serious. She wants to ask them to pray with her. How to say it? "Will you not unite with me in earnest petitions . . ." She stops again. How can she express what she's lost and only God can give her back? "The incalculable blessings of the power of speech . . ." She considers her pencil, turning it over in her fingers, and then writes, "I should think I could never again converse with you, or even utter a single sentence with ease." She leans toward her cousins in their crease of light, the note in her hand.

nine openings

When I was a child, my mother made a weekly trip to the drugstore for corks. They came in three sizes: giant, medium, and so small I used them for bug furniture on the patio. My mother kept them inside the piano bench. Several times a day I saw a young woman wiggling her fingers in her mouth, trying to position the cork (usually medium) between her upper and lower molars. If my mother was out of corks, she'd ask the student to stick two fingers in her mouth instead. All of this maneuvering, I figured out, was meant to teach the budding singer to keep her mouth open. "Resonance," my mother said. After the girl with the long red nails swallowed a cork by mistake, I never saw them again.

During my squawking adolescence, I tried to sing with my fingers in my mouth. Maybe *this* would make me sound like myself, the voice I knew I had inside, somewhere. Open, open, open. But now I couldn't sing words. And my tongue got scared of my fingers and curled up in my throat. More lessons with my mother. "Now I think you're pushing a little bit on your high notes," she said, as kindly as she could, or "The voice sounds hollow." She was right. "The voice," not my voice. I tried singing upside down. I tried sticking my fingers in the front of my mouth, instead of the side. "Maybe you need braces," said my mother, noting my cross-bite.

In college my voice teacher told me I was singing from inside a cocoon. She tried to coax me out of it, showing me how to "gasp" my mouth open, teaching me to "play all the resonators" from my skull to the cusps of my teeth. She touched my jaw, my shoulders, my hips. She had me sing with my back against the wall or my sacrum rolled into the piano bench. She gave me movement exercises to connect my left brain with my right. She gave me every possible consonant to sing, to help me feel vibrations in my mouth, nose, and forehead. When I look at the pages of manuscript paper she filled with *vocalises,* I find notes in her sweeping cursive: *Keep walls pushed out! Play your face! Hoot! Air! Vomit!* Then, in red ink, circled in giant capitals, *FUN!* She tried so hard. I tried so hard. But I wasn't even twenty, and not ready to open up.

Ten years later, I stood in an upstairs studio at Sarah Lawrence College. An Atlantic chill blew in through a window stuck half-open. Who knew what else might be blowing around in this room; this building had been the Marshall Field family's summer home, and it was said to be haunted. A friend had told me she'd once seen a woman in a gauzy white dress, gazing at her in the music library late at night. I stood in front of the mantelpiece mirror. I didn't see anything strange. Only myself, as uneasy in my body as a ghost in this world.

Am I a singer? I wondered. I hadn't planned to take voice lessons in graduate school. I was here to write poetry. All I'd done was register for an elective called "Words and Music," and the Music Department head informed me I was required to take private lessons as well. I drove home in a panic. How would I pack *this* into my schedule and find the child care to cover it? Somehow, I did. I sang for a placement audition. I interviewed every member of the vocal faculty, according to Sarah Lawrence tradition, to find the best fit. On the last day of interviews I found my way up to the attic of the Marshall Field building, for my brief—I thought—meeting with tenor Thomas Young. I came out two hours later, so shaken I had to grip the wall on my way downstairs. No other teacher would do.

At my first lesson, Thomas stood behind me, so fully present, he seemed to fill the room. I was learning, or relearning, how to breathe. As air sang through the window, I let it in, enough to push back Thomas's thumbs that rested on my back. I felt like an adolescent at her first voice lesson. Fear rose into my throat. What would happen if I let my feet feel the floor, if I opened my mouth to this October air, if I pushed back Thomas's thumbs with my breath? Would his enormous energy field absorb me? Would I find enough energy in myself to meet him? What would happen if I actually inhabited my body, even for five minutes? I was afraid I might want to stay.

During many lessons with Thomas, all we did was talk. About

Gaugin's first encounter with the colors of Tahiti. About what it means to be an artist who is, as most people suspect, "a freak." "Don't be afraid to be exceptional," Thomas said. We talked about women and men, sexism and racism. We talked about language. Thomas quoted Shakespeare from memory:

Some glory in their birth, some in their skill,
Some in their wealth, some in their bodies' force;
Some in their garments, though new-fangled ill;
Some in their hawks and hounds . . .

Every syllable of the sonnet turned in the air, a gleaming stone I wanted to touch. I found myself wanting to form words of my own in return. What did all this have to do with singing? Everything, I knew, though I didn't yet know why.

One day, after my breath work, Thomas started picking up furniture. Two metal chairs. A floor lamp. Without speaking, he lined them up between us. "This is the barrier you put up when we talked for the first time," he said. "This is what comes between you and your audience."

"I know," I said quietly. I felt my fourteen-year-old fingers crammed in my mouth. The wet cork. Barriers, stopping the flow.

Thomas straddled the piano bench, his hands on his knees. I'd been around voice teachers all my life, but I'd never met one like this. Could I trust him? I wanted to. I listened as he gave me permission to do what I had not been able to since early childhood: "Claim your voice. Claim your body. Claim your language." He gave me a *vocalise:* the sounds of American English, *ma, may, mee, mow, moo.* I remembered singing these syllables for my teacher in college. She'd wanted me to feel the *m* open up in my head. Thomas asked me to let the vowels out into the world. I sang them on one pitch. He asked me to use my mouth to shape each vowel, and not to be afraid of the American diphthongs I'd worked so hard to eliminate when singing Italian or French. We spent five minutes on one note, one syllable. For years, I realized, I'd been neutralizing my vowels for the sake of an open tone. Who knew *mow* held so many colors? I stayed on this low note, I felt the sounds roll in my mouth. "Now you're singing in the core of the voice," Thomas said. "Don't worry about the periphery. Your high notes aren't going anywhere. Work on developing the core, the part of your voice that is closest to the range of speech." Then he added something I'd never thought I could believe, after my mother's attempts to take me to a speech pathologist: "You have a low, rich speaking voice. Start there."

I understood at last. *The range of speech.* Singing was not so different from our long talks in the studio. "Sing to express, not to impress," Thomas said. And I'd spent most of my life fretting about my jaw and tongue and soft palate, about the "right way" to make sound, and what people would think of me when I opened my mouth. I hadn't even considered what I could say to them.

That night I sat down at my piano and sang a scale. I started on the G below middle C and moved up through my speaking range. I sang in open chest, letting my sound resonate below my collarbone. This was the sound my college voice teacher had called "heavy mechanism." I'd never been able to do it without forcing the tone. No, there had been one time: a funeral, where I'd sung "Amazing Grace." And another time, recently, when I'd sung the first song in a Schumann cycle with Kate, whose music was in a lower key than I expected. But after that I hadn't been able to reclaim the soul voice buried in my chest. Now I could. *I sound like a big mama,* I said inwardly, *and I like it.* I sang the American vowels Thomas had modeled for me. I sang the first line of a song by Ned Rorem, a setting of Theodore Roethke's "Night Crow." The first notes came out rich and full. But now, when I tried to reach into my middle zone, I felt I'd entered foreign territory. Whose voice was this? I remembered what Thomas had said the week before, quoting Miles Davis: "It takes a lifetime to sound like yourself."

At my next lesson, I pulled "Night Crow" from my bag. But Thomas didn't want me to sing it, not yet. He stood facing me in front of the window. "I want you to speak the first line," he said. *When I saw that clumsy crow / Flap from a wasted tree* . . . "No. Close your eyes. See what is happening." I tried. "No." I tried again. And again, and again. "What's the most important word in the phrase?"

I switched on my poet mind: *Flap*. Thomas nodded. I spoke the line again. This time, something opened in my body. I felt the crow break from the branch. Thomas's face lit up. With one finger, he drew the shape of a triangle on his chest. He opened the imaginary window. "When you sing," he said, "you reveal."

chant

The Zuni of New Mexico tell a story about a woman who disappears into a flute. The tale goes like this. Long ago, a flute player named Nepayatamu journeyed through the desert on his way to the eastern sea. He was gifted; he could summon the spirits with a hollow cottonwood branch. All along his journey, he stopped by the rivers and streams and made flutes from the trees' branches. A woman walked beside him. She did not speak, and she carried no flute. People said that Nepayatamu had raped her and that she had cut off his head, which a medicine man had sealed back to his body. The couple walked in silence. They followed the river past White Rocks and Wind Place, past the place Where the Bottle Gourd Stands on Top, past the river's fork to the place called Striped House, in the cottonwoods and willows. The woman was tired. Nepayatamu sat down next to her and sucked her into his flute. Then he gathered up his breath and began to play. Out of the holes in the flute flew a swarm of white moths.

When I came to Zuni Pueblo as an eleven year old, I'd never heard this story. I didn't know the ancient names for landmarks on the desert plateau: White Rocks, Wind Place, Hanging Wool, Circling Water, Hanging Mealbag. I didn't know that where the Zuni and the Little Colorado Rivers meet, pilgrims have reported hearing the faint voices of kachinas, spirits singing under the Whispering Waters. I didn't know what the Zuni know, that there are many states of being between the dry surface of the land and the moist, mossy world of spirits, animals, and newborn children. I didn't have the words to say that I was only half alive. Since my family's return from Germany six months before, I felt as though someone had turned off the tap to my emotions. I couldn't even look forward to Christmas.

On a day in mid-December, I found myself on the outskirts of the pueblo. I had traveled in a twin-engine plane with my parents and my father's law partner, who would later take the Zuni land-claims lawsuit to federal court. We landed on a windy airstrip surrounded by pinyon and juniper—a surprise after our last stop, the red desert floor at the base of the Hopi mesas in eastern Arizona. The day before, we had hiked to a Hopi village with Hal, the plane's pilot, who knew by name the women looking at us from their dark doorways, offering pottery for sale. He told us stories of young men who returned to the village after being schooled in Flagstaff or Phoenix, how they jumped to their deaths from the edge of the mesa. I stood in the wind and imagined one of them falling. A hole in the air. Then my body falling. The wind cried with a woman's voice. The red ground below me looked soft. I wondered if I would feel it.

Today, while my father and his partner met with the tribal council, Hal introduced my mother and me to Zuni Pueblo. A tribal official dropped us off behind some adobe houses. When I opened the car door, a scent assaulted me. Hal said it was pinyon smoke. I opened my mouth, wanting to taste it. I smelled it everywhere in the almost-cold December air, as we walked past three turquoise shops, more adobe houses cluttered with TV antennas and laundry hung out to dry, and mud ovens called *hornos,* where women stood in twos or threes, baking bread. Bundles of pinyon wood lay in front of the houses. Smoke rose from the ovens, shimmering in the blue air. I walked behind Hal and my mother. I heard the crunch of my shoes on the dirt. I breathed pinyon smoke. I watched Corn Mountain mesa change color in the distance, as a cloud passed between it and the sun. I wanted to stay here forever. For the first time since our return from Germany, I felt alive. The day we'd moved back into our house in Salt Lake City, I'd looked out the east kitchen window, expecting the sun to blare in my eyes with the promise of a summer day. The sun hung over the mountains, as usual, but it didn't reach me. *It's like a curtain has come down,* I thought. A curtain between me and the world. For months I moved through the house and through the halls at school, hardly speaking. I felt stuck in a shape that surrounded the shape of my body, a casing invisible to everyone else. I didn't know the word *depression.* I didn't know the Zuni story of the wounded, silent woman who finds herself caught in a cottonwood flute.

Today I stood in front of the adobe church, Our Lady of Guadalupe. It looked soft and alive. Its two spires seemed to grow out of the ground. "Do you want to see inside?" Hal asked, and I nodded. My father had told me about the Zunis' blending of religions in this church. As we walked in, I saw on both walls an unfinished mural of Zuni kachinas, masked human figures wearing skins and feathers. Underneath these life-size figures hung small framed pictures of the Stations of the Cross. Rain Priest. Jesus. Little Fire God. Jesus. I wasn't interested in the pictures of the Cross. I stared at the kachinas with their brilliant feathered masks. Many of them held rhythm instruments in their hands, and I could almost hear them rattling. If I looked away for half a second, I thought, one of the six-foot-tall figures might move. I sat down on a wooden pew and tried not to blink. One kachina, a warrior, wore a collar of crow feathers that hid his face. Another wore mountain lion skins over his right shoulder. Some held pinyon branches or prayer sticks. A female rain dancer (a man dressed as a woman, Hal said) wore white feathers on her blue, slit-eyed mask. An unfinished human face, wrinkled and severe, looked out of the pale plaster. None of these figures frightened me, like the life-size crucifixes I'd seen in Europe. I'd once had a kachina doll, white-masked, black-feathered, that my father brought home from a trip to Zuni. I'd talked to it. I'd moved it in rhythm to the cassette tape of ceremonial chant that one of the law firm's expert witnesses had made. I remembered the pulsing voices, singing from memory. My father had explained that real kachina spirits no longer visit Zuni Pueblo but can enter through the people who wear masks and perform sacred dances. He said these dancers become messengers between the living and the dead, and between "cooked" human civilization and the "raw" forces of nature. Today, as I watched them ready to leap from the walls, I missed my kachina doll. I'd lost it somewhere between Salt Lake and Frankfurt, somewhere on my own journey from childhood to this numb, half-living state.

"Do you want to see some live kachinas?" Hal asked. He must have seen me staring at the dancers on the mural. I nodded again.

My mother and I followed him outside, through a narrow passage between adobe houses, and into the plaza, where the whole community had gathered for the winter solstice ceremony. Hal explained that this festival occasion, called Sha'La/Ko', brings six bird-headed kachinas, men chosen by the kiva leaders, to the pueblo. They stay with host families in the village and perform hours-long prayers and dances to bring abundance to the land. "Watch, the kachinas will throw gifts of food to the Zuni people," Hal whispered to me.

I stood on the edge of the plaza. The shade chilled me. If I stretched out one hand, I could feel the square of sun that illuminated the kachina dancers on the plaza. Drums pounded. The sound seemed to come from under my feet. My father had once told me it sounded like the heartbeat of the earth. I watched the kachinas, pelts and feathers and pinyon branches flying. Some were taller than any human being I'd seen. I couldn't tell the dead from the living, the human from the bird. Voices chanted. Feet hammered the ground. The rhythm beat deeper and deeper into the invisible casing around me. I felt with my whole body. I wanted to open my mouth as the chant accelerated. The dancers flung their gifts into the air. Ears of corn flew overhead, children screamed and darted after them, the drums heaved *one two three four one two three four,* and a package of Twinkies landed at my feet. I was as quiet as a moth.

passaggio

Kate has left her back door open. She'll be home soon. I walk through the hallway and into the living room, where I leaf through the music on her Steinway: Schubert and Brahms, the first songs we learned together in Connecticut. She's been sorting through music, looking for some Schumann we want to learn. I sit down and set the Brahms in front of me. A song called "Immer leiser wird mein Schlummer," "Ever Softer Grows My Sleep." We once performed it for a master class with pianist Dalton Baldwin, who leaned over the keyboard, hummed the melody with great feeling and said, "Remember, this is a Hungarian lament." I hear his humming as I start to play.

"Brahms!" comes Kate's voice from the back door. "Wasn't there something hard about that song?" Soon she's sitting on the piano bench, playing the music her fingers still remember. I come in halfway through the first line. The sound washes through me and out into her living room, which resonates like a church. The hard part, a delicate, syncopated phrase that is not only supposed to be sung pianissimo but also lies in my *passaggio,* comes out of my mouth without thought. When I sing the high note, it blooms. The song is part of me now. "Now *where* was the hard part?" Kate says when we finish, laughing.

I think back five years to our first rehearsal together. It was nothing like this. My family had just moved to Stamford, and I'd started commuting to Sarah Lawrence a week later. I'd phoned Kate one day to ask about piano tuners, "because you seem like the kind of person who would own a piano." She said, "Oh, I have two!" Shortly after that she called, without even having heard my voice, to ask if I wanted to sing for the Dalton Baldwin master class. I sank, speechless, into my bed. I'd listened to recordings of this pianist, playing French songs with my favorite singers, for years. I'd heard him called the finest accompanist in the world. But I hadn't sung a note in six months. I hadn't planned on using my voice at all during graduate school. There were more than enough singers in this part of the country (my mother had always said, "Drop a dime from any building in Manhattan and it will land on a soprano"), and I was supposed to be writing poetry. Besides, I'd just had a baby and moved three thousand miles. Who knew what would come out when I opened my mouth?

I said yes.

Several days later, we met at my condo to practice. Kate came loaded with flowers, tomatoes, and corn from the Stamford farmers' market. She wore a bright-yellow sweat suit. Entering our condo, where the washer and refrigerator had just shut down, where Kent spent hours on the phone looking for work, where the baby was refusing his bottles when I went to school, she brought more cheer than she knew. She sat down to play the Brahms while I cut the huge-headed zinnias and sunflowers and arranged them in a vase. I put off singing for as long as I could.

"Okay, I'm ready," I said. I didn't feel ready at all, though I'd warmed up my voice earlier in the day. Kate played my pitch: the C above middle C, the note I'd dreaded since I was eleven. I opened my mouth and wavered on the first note. I heard German words, but they didn't seem to come from my body: *Ever softer grows my sleep* . . . My voice was asleep, though my brain had known this song for years. I was singing in a fog. *Often in dreams I hear you calling out-side my door.* . . . The voice sounded far away. Then came the tricky syncopation, which Kate counted out again and again. *No one wakes and opens for you* . . . I was sure she regretted having asked me to sing.

We met the next week at her house, where I stood on the doorstep, listening to her piano inside, listening to the rain on the rhododendron leaves, not ready to knock on the dark-red door. I wanted to stay in this moment. I felt I was coming home to some-thing. Even if I couldn't do Brahms justice, I wanted to be here. Kate opened the door, looking so glad to see me that I knew it didn't matter if my voice sounded glorious or not. She asked if I'd brought any poetry. I had, and she opened her hands to take it. She had a stack of papers for me, too: poems she'd photocopied, a recipe for cranberry caramel cake, a review of a vocal recital at Carnegie Hall. We sat down and talked. We ate strawberries, juice staining our fingers. An hour later, when Kate sat down to play, Brahms's Hun-garian lament flowed into the room. I wasn't afraid. I put my music down and sang from memory. This time the sound came from inside my body because, though I could hardly believe it, Kate knew who lived there.

From that day on, we were never without a musical project. My new friend became the first reader for all my work. I showed her poems I'd thought I could never let out into the world. We went to concerts and walked on the beach. As we talked late one night in her car, she asked about my grandparents, and kept asking; I started to spill my family's story and could not stop. In Kate's presence, my frightened heart opened. When she became seriously ill with pneu-monia and then with an infection in her leg, I was beside myself. But her illness—and a string of cancelled classes at Sarah Lawrence—gave

us the luxury of time: I brought food and books into her ro
where we spent long afternoons catching up on all the years
hadn't known each other. This sickroom was a place of comfort a __
renewal. As Kate's health improved, we confided, we laughed, we
read poetry aloud. "Friends forever," we promised. After Kate's hus-
band retired and mine lost his job, we moved to Salt Lake at the
same time. The coincidence seemed inevitable.

Often in dreams I hear you calling outside my door. No one wakes
and opens for you. I wake and weep bitterly. These words have been
part of me for so many years that I can't remember exactly when I
first encountered them. Tonight, as I sing in Kate's house deep in a
canyon above Salt Lake City, as night air blows in through the win-
dow, the words take on more meaning. Until we met, I was full of
closed doors. In my midtwenties I had found the courage to work
and to go to graduate school; my sons had broken me open with
more love than I'd thought possible; but I had not felt truly known.
If anyone stood outside and called to the singer in me, the poet in
me, the deepest soul in me, I rarely heard. I did not reveal to anyone
my heart full of hurts. Now that I have, I can ask why it took me so
long, and why, sometimes, I still resist. If I am to understand my
own history of silence, I have to become a *passaggio,* that word that
means both corridor and journey. I have to move backward and try
all the doors.

After music and talk and ice cream with Kate and her husband,
who has kindly shared his favorite Häagen Dazs with me, I start for
home. As I drive down the canyon, dark mountain slopes rising on
either side of the road, I start down the passageway in my mind.
When was the first time I heard Brahms's "Immer leiser"? It must
have been in my college voice teacher's studio on the top floor of the
music building, always too hot, even in winter. Was it the day I read
through the song and gave up, my voice tired at the end of a lesson?
No, I must have heard it before. I remember I'd brought the photo-
copied music from home. Yes. I did hear the song in that building—
from outside the same studio. I can see the windowless hallway, echo-
ing with students' voices. I sat on a folding chair outside the door,
waiting for my mother to finish her lesson. She was in graduate

school. I must have been twelve. She was studying with the same teacher she'd had since high school, who retired before my teacher moved into that studio. I could hear the accompanist give my mother her pitch. She started to sing the longing, swinging melody. I remembered enough German to know that the poem was about someone in a sickroom, waiting for death to turn her "pale and cold," waiting for a loved one to come to the door. *Come, oh come soon!* And here I sat outside the studio door, as I'd sat outside my mother's real-life sickroom two years before in Germany. How and when did the doors start closing?

To find the answer, I move further down the passage, down to the last glimmer of my childhood, light under a door. Down the dark hallway that took up most of our duplex in Germany. Doors on both sides: furnace room, kitchen, my bedroom, my parents' room. My father tried to make it seem more cheerful by naming it Badger's End, after that curmudgeonly creature's house in *The Wind in the Willows*. It didn't work. Often my mother stayed in bed all day, sick from the mold that crept from the woods into our window wells and walls. I sat in my room and looked out the window at the pines that loomed overhead. The girl next door had told me not to go in the woods in October; tiny spiders would fall from the trees and into your clothes and you'd have a rash forever. I wanted to ask her to play stuffed animals with me, but somehow I knew she wasn't interested in pretending. So I looked up through my basement window. The clouds never seemed to move. The girl's family, who lived upstairs where light could reach them, played the BeeGees and *The Sound of Music* and spoke in perky tones whenever we saw them.

Another neighbor, also from Salt Lake City, often appeared on our doorstep to take us swimming or shopping, anything to make my mother feel more at home. For a while, until she and her husband moved back to the States, she made me feel more at home, too. I liked her big voice and her easy laugh. She was the first person I'd met who wasn't afraid to talk about sex and death and miracles, even when she knew I could hear. I listened from the hallway as she sat at the kitchen table with my mother, confiding and telling stories. My mother shared no secrets of her own; she simply listened. I overheard fragments of our neighbor's musings and narratives: "I think my son is getting too old to sleep in my bed . . . so lonely when my husband's traveling. . . . When we first came here, I couldn't speak a word of German . . . you know how people talk about the 'gift of tongues'? Well, I found myself having this conversation in German, and somehow the woman understood me." Sometimes the words made my heart pound. "I was the only one who could dress the body for the funeral. . . . I'd never met this woman. . . . They found my mother hanging from a tree . . . her handkerchief. . . . During the war he was in a prison camp with nothing to eat . . . still keeps an apple by his bed. . . . The women came back to the village to find all the men hanging from telephone poles." I walked down the hall to my room and, trembling, shut the door. I picked up the green Utah shape I'd cut out from my atlas, and pictured the maple-lined streets of my neighborhood back home. The grape hyacinth that invaded our garden in the spring. The orange-red berries that had kept me alive on my jungle island. The corner where I'd dug four feet down, hoping for bones. The porch where I'd perched, dressed in overalls with two lacy dresses on top, playing princess and ship's captain all at once. The stairs where I'd listened to my mother practicing. The basement room where my friend and I had built tents for our stuffed animals as they journeyed across the Arabian desert. I was in my own desert now. I'd left my childhood, adventurous and protected at the same time, forever. The world was a darker place than I'd ever imagined, and I was in it alone. *No one comes and opens for you . . .*

One day after school, our neighbor was waiting for me inside the door. "Your mom was going to have a baby, but she lost it," she said. "Your dad's at the hospital. He'll come get you later." And then she left.

I found myself in the dark hallway. I paced up and down, my hands over my face, a hard black thing in my stomach, ready to explode. I already knew my mother was going to have a baby. I'd listened to my father talking to the doctor on the phone, and then telling my mother to stay in bed. I hadn't asked her about it. I'd said no when she asked me to get her a drink. I hadn't spoken to her when I'd come home from school. I'd sat outside her sickroom, afraid to go in, afraid to go anywhere else. I hadn't wanted that baby, the one my mother had longed for since my birth, the absent one I thought she really loved—and now I'd killed it. I paced the hallway until the sun went down, and it got even darker. For a while I sat on the toilet and sobbed. The black thing in my stomach rose higher and higher but wouldn't come out. I said nothing to my father when he picked me up. We drove to the hospital in silence. As my mother reached out to me from her narrow bed, I stayed near the window. I didn't hear her voice. I looked out at the night-lit city, which my parents said had been "ravaged" in the war. Words wouldn't come out of my mouth.

Soon we moved next door to an upstairs unit. Less mold, bigger windows, but still the long dark hallway between the kitchen and our bedrooms. And still my mother lay in bed, her nose and throat so infected that she could hardly breathe.

No one wakes and opens for you. No one wakes and opens for you. I didn't open the sickroom door. I closed my door and studied my mother's French grammar book in secret. I closed my door and built elaborate tents for my stuffed animals. No one shared my fantasy. Even when my mother felt well enough to cook or plan church activities for the teenage girls she was assigned to teach, I shut her out. "I want to talk to you about how babies are made," my mother said. I ran down the hall and shut myself in my room. "I have a confession to make. I just read the story you've been writing," my mother said. I ran down the hall and slammed the door. I buried the story, meticulously typed, in the mess under my bed. "What are you writing now?" my mother wanted to know. I shut the door and went on writing my script for *The Marriage of Figaro,* based on the school library's *Opera Stories for Children.* "Would you like to clean your room this week?" my mother ventured. I shut the door and curled up on my bed as ants scattered over the carpet, which I hadn't vacuumed in more than a month.

Sometimes I came out of my room. I eavesdropped as my parents talked. *Bureaucracy . . . bureaucracy . . .* That cold word, hidden in the soft word *Mormon.* I heard it over and over. My father, like all the other fathers on our street, worked in the church offices in

Frankfurt. I didn't like to go there, though the secretaries, young women from England and Germany, were kind to me. I didn't like to go to church in our American military congregation, either. The familiar songs about God's house and the Holy Ghost didn't soothe me anymore. Now that I was old enough to attend the "Merrie Miss" class for girls, my teacher expected me to complete a sewing project once a month. I stuffed the cotton sampler under my bed. I shut the door.

I came out of my room to take the long bus ride to the International School, whenever I didn't have a sore throat, real or imagined. I came out to eat. And to pace the floor in the bathroom, trying to get up the nerve to change my blood-soaked paper towels. I sat in the hall, listening, when my mother was well enough to sing. She sang the same Schubert song over and over, a Goethe setting, "To the Moon." Did she sing the Brahms song then? I don't think so, though I might have heard the melody as I sat in the corner of the living room, my ear pressed to the speaker of my father's stereo. He loved Wagner and Richard Strauss, but especially Brahms. I remember hearing the "Immer leiser" melody, sometime in high school, in one of Brahms's piano concertos. I remember knowing I'd heard it before.

Which concerto, the first or second? Tonight, home from Kate's house, I sit writing at the computer after midnight. I slide a CD into the machine and put on headphones, so I won't wake the boys in the next room. Maurizio Pollini playing the first piano concerto. I listen to the slow movement: no familiar melody. I put in the second disc, Concerto no. 2. It begins with a kind of entreaty, played by a French horn. My father may well have played this on his stereo in Germany. He'd sold his horn before we moved, and I know he missed it. I click away at the keyboard. Did Brahms write this out of longing for Clara Schumann? Or simply to explore the passage between major and minor keys? As I listen I can smell our humid living room in the Frankfurt suburbs. I can see the hazy sky outside, the top-heavy pines, the mustard and puke-green row houses down the hill, and in the distance the train tracks and the Nidda River. I can hear the children playing in the street. Words appear on the screen. I stop, my brain sticking in place. A silence. Now the third movement, andante, unusual for a piano concerto to have four movements. . . . And then I hear it. *Ever softer grows my sleep* . . . Our Hungarian lament, played by the strings, then by a single cello. This version breaks apart after the first phrase. I can't wait to tell Kate. She'll want to know which was written first, the concerto or the song. I check the CD jacket. This is opus 83. The song that has shadowed me through the passage from childhood to adulthood was written later, part of opus 105. What I'm hearing is the germ, longing without words. The music circles back to this principal theme again and again. I circle back to Kate's canyon house, to her rain-damp doorstep in Connecticut, to the corridor outside the studio where my mother sang, to the duplex in Germany, the hallway of closed doors. Does the story reach back further?

I close my eyes. I see my mother sitting across from me in the therapist's office. We've come to learn how to speak to each other. It's a recent memory: I can see my mother looking straight at me, her eyes full of tears. I can see myself, turned partially away from her, my voice sticking in my throat as I try to name my hurt. The counselor has to remind me to say "you" instead of "she." Now this gentle-voiced woman turns to my mother and asks, "How did your daughter hurt you?"

My mother faces me. She speaks to me directly. "When you were little, I used to play with you and your friends. I wanted to be close to you, but I didn't know how to be a mother. When you were about seven, you started closing your bedroom door. You asked me not to come in without knocking, a perfectly appropriate thing to ask. But it hurt me. I felt like an intruder. I'd felt like an intruder growing up, too, because my older sister was the queen, and my mother was so ill."

I don't remember the first time I shut the door to my room. I don't remember my mother playing with my friends and me. All I remember is feeling, as I talked to myself in my room as a child, that no one in the world knew my heart. *Sometimes in dreams I hear you calling outside my door. No one wakes and opens for you.* My mother and I have been singing this song all our lives, all those years we were too disconnected from ourselves to love and be loved; we're singing it even in this moment, when I have to move through thick inertia to turn my body toward her. I can hear her saying, "I want to know you." Our common wound. The door at the end of the passage, which we both want to open but don't yet know how.

conversation

I found the broom in the laundry room. I carried it, bigger than I was, across the basement hallway and to the shut door of my father's study. I looked one more time at the note I held in my other hand, words scratched in my second-grade hand-writing: *Dear Dad, I am very sorry.* I laid the note on the threshold, which was wide enough for light to come through. I pushed it under with the broom, as far into my father's sanctum sanctorum as it would go.

I don't remember what naughtiness prompted this formal apology. I do remember my father's silent retreat down the stairs, and my mother's whisper: "I think you hurt your dad's feelings." The sting of embarrassment went right through my skin to my bones. How could I have committed such an offense? I idolized my father. I thought he was the handsomest, smartest person in the world. I loved the way he talked to me about politics and Greek philosophy, as though I actually understood. I loved our Sunday walks at the university, when I would struggle to keep up with his brisk pace as he told me his plans for a new work schedule, a new house, a trip to Rome, plans that rarely became reality but that sounded wonderful to me. Now my father was giving me the same silence he gave my mother, whether because he was in a particularly black mood or because she'd spent too much money, I was never sure. Apologizing face-to-face did not seem like an option to me.

My father never commented on the note. I have never wanted to tell this story. But if I am to follow the passage backward into the shut doors of my childhood, I can't ignore this one. For years it kept me from speaking a word to my father about my emotional life. It set the stage for my marriage.

Once when I was in high school, my mother said, speaking of my father's parents, "Grandma hates it when Grandpa gives her the silent treatment." So that's what it was called. In the house where I grew up, the silence went both ways—Dad in his locked study, Mom tiptoeing through the house, not sure what she'd done wrong, trying to make her offensive self disappear. I don't think my father was chemically depressed. I believe his depression was a literal pushing under of his true passions. He controlled himself, and his environment, with silence.

If it's true that people find partners who expose the work they must do in order to grow, I found someone whose silences asked me, though I didn't know it at first, to learn to break them. In the apartments and houses where Kent and I spent the first decade of our marriage, we played out the same pattern my parents had during my childhood—but with me behind the locked door. In our first apartment, I chose the bathroom. Like my adolescent sickroom, it served as both refuge and escape. When Kent sulked because I'd left crumbs on the counter or forgotten to shop with coupons, his silence filled the rooms like water. The bathroom door was the only one with a lock. I stayed in there to stem the flood. Before my wedding, my mother's only words of wisdom had been "You'll cry every day for the first year." I did.

Kent had warned me, before our engagement, "I'm a tightwad and a control freak." I hadn't taken him seriously. I'd simply laughed when he told me that, as a Mormon missionary in Norway, he had insisted his companions obey every mission rule to the nth degree. I didn't know Kent's family well enough to see how much pressure he'd felt to clean the bathtub just so, and how much he depended on the security of a predictable home life. I didn't know myself well enough to see the absentminded way I drifted through the world, as my own mother did. I didn't realize that I'd never learned to deal with conflict, in a family that denied having any. And then there was Kent's depression, the dark tide inherited from his Norwegian grandmother, who would sit in silence in her chair for hours at a time. Kent did not show the classic signs of depression—emotional numbness, sleeping all day—and so neither of us recognized the ill-

ness, though his mother and sisters had recently gone on
When I offended Kent's frugal sensibilities or failed to meet h
for control, he could not pull himself out of his spiral of self-p
believed, as he tells me now, "it was just a personality defect" _____ ___
could overcome with enough willpower and trust in God. He recently showed me a journal entry from ten years ago, in which he
vented his anger at me for "being too free with postage" and, at the
same time, admonished himself not to give into these negative
thoughts. "I wish I had more faith!" he wrote.

The first time I found him in an impenetrable sulk, I was as
stunned as I'd been the day my father retreated to his study after my
childhood offense. *This* was the man I loved for his humor and gentleness? This was the man I'd married because I felt at ease with him?
This was the man I thought adored me? I forgave him this time, because that was easier than speaking my mind. But the more he withdrew, the more I closed my heart and only pretended to forgive. My
mother had been right: you got married, you cried every day, and
then you just got used to it.

In the privacy of our prewar bathroom with its chipped mirror
and blackened grout, I developed a saving ritual. I had just finished
reading Willa Cather's *Song of the Lark* for a college literature class.
The first time I'd read the novel, in junior high, I had not appreciated the heroine's journey into independent selfhood as an opera
singer. This time, the story burned me. During slow periods at work,
I memorized passages in the book. My favorite chapter was "The
Ancient People," in which Thea Kronborg spends slow days alone in
a cliff-dweller canyon in Arizona, splashing in a cottonwood-
screened pool, or lying in a sunny, windswept rock room, her body
filling with "fragrance and color and sound" as it empties of her life's
cultural accumulations: "Here she must throw this lumber away. The
things that were really hers separated themselves from the rest. Her
ideas were simplified, becoming sharper and clearer. She felt united
and strong."

Alone in the bathroom, I thought these words as I took off my
clothes and Mormon undergarments. One night, despite my grandmother's warning to never, ever remove my wedding ring, I did. I

laid it on the edge of the sink. I knew it could fall in and swirl down the drain. ("How could you be so careless?" my great-grandmother had scolded her daughter-in-law, early in her marriage, for doing the same thing—the scarring event that must have prompted Grandma's warning to me. Maybe she had taken off her wedding ring because she longed to escape the silent treatment, too.) Without my lovely marquise setting, I felt united and strong, like Thea Kronborg alone in her canyon room. I looked at myself in the mirror. Kent's silence couldn't reach me here. This was the one place in the world where I could be truly myself. From that night on, I took my ring off every time I had a bath. And every night, I stood in front of the mirror and saw a person I knew, as free as a child, belonging to no one. Some nights I opened my mouth and pretended to sing.

Outside the bathroom, I played the part my mother had in the first decades of her marriage, and tried to disappear. I tiptoed. I packed Kent's lunches. Sometimes I wrote him a note of apology and left it on his pillow. Sometimes we spent hours talking on the couch, the same conversation over and over for years: I pried out of him what I'd done to offend; he listed five or six things that had "built up" in the past few days; I promised to do better; he told me he didn't want me to have to promise, he wanted me to do these things because I loved him. Afterward, enraged and mute, I'd lock myself in the bathroom and weep until I felt strong enough to wrench the ring from my finger.

In our decade of silence, we did try to break the habit. One day, after we'd been married a year and a half, I phoned Kent at work and told him, my voice trembling, that I'd no longer make his lunches for him. "I resent it," I said. "I feel like my mother." He said this made him sad, but he could accept it. He did not sulk. Many times Kent told me he wouldn't hold me back, couldn't, in fact, from accomplishing whatever lifework I wanted to do. We had times of great tenderness: our quiet days together after each of our sons was born; our move across the country, after Kent left his job to support me in school; the days we walked Manhattan, juggling our boys in stroller and backpack. Kent fought hard against his neglected-child feelings when he saw me taking more and more pleasure in my graduate

studies. And sometimes, when he gave in to his depressive's rese
silence, I actually spoke my mind. "If I love my work, it doe
mean I don't love you," I said more than once. But most of the ti.
I gave up trying to speak and retreated further into my own silence,
and into the late-night writing that consumed me. Again and again,
Kent tried to conquer his inner darkness by sheer willpower. Again
and again, no matter how he prayed or studied the Scriptures or did
his temple work, all the things he'd been taught would solve any
problem, the darkness conquered him. We were on the way to fulfilling each other's worst fears.

For years I told no one about the paralyzing hurts in my marriage. I couldn't tell my parents, my closest friend from high school,
or several younger cousins who married shortly after I did, also just
out of their teens. We didn't know we shared the same secret unhappiness. "I was so ashamed," one of them tells me now. "I didn't
think it would be appropriate to say anything." Now my cousins and
I talk freely, in my kitchen or via e-mail, about the fear, anger, and silence we lived with for so long. One decided she was worth more
than the family's good name, gathered all the courage she had, and
left her emotionally abusive husband. She is now finishing a Ph.D. in
women's history, with a supportive second husband by her side. Another has struggled, like me, to mend a marriage that started with
what she called, in a recent e-mail, "newlywed hell."

Kent and I reached a crisis in December 2001. I have blocked
out of my mind the item I forgot to bring to a family gathering at his
parents' house. He met me when I pulled into the driveway. One
look at him and I remembered what I'd left at home; one look at me
and he withdrew. I knew we wouldn't speak for hours. "I'll go back
and get it," I said through my teeth. I backed the car into the icy
street, spinning the tires. All the way home, as sleet hit the wind-
shield, I pushed the gas as hard as I could. I ran two red lights. I
swerved onto the freeway. I longed to spin out of control and into
oblivion. Why my tires gripped the black ice, I still don't know. For
the first time in my life, I was willing to end it all; the second I saw
this, I knew it was time to speak up or leave my marriage. I wanted
to survive.

The next night, Kent and I sat in the car in a parking garage, late for his office Christmas party. I told him I couldn't live with him this way. I told him I thought he was depressed. I told him we both needed help. I asked him to go to the doctor and come with me to counseling. I told him I could not stay unless we tried this. The words fell out of my mouth like pieces of broken glass. I thought of our boys at home with their sitter, expecting us to be there when they woke up. I knew one of us might not be. Kent reached across the parking brake and took my hand. "I've tried for so long to fix this by myself, and I can't anymore," he said. "I'll do anything."

The next week he saw his doctor, who diagnosed depression and wrote out a prescription. In the month it took for the Prozac to take effect, we had more dark days than ever. But just when I thought the silence in our house might crush us both, it began to lift. "Hey, I didn't get mad at you this time," Kent said after I'd worked late at the computer two nights in a row. I realized I looked forward to seeing him at the end of the day. Some troubling side effects took Kent back to the doctor, who tried another antidepressant; here came another adjustment period, and more downward spirals. One night we sat on the Story Couch and talked about divorce. I spent a long, silent moment staring at the dining-room table. I pictured the house without me, or without Kent. I pictured our boys being driven from parent to parent, their sleepover bag and favorite stuffed dogs between them in the backseat. I remembered our "Prozac month" and how at ease we'd felt together, for the first time since our courtship. Something like hope surfaced inside me, though I still shook when I said, "I want to try to stay together."

The second antidepressant had no effect at all. Kent went back on Prozac, willing to endure stomach discomfort, sleepless nights, and unending drowsiness at work. Since then, his doctor has changed his dosage several times and tried a number of medications to alleviate the side effects. Kent has found a psychiatrist who takes the time to thoroughly research his case. We've read books on depression and begun to understand how complex and difficult to treat it can be. Unlike some sufferers, Kent has found an antidepressant that gives him enough psychological autonomy to say, "I could let this get me down, but I won't." An insightful counselor has helped Kent let go of his need to control, and has given me tools to speak authentically to him.

Tonight, I emerge from the bathroom warm and wet-haired. "It sounded like a committee meeting in there," Kent says, looking up from his newspaper. I laugh. He knows what I do when I retreat to my sanctuary for a bath: I memorize music while splashing in the claw-foot tub; I meditate while sitting on the toilet in my towel; I speak lines of poetry, trying for the right rhythm. The bathroom is still my refuge, but no longer an escape. I go in after Kent and I have had our nightly talk on the Story Couch, something we rarely did—except to have our what-did-I-do-this-time conversation—during our years of hostile silence. We've created this structure for our relationship at the suggestion of our counselor. Now, after the boys are in bed, we sit together and discuss the day. If I've done the shopping that week and haven't used a single coupon, Kent no longer withdraws. He has bigger things on his mind—a client's heavy sentence, our son's playground crisis, our plans for the weekend. Now, in those rare moments when the old silence rises in our house, I fight the temptation to cower and tiptoe. Recently, after I told Kent his silent treatment was unacceptable behavior, he thanked me. "You don't know how it helps me when you speak up," he said. I told him it had taken me my whole life to learn how.

silence

"I need to talk to you about something," my mother said.

I knew what was coming. I skulked into the bathroom, where she stood in front of the mirror, swirling dark foundation over her face and down her neck. She used her fourth finger, the weakest, to keep from wrinkling the skin around her eyes. I knew she'd look like a different person when she was done. "What?" I said, trying not to sound resentful.

"I think you said something inappropriate in church yesterday." My mind scrambled back twenty-four hours—summer heat in the Sunday-school classroom where I'd sat with the other seven year olds, my legs sticking to the metal folding chair, the mosquito bite behind my knee itching ferociously, and in the chapel, the usual buzz of voices. I couldn't remember talking to anyone.

My mother leaned into her hand mirror and made a slow, meticulous curve with liquid eyeliner. She pulled back and examined her work. "When someone asks how you're doing," she informed me, "it's best to say, 'I'm fine.'"

My error came back in a torrent—the lady with shiny black hair, walking out of the grownups' Sunday-school class, had asked me how I was; I'd said, "I'm too hot, and I have a mosquito bite." Or had I forgotten to tell her about my terrible itching? I hoped so. How could I not have known? I'd heard my mother say, "I'm fine" all the time, even when she wasn't. I prided myself on my social skills with adults. Now I felt as humiliated as I had the day when I was four and Sister Gulbransen phoned my mother to say I'd come to church without my underwear.

I skulked out of the bathroom, saying nothing. I promised myself I'd never tell the hot, itchy truth again. But somehow, every few months, my mother called me into her pink-tiled inner sanctum and corrected me again. For teasing my grandmother about something, I couldn't even remember what. For dancing around a kerosene lamp at the cabin with my friend, pretending to be Egyptian priestesses ("Remember what Heavenly Father told Moses about idol worship," my mother said). For tapping my toe at the symphony. Again and again, I promised myself I'd keep my body still and my mouth shut.

Inappropriate. Inappropriate. The word sings in my head as I sit in Quaker meeting, my eyes closed, other bodies creaking in the chairs around me. I've never spoken in meeting before. Am I afraid of what will come out of my mouth, afraid of saying something Quakers just don't say, or afraid, as Catharine once put it in her diary, of "professing more than I possess"? In Mormon testimony meetings, I've heard people say they can tell by their pounding hearts that the Spirit wants them to speak. My heart has never pounded in those meetings. It isn't pounding now. How will I know?

grace notes

I let this question go. I'm new at "quaking," as my husband calls it, and I don't have to know right now. Whatever happens, I don't want to fret about saying the right thing. It comforts me to think that most people who stand to speak in meeting do so hesitantly, letting the words out a few at a time. Unlike most Mormon testimony bearers, who speak of what they know to be true, Quakers tend to leave their questions in the air. I hear phrases like "I'm wondering about . . ." and "This puzzles me . . ." and "I'm not sure what to do with this." Some people don't stand to speak but stay in their chairs, eyes closed or focused on the floorboards, their words rising into the square.

I shift my weight in my chair. It creaks. Not to worry, everyone else's does, too. Now another word floats into my head: *reverence.* As a child in Mormon meetings, and in the children's meetings I supervised until I asked to be released last month, adults murmured, "Be reverent" over and over. This phrase carried several meanings: "This is God's house," "Stop talking right now," "Fold your arms and sit still." Reverence, the way I learned it, had little to do with awe. I didn't *feel* different from my playground self when I entered the church; I behaved differently. I folded my arms and bowed my head. I performed. Now I want to learn reverence from the inside out, and be still not because it would be "inappropriate" to tap my toe, but because I really don't feel like tapping my toe right now.

What did my mother feel, sitting in church meetings, speaking platitudes when people asked her why she hadn't been there the week before or why she wasn't having more children? "I'm fine," she would say, or "We'll just have to see what happens." I don't remember her confiding her pain to anyone. Outside our family's protected bubble, no one saw her sickroom, the hours of white-knuckled prayer, the ovulation chart and thermometer next to the bed, the words she scribbled on notebook paper (*I am an empty vessel . . .*), the nights she sat on the bathroom heat vent and read Numbers and Deuteronomy—doing what, trying to submit to an unfriendly God? People saw the woman with the beautiful face, sitting with her arms folded in church. The woman in costume, singing onstage. The woman who never offended anyone—or if she did, or thought she had, paced the floors at night, worrying about it. This is the legacy I'm struggling out of, like a film of makeup that resists my scrubbing.

I picture my mother now, letting my sister's teenage onslaughts sail over her head and around the room. My sister uses words that would have put her in a coma when I was fifteen. I don't think my mother frets anymore about what she said or didn't say at a dinner party; she's experienced enough real worry to know the difference. Do I know it? If I stand to speak in this meeting, and if what comes out makes someone turn and raise her eyebrows at me, can I let it go?

"During this past week, I've been thinking a lot about something," says a voice. I open my eyes wide enough to see the woman who teaches English as a second language speaking from her chair, her eyes on the floor. "I've been thinking about how difficult it is to say what we mean to each other." I hear her words, her story about an experience in the classroom; words of my own are forming in my throat. I'd thought, if I ever stood to speak, I would think of something profound to quote, someone else's words about God or peacemaking or human suffering. But I'm thinking about my husband, and the strange sounds he made in the middle of the night.

Silence. Why am I thinking of this? Kent's esophagal clogging is something we're used to; "I have small orifices," he always says. I brought him water; he doesn't even remember his gasps for air. What does this have to do with peace or faith or forgiveness? I am standing up. "Something happened last night that made me think about how hard it is to really know each other," my voice says. "I woke up hearing my husband trying to breathe. He made the strangest sounds. I didn't know if he was trying to talk, or if he could hear me telling him to take a drink. He was all right, and he went back to sleep. I felt great love for him, hearing him in that struggle, and wondering what I'd do if anything happened to him. I understood something new about him in those sounds he made. It makes me think about whether we're really learning to know another person, even when we're using words."

Silence. I sit down. I have made no sense at all. Real Quakers speak to one another's condition, even to the world's condition; I just rambled on about gagging noises. *Inappropriate?* Not very articulate, anyway. Now I realize what it was I understood about Kent last night: his mortality, his vulnerability to a catch in the throat, my realization that after all we'd been through, I loved him. Why couldn't I have said that? And why did I need to say anything? Nobody else needed to hear my words. *But maybe,* comes a voice in my head, *you needed to risk saying them.*

three

diary

"As I become more like her, she becomes more like me," my mother says. I stop pacing the bedroom, phone to my ear, and sit down on the bed. My mother is speaking about her close friend. Her words stir me. Throughout my childhood and adolescence, I never saw her confide in another woman. I could hardly imagine such intimacy, such revealing of self, for the polished lady who listened to her students' troubles but never mentioned her own. Now, as she speaks to me on the phone, I imagine her facing her friend. One whispers across the table; the other knows exactly what she means. The picture looks so strange that I shiver.

As a young girl, I could not imagine this scene for myself, any more than I could for my mother. I spent hours with a friend in high school, talking about our favorite books and pet peeves, but the sense of competition that often surfaced between us made me guarded. As adults, we're learning to open our hearts to each other with new freedom and trust. Other nurturing female friendships in my life center around shared history, around writing or music, or around moments of "Yes, yes, I feel that, too." One entered my life at such a depth that I stopped keeping a journal.

It happened the week my friend was away for Christmas. I sat on my bed, about to tell my journal what I longed to tell her. I stared at the page in my pretty bound book. No. I would not write it. I no longer feared a committee of diary-reading angels; I'd been scribbling my secrets for nearly twenty years. But I knew if I put these words on paper, I might never say them aloud. My journal was starting to feel as claustrophobic as my adolescent sickroom. Written words seemed too limiting for this new, sacred friendship. "No more chattering in here," I wrote in my final entry. "No more tending my emotional hothouse. I want to speak in poems and in person." I shut the book, leaving the last twenty pages blank. In the next several months, I spoke words I'd never thought I could. The confidante I'd imagined at thirteen had entered my life at last. My voice broke out of its paper walls.

From the other end of the phone line, my mother listens as I tell her this. We understand each other. Until today, I didn't know my mother had a friend even remotely like the one to whom I still reveal my soul. I'm glad. Each of us has found a place on the spectrum of relationship where women choose to cherish, not compete with, each other. We have something in common with our relative Catharine, and with other nineteenth-century women who relished their passionate friendships.

Today, after talking with my mother, I want to read Catharine's words again. I settle into the Story Couch and let the photocopied pages spill across my lap. "More care would be taken if I were writing for the perusal of others," wrote Catharine at sixteen, "but that is not my intention. It is the simple feelings of my heart, very imperfectly set down for my own improvement." In this same diary entry, she apologizes for writing so hurriedly and "with an unsettled mind." Catharine is addressing herself, a confidence from inner voice to inner ear. I keep reading. Every time I pick up these pages, I get a little thrill. After reading Thomas Mann's diaries (the ones he never got around to destroying), Polish poet Wislawa Szymborska admitted to the "great if ambiguous pleasure of spying and eavesdropping on someone else's secrets." So do I. But it's more than eavesdropping I'm after: it's the unseen membrane that joins one woman to another. I want to listen when my bedridden relative speaks of her closest friendship. I'm glad, for purely selfish reasons, that she carried on the Quaker tradition of diary-keeping until her death.

As a young girl, Catharine longed to tell someone about the deaths of her mother and her brother, about the God she hoped would "arouse and warm the cold and stupid, the world over," and about her illness in 1815, when she felt "changed from hardness of heart, to such tenderness, composure, and engagedness." At the time, she recalled later, she "had not freedom to express my feelings to anyone." But from her early twenties until her death, Catharine found that freedom: the confidences she shared with her bosom friend were spoken in person and are, as they should be, lost to the rest of us.

The book I opened in the basement of the court building in Hartford is not Catharine's alone. Another woman's diary is included at the back. I can't imagine the book otherwise, since Catharine and her cousin Deborah were inseparable for most of their adult lives. Their relationship reminds me of Emily Dickinson's lifelong attachment to her sister-in-law Susan, the friend who exchanged ardent letters with her even when they lived next door, the woman of whom she wrote,

> When my Hands
> are Cut, Her
> fingers will be
> found inside—.

Reading Catharine's and Deborah's diaries, I can only glimpse what Catharine once described, to another friend, as "an interchange of thought, a union of soul." These women appear to have inhabited what historian Carroll Smith-Rosenberg calls "the female world of love and ritual" in the nineteenth century. "Women expressed their attachments to other women both physically and verbally," writes Adrienne Rich in her essay on Emily Dickinson. "A marriage did not dilute the strength of a female friendship, in which two women often shared the same bed during long visits, and wrote letters articulate with both physical and emotional longing. None of this was perceived or condemned as 'lesbianism.'" Quaker historian Margaret Hope Bacon notes that in the mid-nineteenth century, "it was not unusual for two single Quaker women to share a home and a warm devotion to one another."

Still, Catharine bristled at criticism of her relationship with Deborah. Shortly before her death, she wrote that "some unfeeling minds" had censured her cousin, "who is as a mother and sister to me," for living with her. I don't know how much of their closeness the two revealed in public, but it must have touched off some gossip, even in an age that accepted "romantic friendships." The situation may not be so different today. For all the fashionable girl-kissing on our TV sitcoms and college campuses, we're still recovering from the twentieth century's culture wars. Even now, a bond like Catharine and Deborah's might be whispered about or trivialized, judged too queer or not queer enough.

A therapist friend once told me, "When I taught a workshop for women, almost everyone in the class said she'd had a passionate friendship with another woman. These relationships aren't talked about. They defy the usual labels." Sometimes, in private, they *are* talked about. Recently a friend broke down in tears when she told me a young girl she loves had not called back after their late-night phone talk was disrupted. "I don't even know how to talk about this, why I need to know she loves me—it's too hard to explain," she said. I understood. As a writer tempted to force every gust of wind into words, I've been humbled by close friendship. When I try to describe it to Kent, I lack the eloquence of the woman in the French film *Entre Nous* who says, speaking to her husband about her best friend, "Madeleine helps me live. Without her I suffocate." Even between my friend and me—though Kent teases us for being "Siamese twins"—the invisible tissue that binds us is hard to name. "We don't have to define this," I once told her. "It is what it is, and it's ours." Sometimes, when we do try to describe our friendship, it feels like singing, as the words pour out; sometimes it feels more like coaxing open a poem's central metaphor. Sometimes a look or a laugh is enough. I'm learning I don't have to name every nuance. I'm learning to value the soft, private core of relationship more than anything I can say about it, to myself or the world.

Emily Dickinson guarded her communion with Susan with a ferocity I admire. Her famous poem that begins

> The Soul selects
> her own Society
> Then shuts the
> Door

appears in a letter to Susan, on a paper whose multiple creases suggest it may have passed more than once between the two women. In another letter to Susan, Dickinson wrote,

> Whatever throng
> the Lock is
> firm upon your
> Diamond Door.

Even in our confession-obsessed culture, this guardian instinct survives. I felt it the night I stopped keeping a journal. I feel it as I write about my marriage, family, and friendships, weighing how much to reveal. Some things I save for confidence, for poetry, for song, or for silence. As Nabokov wrote in his short story "Sounds," "All silence is the recognition of a mystery."

Catharine and Deborah's private conversations are a mystery to me. Silence guards the words and quiet moments that passed between these long-dead friends. But I have their diaries, which have become as public as the Connecticut State Library will allow them to be. Reading the pages in my lap, I imagine the sound of the women's voices.

Catharine's written speech sounds gentle and measured to me. Deborah's words burst with curiosity and strong opinion. She sings her spiritual enthusiasm. She calls a conversation with a woman minister "a refreshing shower to my thirsty soul." She decides, having "considered the situation of the poor oppressed Africans," to "decline the product of their labor." She longs to make some *"great sacrifice"* (emphasis hers) and tries to make her hairstyle "as plain as I thought necessary for a young person"; then she realizes that this might be just another form of showing off. She prays, with her pen, that she will be preserved from "mere traditional religion" and find "the true life." She describes the "deep and lonely places" her mind travels. And here, on page 223, is a reference to the first Friends' meeting in Catharine's room, the same words I copied in my notebook in Stamford, quoted in what book I can't remember. Deborah goes on to say that "reverent solemnity covered our minds under the consideration of the important step we had taken." I love the idea of two young women initiating worship in a private bedroom. According to the diary, their decision was approved, more Friends joined them, and Catharine's sickroom became their regular meeting place for the last ten years of her life.

Though the two women rarely needed to write letters to each other, the words they did send by post allow me to see, a little, into the interstices of their lives. Catharine's diary includes part of a letter Deborah wrote to another friend in 1824, describing the hours spent tending to her cousin. "Sometimes friction, bathing with warm brandy, internal stimulants, &c., appear to be beneficial; at others, nothing but peace and quiet around her will answer." Deborah's diary contains some of the letters that passed between the two women when Deborah traveled to New York for her own medical treatment in 1829. In the first, Deborah describes her "five large blisters" and her longing to go home to her friend. "The tumult of a busy city cannot attract my attention nor erase from my heart that affection," she writes. Catharine writes back about her father's death, "a deeper sorrow than any heart can fathom but thine." Deborah responds, "Oh, my dear, sensible am I of the total insufficiency of words."

Reading this, I picture Deborah alone in a room in New York, the clatter of horses under her window. Her mouth tries on a phrase and lapses into a sigh. She'll never find language for what she means. I see moments like this in my own life: I sit at my friend's feet, the day after my grandmother's death; she says, "I tried so hard to write you a note, but I couldn't express what I meant. Is it all right if we just sit like this?" One day my friend lets loose her life's greatest sorrow, too much for words; all I can do is hold her as she weeps.

Catharine could not speak aloud to her friend for much of her life. As the scrofula worsened, Deborah moved into her house to care for her. In 1835 Catharine wrote that her most private spiritual musings "are close and searching to my heart, and to the heart of my beloved D.S.R., yet often do we hold sweet communion together, and no hours are more delightful than those in which we are alone by ourselves." Later this same year she wrote, "My dear D.S.R. was sick and unable to sit up, but did not feel easy to leave my room, as she could see my motions, and tell my nurse when she did not understand me." The two women must have developed an understanding beyond the formal written words they felt to be "insufficient," even beyond their spoken words. A shared code for voiceless Catharine.

A year before her death in 1838, Catharine was troubled about the coming separation from her friend. Sitting in the Connecticut State Library, I turned a page in her diary and saw the heading "A Dream." I shivered. The title formed a doorway to privileged space, but a space meant to be entered. Catharine needed to tell her dream to someone, and here I was receiving it. "I was standing on elevated ground with my face towards the east, and a most brilliant and beautiful face or sun . . . stood in the firmament a little north of me." She saw "a light to which that of our natural sun would bear no comparison." She stood with her brother, Sands, who had died twenty-six years before; he spoke to her, but she could not reply, she was so "riveted to the source of light." Her brother told her the light she was seeing came from an angel, who would take her with him on his next passing. She woke from the dream filled with "clearness and brightness," and believed she and her friend would not "be separated in so important a journey as lies before us."

During Catharine's last illness, Deborah contracted typhus and had to be moved back to her own home. After her things had been packed, she asked that she be lifted onto the bed next to her friend, and that the two be left alone. They were. Catharine died shortly after this, on October 27. Deborah had shown signs of recovery, but when she heard of Catharine's death, she told her family that she had no more desire to live. She died on November 2 and was buried next to her friend.

I don't know what the two women said to each other in their last conversation, or if it even took the form of words. I don't want to know, any more than I want the world to overhear my own moments of quiet confidence. I gather up the pages of Catharine's diary. I close that "Diamond Door" as gently as I can.

nine openings

Chiff. The word is my favorite example of onomatopoeia. I discovered it when, as a despondent newlywed, I asked my friend Sharla for organ lessons. When the instrument made a "chiff," a simulated sound of opening pipes, hope opened in me.

One morning a week, I packed up my organ books and walked a block to the Mormon chapel in Gardnerville, Nevada. It was a good thing we lived close; we only had one car, and Kent drove it to work in Carson City every day. He'd taken his first job out of law school at the Nevada Supreme Court. I spent my days wandering around our thin-walled apartment, waiting to get pregnant. Many evenings, my lethargy met Kent's depression and we couldn't speak a word to each other. On his good days Kent prodded me to get a job or take classes, to "Do what it is you most want to do." But I didn't even know what I wanted anymore.

Kent worried about me. He was a paradox: he'd always been attracted to bright, resolute women, though he once—he can hardly believe it now—advised one college girlfriend to "follow the prophet" and be a wife and mother instead of going to medical school. A year into our marriage, he wondered what had happened to the "passionate and ambitious" person he'd thought I was. The night we met, on a blind date organized by the Mormon sorority-fraternity system, he heard me talk about poetry and music and my study-abroad summer in Italy; he didn't know I'd chosen an impractical education on purpose. Like many girls in my community, I assumed that I would marry young and be taken care of. At nineteen I lived out my pubescent fantasy and chose a wedding dress as tight as a Victorian winding-sheet. I stopped writing. Shortly before my wedding, I came home one night to find an embossed envelope on my desk: an invitation to a poetry reading by Mark Strand. My father must have put it there. I threw it away. In my mind, the world of language and ideas was closed to me. A year later, I graduated from college ill-qualified to do much more than answer phones. Graduate school did not enter my mind. After I moved with my husband into the desert, I stopped reading the feminist books I'd only recently discovered. I feared what they might tell me: that I was buried alive in my already ended story.

And so I wandered the apartment. When I did try to put pencil to paper, nothing came. I had no piano and no desire to sing. Why couldn't I just get pregnant? I wasn't "baby hungry"; I didn't even think I'd be able to bond with a child. I was simply doing what I'd been told all my life, marrying a "worthy young man," preparing to start a family, fulfilling my "divine role." I'd chosen this role because it was easier than inventing my own life. At least I'd thought it would be easier. Where were my eggs? Was I going to repeat my mother's years of emptiness? Month after month, I bled. The doctor prescribed fertility drugs. I spent my mornings in the bathroom, peering into the test tubes that came with my ovulation kit. Would the solution turn blue this time, or not? Some days I walked to the drugstore and pretended to look for greeting cards, just to have something to do. Most days I paced the living room, wondering what to make for dinner. My organ lesson, though I would never have admitted this to anyone, was the pinnacle of my week.

On my way to the church, I walked through our parking lot and out onto the sidewalk. Canada geese squawked overhead. Sometimes a hot air balloon huffed above me. I could see the wall of the Sierra to the west, and the dry switchback road to Lake Tahoe. If the wind blew from the west, as it often did, crying in our windows at night,

I could smell garlic—one of the few crops that grew in this place. Cottonwood leaves flipped white in the wind, a harbinger of rain that rarely came. When it did come, I smelled sagebrush. This was the high desert, in the state with the lowest annual rainfall in the country. By coming here I'd also entered the desert of biblical story, full of tombs and miracles.

In the church parking lot next to the garlic fields, my friend Sharla climbed out of her blue van. She smiled and waved. She had keys to the church, where we'd met a few months before. I admired her because, unlike most Mormon mothers I knew, she'd gone to law school, relished her part-time work as an attorney, and didn't seem constrained by her religious culture. Her house was full of books. Her small sons were cheerful and articulate. She invited me to hang wallpaper with her, to go shopping in Reno, and to join her book club. Her calm presence, whether she was smoothing my bubbly stretch of wallpaper or talking politics or reading Emily Dickinson aloud at book club, made me think I might be capable of raising a family and pursuing my passions, too.

Before each organ lesson, Sharla unlocked the instrument's rolling cover with a tiny gold key. She didn't know she was unlocking something in me. As I perched on the bench, the organ's two keyboards ready for my hands, my childhood sense of belonging in the world returned. At six or seven, my fingers poised over the black keys on the piano, I'd spent hours spinning songs in the pentatonic scale, which makes any combination of notes sound inevitably matched. I'd pounded my "Dance of the Cobra" until my parents shouted down from the kitchen for me to stop.

Sharla taught me to concentrate on my fingering. I worked my hands into contortions I'd never tried at the piano. "Hold your thumb down," she said. "Remember you don't have a sustain pedal, and if you let go, the sound goes, too." I held my thumb down, I crossed over, I imagined my fingers glued to the keys. Sharla reminded me to breathe. If I didn't, she said, the sound would be stifling. In my slippery stocking feet, I battled with the pedals, learning them by feel. Slowly, with many halts and wrong bass notes, a familiar hymn rose out of the big brown box. I learned which stops sounded like a trumpet, a flute, or a violin. But the button I liked best was the one that said *Chiff.* Because I practiced on an electronic organ with no real pipes, this button imitated the sound of a pipe-mouth opening. With the chiff function on, every note I played began with an intake of breath.

In organ slang, a pipe "speaks" when it opens and sound comes out. An organ's voice is not so different from a human's; it runs on air pressure. The famous Mormon Tabernacle organ once ran on bellows powered by an underground creek. My cousins and I used to work up a sweat at an old pump organ in the Old Home where my grandmother led summer tours. If our feet slowed their pumping, the sound would die under our fingers within a few seconds.

Organ builders have anthropomorphized this instrument for centuries. Flue pipes, which contain a set of "lips," as well as a "mouth" and an "ear," make the organ's principal, foundation sounds. A flue pipe's pitch depends on its "speaking length": the longer the pipe, the lower the sound. Reed pipes, which contain vibrating "tongues," imitate the sounds of other instruments, such as the trumpet. As a beginning organ student, I didn't have real pipes to open and close. I didn't even have draw knobs to pull. This organ's stops were programmed into a computer, which I accessed by pressing long cream-colored keys. From somewhere in this electronic organ, I heard an imitation of a pipe organ, which imitates the sound of a flute or trumpet. Whenever I pressed the chiff button, I heard what sounded like, but wasn't, a breath. I felt a little like the professor hiding behind his curtain in *The Wizard of Oz.* Still, I loved the clean, cold sounds this organ made. Sometimes I cheated and put on the bass coupler, which adds bass pedal notes so the organist doesn't have to use her feet. I turned up the volume. The deep vibrations filled me from my toes to the ends of my hair. I breathed at the end of a phrase, lifting my fingers from the keys. I imagined pipes opening and closing all around me. I felt I'd entered a giant breathing, singing body. I needed this instrument's body to sing through, since I wasn't ready to inhabit my own.

Soon I was able to play a whole organ solo, pedals and all. I practiced it every Saturday morning, when Kent played basketball with other young men behind the partition that separated the chapel from the gym. I played it for Sharla in our lessons. She believed in me. In her presence, I felt the same surge of confidence I'd felt playing Bach on the piano years before, letting my fingers work their counterpoint, letting the music play itself. This confidence fed me. I felt it rise in my rib cage when I attended a writers' group meeting in Carson City and asked a freelance writer named Kay if she wanted to go to lunch. She did, and we met every week from then on. When she connected me with a newspaper editor who offered me work, I breathed deeply. *Chiff.* My new courage worked like a bellows, pushing air through my body. When I had to phone strangers to set up interviews, I opened my mouth. *Chiff.* When I took a job with Reno's alternative weekly paper and found myself ringside at a women's boxing match, inside the gas chamber in the Nevada State Prison, or checking out the "Bondage Room" at the Mustang Ranch brothel, I breathed, I asked questions, my words rolled out onto newsprint. *Chiff.* I started reviewing books of poetry. I went to readings and drank in musical language, the way I'd taken in poetry as a child, hearing my mother's students sing Dickinson or e. e. cummings. I bought a new notebook and recorded the images and rhythms that passed through me. *Chiff.* When I heaved myself up on a hospital bed in Carson City, my first child coming so fast I had no time to even think about an epidural, I breathed to keep from screaming. When Anders lay in my arms, red-haired and wide-eyed, the "bonding myth" I'd never believed in came true. Clouds had broken over the desert; rain splashed the hospital windows. Anders stared. I loved him more ferociously than any speech about "the divine role of women" would ever dare acknowledge. The tomb had opened a crack, and I had no desire to seal it up again.

chant

At sixteen, composer Ruth Crawford wrote in her diary: "What is the soul? When it leaves the body we do not see it. And where is God? Everywhere? But where is he? Why can't I know all these things?"

In 1930, after studying composition in Chicago and finding some success in New York, twenty-nine-year-old Ruth traveled to Berlin. She wanted to express her spiritual questions in music. She read the Bhagavad Gita and wanted to set fragments of it to three chants for women's voices, but she was unable to find an English translation. Instead, she made up a language of her own. At first she titled the first two chants "To an Unkind God" and "To an Angel," but by the time she got to the third, she abandoned the titles altogether. One scholar has called the language of the chants "meaningless phonemes," but when I hear the choir's chromatic swerves around a single pitch center, that ancient form Hildegard von Bingen used in some of her music, no sound the voices make is meaningless. As the soprano and alto lines break apart and balance each other on either side of the pitch center, as they overlap and press together, I hear a wild discourse that speaks of the unspeakable. At the end of the chant, the lower parts sink into quiet, while the sopranos hold a high A, fortissimo, on the vowel *o*. I press the backward arrow on my CD player and play it again.

And then I listen to Chant no. 2. When I hear the opening "oo" in the soprano-alto duet, it sounds like a question, even though it's a brief, descending phrase, unlike the rising tones of a spoken question. I don't hear an answer. The phrase answers itself with a mirror phrase, another question. Who is speaking? Who is the angel?

Unlike Crawford's first chant, a puzzle of made-up syllables, this piece weaves four melodic lines on continuous vowel sounds. When I played my recording of the chant for Kent, he said, "It's oo-ey music! It's preexistence music!" I knew what he was hearing in his head: the soundtracks attached to some Mormon films about premortal life in Heaven. I could see his point, though Crawford's chant is sparer and more dissonant than these choruses. A continuous question without an answer, and, as I hear it, a longing for relationship.

Until I was twenty-nine, I avoided asking questions about God and angels in my own writing. They seemed too far away for me to know intimately. Though I longed for a female divinity who would know my secrets and answer my prayers, I never addressed her on paper. Learning to write honestly about my real-life experiences was hard enough. And then one Sunday afternoon, I came home to a phone message from my friend Jennifer, a poet in New York. "I have an idea," was all she said. When we talked, she told me she wanted to collaborate on a series of psalms. I could hardly wait to tell her that, just a few days before, a composer friend had suggested a similar project.

After weeks of brainstorming via phone and e-mail, Jennifer and I came up with a list of images we felt held meaning in our lives. Stones. Birds. Water. Like Crawford's pitch centers, these motifs worked at the core of our project. Throughout the process, Jennifer placed resonant words in her e-mails, with huge spaces in between. I printed the pages and kept them; looking at them now, I see words I highlighted in yellow: *Threshold. Awakening.* I sent her a list of opening phrases I'd collected from the Psalms in the Old Testament: *Why standest thou afar off. . . . When I kept silence. . . . I will open my dark saying. . . . Be not still, O God. . . . Hide not thy face.* The lines that drew me had to do with God's distance, not divine nearness or love.

Our project evolved into a three-part work, *Psalms of Water and Stone,* with interior titles like "Saltwater Psalm," "Frost Psalm," and "Egg Psalm." We wrote our psalms separately, and then arranged them with spoken words and silences in between. Jennifer's words question themselves in a circular pattern: *You are god. / You are not god.* I found myself asking this "god/not-god" to touch me. My psalms are full of imperatives like *Startle us, Cover me, Take this stone in me,* and even *Let me touch your hand.* I sound like a petulant child, demanding my heavenly parent's attention.

Jennifer attended strict Catholic schools as a child. In one of her poems, she remembers picturing God as

> the tall man
> up the hill . . .
> White shirt, leather belt.

As an adult, her spiritual journey has been a search for gentleness, a dance around the invisible presence that may or may not, as she says in the psalms, "unbolt my heart." Reading my psalm texts several years after writing them, I see my own longing for connection with the God I grew up believing was real, made of flesh and bone, but who seemed as distant as my grandfather, a Mormon General Authority who wore his white dress shirt even to mow the grass at the family cabin. I used the word *Lord* in many of the psalms. Now, thumbing through the pages in my folder, I feel that word as an ache in my head. It makes me think of a landlord, a man in a dark suit, not so different from Jennifer's leather-belted figure. I wrote the psalms before I left the church. What kind of God would I address now? Would I speak to the invisible Mother in Heaven I used to imagine? Probably not. I see her now as a mirror of the human connection I once lacked, in my religion and in my life. Now that connection is real; I don't have to look for it in the sky. And so I bend my thoughts toward Ruth Crawford's "unknown god." He/She/It could be anywhere. I picture the snowy egret I once watched on my favorite beach in Connecticut, as it lifted from the ground and seemed to carry away all the grief I'd ever felt. I hear in my head Bach's *St. Matthew Passion,* every aria and chorus composed in dance rhythm, a physical, this-worldly song of sorrow. I try to imagine God as whatever in us is capable of kindness and hope, and see how that feels. One human hand, reaching for another.

When I wrote the psalms, I wasn't ready to open myself to these possibilities, though I wanted to. One Sunday at church I gave several drafts to Rich, the composer. He phoned me that afternoon and said, "Someday, if you want to, I hope you'll tell me what made you write these words." He said he could sense a crisis in them. He was right, though I didn't feel I could tell him at the time. I was trying to decide whether to leave the church. Several of my women friends were on their way out. Another confided to me that she'd leave in a minute if her family could handle it, but she knew such a choice would devastate them. I stood on that threshold, the word Jennifer had sent, the one that came before *awakening.* I was afraid of what I might wake up to.

I had recently talked with my bishop. I hadn't renewed my annual temple recommend, the document that allows members "in good standing" to enter the temple. The bishop phoned me, concerned. When we met, I was relieved to find that I could speak frankly with him. In most meetings of this kind, I'd told bishops what they wanted to hear, and then hurried away. This time, facing the bishop behind his bulky desk, I expressed my doubts about our religion's claim to be "the only true church on the earth." I told him the church didn't feed my spiritual hunger, the way Bach or Emily Dickinson or pounding ocean waves did. I voiced my concerns about the church's stand on women and the priesthood, and its aggressive campaign against a same-sex marriage referendum in California. I explained that I didn't feel at home in a church that provides tidy answers to life's most perplexing questions. "I *like* ambiguity!" I said. I told the bishop I didn't think a person with all my doubts should go to the temple. He listened. He knew better than to pressure me. All he said was, "I don't want my friends to give up."

That night, I decided to speak my own private psalm. *I will open my dark saying.* . . . I shut the door to my bedroom, turned out the light, and knelt by the bed. All the things I'd been taught to do in Sunday school. I was going to pray, until my knees hurt, to whatever Father or Mother in Heaven might be listening. I wanted to know if the time had come for me to leave the church. I remembered the overwhelming peace I'd felt when I'd prayed about taking a newspaper job in Nevada or moving to the East Coast. I thought of Thomas Merton's notion that answers to prayer may be the Providence within us, not something alien but "what is inmost in our own selves, the very depth of our own being." I breathed deeply and said a silent prayer.

I don't remember what I said in my mind. I didn't form words. My thoughts were all vowel, the language of longing. And as the sound flowed through my brain, I knew what the depth of my being needed. It was time to leave.

I didn't know this because heavenly beings appeared, or lightning flashed, or fire filled my rib cage. I felt peace. My heart was not bound. I could be free of the institution that had made my faith a rote performance. I did not have to stay because the church needed me. The changes I longed to see were so radical that they seemed at least a hundred years away. I needed to live in the present. I needed to take responsibility for my spiritual life.

I stood up shaking. I didn't want to know all this. It was easier to stay, to speak the religious language I'd been taught. I knew the cost of leaving the insular world of the Mormon Church: some people would say I was trampling my sacred temple covenants, giving up any hope of exaltation, leaving "an empty chair in Heaven." People would worry about my children: Would they be baptized, go on missions, marry in the temple? Would I compromise their hope of exaltation, too? I'd seen what happened to one of my friends who left the Mormon "side" in this divided city: she told me, "I found out in a hurry who my real friends were, and they weren't many." No. It was easier not to leave, not to disappoint my neighbors, and especially not to hurt my husband and his family, all devout members of the church. I knew I couldn't do it, not yet.

When I kept silence . . . I said nothing to Kent. I kept going to church. I taught a class of sixteen-year-old girls, sneaking in subversive advice where I could ("Don't marry young. Prepare to support yourself. Find out what your passion is."). I kept working on the psalms. Jennifer sent me hers. I spread them all out on the floor and spoke them aloud. Here, at least, I could speak a portion of what I felt. I e-mailed Jennifer an idea for ordering the psalms. She e-mailed back. I printed the psalms and put them in a folder. My friend Rich came to my house and took the papers from me, pressing them to his heart. He got to work.

Every month or so, as I grew further from the church that had raised me, Rich appeared on my doorstep with a green folder; I rushed to the piano to play the new psalm. I heard a change in Rich's music, the kind of change I was hearing in myself: more allowance for silence and dissonance, more exposed vocal lines, less easy chord resolution. I noticed that Rich sometimes asked the voice to stretch beyond its comfortable range; in one bass line, the voice reached its upper limits, as lightly as possible, on Jennifer's words *We rise / Ashamed of your embrace.* As my fingers felt out the melody on the keyboard, I imagined a bass voice lifting to a high F, womanlike, flutelike, new. How I wanted my voice to do this. To make new sound, to speak what I still didn't dare.

One morning, Rich phoned me and apologized for taking so

long on the psalms. "Some things just *throw up* on the page," he said. I could picture him flinging out his arms to make his point. Then his voice grew quiet. "I can't just toss these off. They're too emotionally complex."

"*I'm* too emotionally complex," I wanted to tell him. I was living a double life. I went to church and told myself, *I know I don't belong here, but I'm doing it for my marriage, and my in-laws, and the people who are counting on me to be here. I can do this. I can stay and still have my separate spiritual life. Maybe I can even make a difference.* I was lying, and I knew it. Week after week, I came home from church exhausted.

Now, two years later, I attend sacrament meeting with Kent and the boys once a month. The rest of my Sundays, I come home from Quaker meeting renewed. Kent and I can't wait to ask each other, as he changes out of his white shirt and tie and I curl up on the bed in the jeans I've worn to church, "What happened in your meeting?" The boys listen as we talk. "We heard about getting out of debt again," Kent said recently; I told him someone in Quaker meeting had spoken about "living below our means." "Today in church I really thought about the Atonement," Kent explained last week; "We riffed on forgiveness," I said. Together, we discuss the adult Sunday-school lessons Kent prepares each week. He listens openly to whatever extracurricular readings I bring him. He's become known for his willingness to ask challenging questions and invite discussion; the last time I attended his class, the room was so full that I couldn't find a seat. One Sunday Kent came with me to Quaker meeting and came away saying, "You know, that made me appreciate the sacrament more. That's the one quiet time in Mormon meetings, and I want to make better use of it." When a friend said to him, "I feel for you, you know, this must be really hard on your marriage," Kent told him, "Actually, it's made our marriage happier."

For a while the bishop phoned regularly to check on me. One night at the temple, the woman assigned to visit me every month ran into Kent and said, with tears in her eyes, "What could I have done better?" One Sunday, when I did sit with my family in the chapel, an elderly German woman poked me in the ribs and said, "Remember.

Family comes first." Another woman surprised me when she said, "I've always been interested in the Quakers. Can we talk sometime?" Many members of the congregation are as much my friends as ever. One neighbor told me recently, "I think it's so cool what you've done. I love it when people act on what they believe." Another hugged me and cried when I told her my news; she said, "So many people in this culture walk around with masks on, but you don't, and now there are so many things I can tell you." Rich's wife has come with me to Quaker meeting, not because I asked her, but because she wanted to.

Now that Rich knows what pushed the psalms out of me, he wants to hear more of it. Last week, before I left for a trip to northern Nevada, he phoned and begged for a favor. "Can you write more verses to 'Hand Psalm?' You won't believe this, but I'm hearing it as a pop song for the whole choir." All the way to the Carson Valley, as I squinted across the Bonneville Salt Flats, as I cranked up U2's *Joshua Tree* to stay awake, as the boys poked each other mercilessly in the backseat, as Kent took over the wheel in Elko, as night fell and Anders found the Big Dipper right outside his window, I tried to hear what Rich was hearing. *Make our clasp a journey . . . a rope to cross every canyon.* . . . The road ribboned into darkness in front of us as I remembered the words I'd written. The engine hummed. The boys toppled into their pillows, sound asleep. Silence. Miles to go.

This morning I wake up early, a guest in my friend Sharla's house, in the desert valley where I used to wander in circles, waiting for something in me to come to life. Now this place is a refuge. Since our move back to Salt Lake from the East Coast, we've made the trek here every October. My boys look forward all year to seeing those adored Nintendo owners Evan calls "our friends in Avada." Sharla and I talk as we hike the trails above Lake Tahoe, as we chop vegetables in the kitchen, as her seven-year-old daughter leads my boys around the house in her pink princess costume, as we sit with our husbands in the family room late at night. Yesterday, after Kent and I told Sharla about the change in my life this year, she said, "You know people don't love you just because you're Mormon." Our friendship is unchanged.

three

I open the blinds. From this upstairs room, I can see the Carson River, dried to a muddy vein, at the bottom of Sharla and Jim's backyard. I can see across the cattle pastures to Job's Peak, its upper face hidden in clouds. The cottonwoods and scrubby Russian olives that line the riverbed are still slick from last night's rain. This day reminds me of the mornings my sons were born in Carson City. Each time, rain ended months of unbroken sunlight. The hospital staff said this was typical: "When we get rain in this place, everybody goes into labor." Today my only labor is to add three verses to "Hand Psalm." Not as easy as it sounds.

I'd better work while Kent is away at a conference in Reno, Sharla is working out at the gym next door, and the boys are still asleep at the other end of the hall. I find my books and papers on the desk and climb back into bed. I'm still hanging on the threshold of this psalm, not sure how to reenter it. I reach for the orange paperback I couldn't resist at the bookstore last week: a compilation of Meister Eckhart's thought, including his defense against charges of heresy in 1327. I flip through the book to see what I've already underlined. "Nothing is as near to me as God is. God is nearer to me than I am to myself." I'm back at a two-year-old level in my understanding of God, but somehow these words feel right to me. They allow me not to know myself entirely. They allow me to give up reaching across the abyss. They allow me to trust, just as I trust in my human friends. I didn't dare imagine God breathing so close to me when I wrote "Hand Psalm," which begins with the words,

> Come down, Lord, in body,
> let me touch your hand
> across the table.

Lord. The white-shirted one who's always over there, out there, on the other side. "God is within; we are without," said Meister Eckhart. "God is at home; we are abroad." God lives in what Eckhart calls "the little castle of the soul." As I read, I encounter "God/not god," a distinction similar to Jennifer's "god/not-god," a verbal dance around the unnameable. What will I name God now? I think of Eckhart's famous prayer "to God that he may make me free of 'God.'" I hear Ruth Crawford's adolescent questions in my head: *What is the soul? Where is God? Why can't I know all these things?*

I flip back to the introduction of this 1941 translation of Eckhart. Raymond Blakney, the translator, mentions a "'wild' mystical society" that cherished Eckhart's thought after his death, the Friends of God. Blakney calls this group a precursor of the Quakers. No wonder I feel at home in Eckhart's words. No wonder he faced charges of heresy. Eckhart celebrated the "inward Light" and the individual experience of God, without ecclesiastical intermediary. He spoke of breaking the shell of religious symbol and ritual to reach the sacred "kernel" or "spark," similar to the Hasidic idea of Shechinah, the divine presence scattered in gleaming shards throughout the world. Eckhart used the word *friend* to describe God's reciprocal relationship with human beings: "The faithful God often lets his friends fall sick. . . . Friends know all, for that is the nature of friendship." He spoke of "something in the soul so closely akin to God that it is already one with him." What do I call this something?

I make a list of words. *Friend. Blessing. Secret word. Mother.* Why not address, if not a goddess in the sky, real women who have touched me? I think of the white-robed women who anointed me with oil in the temple initiatory. I think of the nineteenth-century Mormon women who gave blessings to the sick in covered wagons crossing the plains, before this practice was limited to male priesthood holders. *Hand to hand, oil in the hair,* I write in my notes. Then I write a question: *Why do I call you?* I remember a line from a blues lyric I once wrote, addressing the "blue devil" people in Renaissance England believed could enter the body and cause melancholy: *You've been inside me all the time.* If I could imagine a gloomy blue gnome inhabiting my body, I can certainly imagine something light and joyous in there. Maybe its name doesn't matter. I tap my pen on the page and look outside. The clouds have fallen farther to the ground, hiding the mountains I know are there, a granite imprint in my mind. The psalm begins to weave itself.

Lord, Friend, Mother, Blessing,
whatever name I name,
why do I call you?

I leave a space.

Closer to me
than my own skin,
hand in my hand, my secret word,
you've been inside me all the time.

I close my eyes and hear a gospel choir clapping the offbeat. They
sway and raise their hands above their heads. They're shaking the
floor. Now they're not singing words, they're wailing their longing,
all vowel, like Ruth Crawford with rhythm. Who knew *this* went on
in the little castle of my soul?

passaggio

I'll call her Leska. This is the name I gave her
in my spiral notebook, when I was a thirteen-year-old voyeur. The
notebook has sat at the bottom of a file box for years. I found it this
morning, downstairs in the Voodoo Room. It wasn't with the blue
binder that holds my saga about Charlie and her shell-shocked
brother. I found it buckled under the "Alien Invader Handbook" my
friend and I wrote when we were nine, cassette tapes of pretend
radio news shows, meticulously traced Egyptian hieroglyphics, a few
remaining pages of the old Miss Lamb stories, and the "Poppy the
Prairie Dog" story I dictated to my mother when I was five. I'm surprised I never destroyed this notebook. The scraps of paper I carried
with me that year, copying every word Leska said in my presence, are
long gone. I transmuted her real-life words into fiction, the opera
singer novel I attempted to write in the privacy of my sickroom.

The notebook sits in my lap. I force myself to leaf through it. It
must have been a later draft; I wanted it perfect, so instead of my
usual scratches and circles and whole paragraphs scribbled in the
margins, I see my cursive sentences laced with white-out. Sometimes

the cursive breaks into print, eerily like my mother's. I used this "italic" writing to indicate Leska's thoughts, since I wrote her story in the first person: *Maybe I should stick to vocalises. . . . My teacher is going to be ashamed of me. . . . I can already feel the tears in my throat. I can't sing like this!* Leska's thoughts, as I imagined them, were my thoughts. Her fears, as she tried to sing with a damaged voice, were my fears. As I shadowed her in the hallways of the university music building, as I wore blue pumps like hers, walking the hallways at school, humming the songs I'd heard her sing, I hovered in liminal space. The passage between her voice and mine.

A graduate student in the same music program as my mother, Leska was what I thought of as a real singer. She had studied in Boston and in Austria, where, people in the Music Department whispered, she had "ruined her voice." Her teacher used the phrase "vocal rehabilitation" when speaking of her. In the hallways of the music building, I heard murmurs about her divorce and the little boy she'd brought with her from Europe. I listened. I watched. Leska's full-bodied bearing, the height she seemed almost ashamed of, moved me. I tried to memorize her face. If I didn't have paper with me, I memorized every self-deprecating comment she made, and wrote it down at home. I tried to imitate the clip of her New England accent. Instead of leafing through magazines or painting my nails with friends after school, I went everywhere with my mother, to master classes, to student opera rehearsals, to coaching sessions—just in case we might run into this woman who, though I wasn't conscious of it, echoed my own lost voice.

In my notebook I find Leska onstage again and again. "My mouth felt like it had been swabbed with cotton," I wrote. "My hands were clammy, shaking like leaves. I could see the pleats of my old red formal doing the same thing, because my knees couldn't keep still." Her stage fright sounds a lot like mine. I find Leska telling herself, *This isn't going to work. I can feel it in my bones; if I attempt that third song, I'll disgrace myself forever.* I find her fretting over a phrase she sings "off the breath" and her lack of abdominal support, the same technical difficulties I had as an adolescent singer. Luckily for the Leska in my story, a nurturing voice teacher and a gruff but deep-feeling theory professor give her exactly what she needs to get her voice back—belief in her abilities, and love. In pages of interminable dialogue, I find them telling her, "Do you know what a fine voice you have?" or "You've been so strong." They sound like people in a made-for-TV movie. They sound like people I must have wished, at thirteen, to have in my life.

As she rediscovered her voice, in life and in the pages of my notebook, Leska sang music I loved. Some songs and arias I heard her sing in person; others I imagined her singing. At one master class I still remember, she sang Donna Elvira's fiery aria from Mozart's *Don Giovanni,* a rant by a woman betrayed. In my version of the scene, her ex-husband appears in the auditorium before she sings, a trigger for her personal rage. Afterward she tells her teacher, "I was drained and upset when we started, but then—I got really mad and let that energy work for me." Sometimes, in the privacy of my room, with the rust-colored curtains drawn, I pretended to sing this aria, too. I put on the cassette tape of *Don Giovanni* my parents had bought in Germany. I stood in front of my mirror. I didn't see myself in the glass; I saw through my body to a grown-up body on an imaginary stage. I lip-synched, though I was too socially maladjusted to even know that term, the whole aria. I knew every word. I felt every word, especially on the days when the tall, dark boy who sat in front of me in English failed to flash me his shy grin, or on the day when the girl I thought was my best friend stopped talking to me. *What contrasting feelings rise in my heart? Why these sighs?* I mouthed in Italian. And then the orchestra launched its heated up-and-down scales: *He betrayed me, ungrateful soul!*

Mouthing a song, hearing Leska's voice in my head in front of the mirror, feeling my own hurt through someone else's, I didn't have to live in my own body. I could imagine myself tall, adult, taking up space in the world. Not stuck at five-foot-one, barely breasted, and so pale I imagined people couldn't see me or hear me humming in the halls at school. Mirroring Leska was the only way I could experience my own woundedness. To feel it fully would have overwhelmed me. The passage I entered, the mirror, the corridor ringing with *vocalises,* seemed inviolate. I believed I could stay there forever.

Near the end of my thick notebook, I find Leska in her voice lesson, singing an aria from Handel's *Giulio Cesare* and saying to her teacher, "Sorry—I can't go on." As I read, as Leska struggles to feel the lightness in her upper voice, the speech I hear hits me with a shock. It's not my thirteen-year-old writerly voice, not Leska's, but the voice of the real woman I called Leska. She said these words under the hot stage lights during a master class. I can still see her hand on the piano lid, and her wide, nervous smile. I can hear her: *That's what all the screeching is about. . . . Yeah, the lightness. . . . I'm getting hot flashes!* I'm sitting next to my mother in the poorly lit auditorium. Her music is open in her lap; she's going up next. With my left hand, I shield the words I'm writing. Leska's words. A note to myself: "Look up 'hot flash.'" I believe my mother doesn't notice. I believe she doesn't think it strange that I'm here with her every afternoon. As I watch Leska step down from the stage and sit next to the curmudgeonly theory professor, I watch them. I believe they don't know I'm watching. I believe if I copy their words, even if I use Leska's real name on paper, no one will know.

Now, almost twenty years later, the notebook sits in my lap. Looking at it, I know it's only one of many stories I wrote about Leska. I did use real names in one version of the narrative. It took the form of a short story. The final draft, which I typed, has disappeared. I couldn't find it this morning in any of the file boxes in the Voodoo Room. This was the version of the story in which Leska gave up her singing to marry the theory professor and become his Angel in the House. The ending felt inevitable to me. Leska's rediscovery of her voice risked too much freedom, too much future. It was easier for me to domesticate her, as I domesticated myself at thirteen, fantasizing about the man who would rescue me from the steps of the Paris Opera and put me where I belonged, in a lacy wedding dress. At the end of every draft I wrote, Leska stood on the cusp of a new, independent life. I wouldn't let her step over that threshold. "Sorry—I can't go on," she said again and again. She was stuck forever on the steps of the opera house. Where is the final version of her story? I probably ripped it to shreds the night my secret passage was invaded.

I kept the typed pages in a manila folder. One night I was proofreading them in my parents' bedroom when a horn honked outside. My grandparents, picking me up to see a film about Scotland at the university. It must have been my father's idea; somehow, quietly, he found ways to get me out of the house. Part of me resented him for phoning his parents to get me a social life; part of me was secretly grateful. I hollered good-bye to my parents and ran out the front door. My grandfather drove, silent as usual. My grandmother asked me about school. "I'm worried about my algebra test," I said.

She looked back from the front seat and smiled. "If you belong to this family," she said, "you can't possibly fail."

Her words didn't comfort me. I couldn't think of anything to say and looked out the window. And then I remembered: I'd left my folder on my parents' bed. My stomach coiled into a ball. I squeezed my eyes shut and prayed in my head: *Don't let them find it. Don't let Mom open it.* She'd done it before, reading one of my Miss Lamb stories in Germany, wanting to break through my silence, the space between our separate sickrooms, in the only way she knew. I'd slammed the door as violently as I could.

The drive to the university seemed to take an hour. Finally we found a parking space in my grandfather's faculty lot. We walked across campus in the blossomy spring darkness. I lifted my feet with effort. In the balcony of the theater where my father had taken me to *The Nutcracker* every year when I was a child, where I'd once heard Leska sing for Concerto Night, I sat through the travel film, hardly registering the images that flashed in front of me. *Don't let them find it. Don't let her open it.* On the way back to the car, I only half heard my grandmother's words about our Scottish ancestors. My typed words pounded in my head: Leska struggling through a *vocalise—I can't go on*—or confiding in the theory professor in his office, tears spilling onto the carpet.

"I have a confession to make," my mother said when I came in.

She held my folder in her hand. I tore it from her and ran down-stairs to my room. I slammed the door. I wanted to throw up. Why did it have to be *this* draft of the story, the only one with real names? Now my mother knew. She'd broken into my private world. I didn't speak to her for days.

What did my mother want with me? Why couldn't I stay invisible, suspended between Leska's world and mine? I believed, though I know better now, that my mother didn't see how troubled I was. Maybe she knew my secret even before she opened that folder. Maybe she broke in on purpose, to shock me back into my life. I almost wish she'd been able to. After that night I retreated further into my room. I wrote myself further into Leska's world, curled on the floor under my desk, or propped in my sickbed. I wrote her into a thickly curtained house. She pulled a vacuum cleaner from the closet. I rarely saw her in person anymore. The thread between us grew so long and fine that I could hardly hear her voice.

Several months later, my mother woke me on a summer morning to tell me Leska's friend, the theory professor, had died of a massive heart attack. All day I stumbled through my room, through the hallway, through the kitchen, as though I'd lost someone I loved. Shortly after, Leska moved back to the East Coast. "I think it was too hard for her to stay here," my mother told someone on the phone.

I stopped singing in front of the mirror. I put my notebook under my bed. As I hold it now, I feel I've encountered an old friend. I wonder where Leska is today, and if she's realized the future I did not dare imagine for her. She never knew that when she vanished from my life, though we'd never said a word to each other, I mourned.

conversation

In the neighborhood where I grew up, there was a shortcut to church. You walked to the bottom of our cul-de-sac and up the bishop's driveway, and then you climbed two flights of rickety wooden steps, passed by Jeannette's balcony on the way up, and emerged several yards from the church parking lot.

I could see Jeannette's balcony from my parents' front yard. I knew she was a distant cousin of my grandfather and had been an English professor. When I saw her at church, I admired her fine white hair, her upright bearing, her long fluttery scarves, and her voice so quiet that every word she spoke sounded important. My mother said Jeannette had never married because her parents disapproved of the man she loved when she was young; he wasn't "of the faith." At least, that's the story I remember.

Before we moved to Germany, my father asked Jeannette to tutor me in German. I walked up the steps to her duplex one afternoon a week. From my seat at her kitchen table, I could see down to my own street and Allen Park behind it. My parents spoke of Allen Park in hushed voices. It wasn't a park at all, but a wooded street lined with white cottages. A creek ran down the middle. "Hippies live there," my parents used to say. "It used to be an aviary," my mother once told me. This explained the tall chain-link cages I could see behind our back fence, when the leaves fell and I had a clear line of vision. Sometimes in my German lessons, I'd look at the slate-roofed cottages among the willows and elms and cottonwoods, and imagine people smoking and playing the guitar. Sometimes, if Jeannette's kitchen window was open, I could hear a peacock's cry.

Each week Jeannette gave me several sheets of onionskin, with meticulously typed vocabulary words and idioms. When I wasn't wondering about hippies and exotic birds, I tried to imitate the sounds Jeannette made in her papery eighty-year-old voice. To make the *ch* sound in the word *Ich,* she said, "Make the first sound in the word *human.*" I tried. It wasn't until I heard German spoken on the bus and in restaurants and in my father's instructions to the plumber that I heard German as a language. For now, it was a catalog of alien sounds.

As I tried to hide my terror of conjugating verbs (something I was surprised to find I did every day in my own language), I wondered how Jeannette had learned German and all the other things she knew. I wondered what she did every day, alone with her collection of ticking clocks and the flocked wallpaper that looked like rows of gaping faces. Once I'd overheard her tell my mother, "I may look eighty, but I still feel eighteen. Sometimes I flap around the house in my old bikini, and it feels *wonderful.*" I bent over the onionskin and tried not to picture this.

Jeannette's German lessons helped demystify the signs and

sounds I heard when my family landed at the Frankfurt airport. They didn't prepare me for the giant SEX SHOP sign that confronted me as I left the passport booth. They didn't prepare me for my lonely hour-long bus rides to school, or for my mother's miscarriage, or for the stories of gas chambers and bodies hanging from telephone poles that I overheard from the hallway outside our kitchen. They didn't prepare me for my own silence.

After our move back to the United States, I spent hours every day alone in my room. My whole being felt crippled. My white walls and rust-colored drapes were all the world I could bear. They became the lining of my chrysalis. When I wasn't ensconced in my sickbed with a Victorian novel, I drove myself even deeper into my cocoon by curling up under my desk. Sometimes this was the place where I wrote about Leska and her damaged voice, read *All Quiet on the Western Front* and fat library books about the French Revolution, and made up dialogue for Charlie and her shell-shocked brother. After several years of this, the summer I was fifteen, my father phoned Jeannette. This time, he announced over dinner, she was going to teach me Shakespeare.

I actually looked forward to climbing the old stairs and ringing Jeannette's doorbell. The familiar flocked wallpaper comforted me. So did the ticking clocks. This time, when we sat down at the table, Jeannette offered me a caffeinated Coke. I accepted, secretly relishing the sight of this elegant elderly woman breaking a Mormon taboo, even if it was a mild one, and subject to debate. Jeannette didn't give me anything typed on onionskin this time; she handed me a thin paperback and said, "We're going to start with the sonnets."

I didn't even know what a sonnet was. I had just started writing poetry for the first time since I was ten, with the help of an English teacher who removed most of my adjectives with a kind, brisk pencil slash (despite the adjectives in this sentence, I still consider this one of the greatest gifts anyone has given me). Jeannette allowed me the freedom of browsing through the book. I could choose a favorite sonnet, she said, and we'd look at it the next week. In the meantime, she gave me a minilecture on Elizabethan England and another book that I still have, Marchette Chute's *Shakespeare of London*.

I took the long way home, down Wilson Avenue and around the corner to my street. I leafed through the book of sonnets as I walked, and whispered one to myself: sonnet 73. Though I walked in June heat, I felt, like the poet, that leaves were falling in me. I murmured my favorite line: *Bare ruined choirs, where late the sweet birds sang.* The words said what I couldn't. They spoke to my inner ruin, the dead limbs of my childhood. They spoke in my own language, in iambic pentameter, the rhythm of the heartbeat.

When I brought the sonnet to Jeannette the next week, she talked about Shakespeare's obsession with time. With fourteen-odd clocks at work in the next room, the idea stuck with me. Falling leaves, wave-worn pebbles, razed towers—all showed signs of "sluttish time." Other people watched their lives go to ruin, too. I wasn't alone. I looked hard at Jeannette, still eighteen inside, never able to marry the man she loved. Somehow she kept going, making breakfast, reading, wafting from room to room in her bikini. She astonished me.

We moved on to *Henry IV, The Tempest,* and *Romeo and Juliet.* At home I pored over my paperback Folger Editions. I read the notes on the facing pages. I murmured lines to myself, trying to feel the language. At Jeannette's table, I listened to her read, her bifocals balanced on her nose, her delicate hair in perfect place as she bent over the book. One day she read me her favorite Shakespeare lines, when Juliet, waiting for Romeo, says:

> Come, night; come, Romeo; come, thou day in night;
> For thou wilt lie upon the wings of night
> Whiter than new snow upon a raven's back.

I can still hear Jeannette's voice almost whispering these words, as though she shared Juliet's wish. I felt I'd intruded on a painfully private thought.

At the end of the summer, Jeannette gave me a skinny strip of paper rolled up like a scroll. "It's a sonnet," she said. When I opened it, I saw one word per line, a thread of a poem, in her spidery handwriting. Years later in graduate school, I remembered this gift when poet Joan Larkin asked our class to "break the back of the sonnet."

I keep Jeannette's broken sonnet in a box of odd items from before my wedding. I found it the other day, buried under the key to our duplex in Germany, a note from the boy I loved in junior high (he wrote, eloquently, "Hi there"), a plastic stegosaurus keychain, a Paris Metro ticket, and scraps of letters I tore up and never sent. The sonnet goes like this:

> I
> through
> blue
> sky
> Fly
> to
> you.
> Why?
> Sweet
> love,
> feet
> move
>> So
>> slow.

silence

"So you sit in silence for an hour and then go home?" my father asked over dinner at my parents' house, after my first Quaker meeting.

"Sometimes, from what they tell me," I said.

"Sounds like my kind of church."

Since then, when people have asked, I've found myself describing unprogrammed Quaker meeting as group meditation, as a testimony meeting with questions instead of answers, or as spiritual improvisation. This interplay of silence and hesitant speech reminds me of Miles Davis's comment about the greatest challenge in jazz improvisation: "*not* to play all the notes you could play, but to wait, hesitate, let space become part of the configuration." A visual artist might describe Quaker meeting in terms of negative space, the in-between places in a painting. Sometimes negative space is all there is. In the social hour after my first meeting, as Friends greeted me kindly and explained what I could expect, one woman told me, "Sometimes nobody stands up to speak, but a lot of us come out of the silence having worked through difficult things." I tried to imagine this. I wondered if people ever fell asleep.

Several months after I started attending Friends' services, I found myself in a speechless meeting. Inside the Ladies' Literary Club, chairs squeaked under shifting bodies. Clouds darkened the windows' stained-glass rectangles. I looked at the floor. If I closed my eyes, I might end up doing some embarrassing head lolling, unable to stay awake. Maybe this is why most churches have rituals, I thought—to keep people from drifting off. To consider everyday life a sacrament, every encounter a potential means of grace, as Quakers do, was harder than I'd expected.

My mind skimmed the scuff marks on the wood floor. My paternal grandmother had probably walked across this room, I realized. She had died the week before. At her funeral my aunt joked that when the wind pulled down two hundred-foot cottonwoods in front of the Old Home in Huntsville, the day after her death, it must have been a sign: her joyful reunion with Grandpa. Another family member whispered to me that no, the trees blew down when she beat the tar out of him in Heaven. Where was she now? Anywhere? Drifting through this room, shocked to know what I could never tell her when she was alive?

Silly me, fantasizing about ghosts. I should feel some relief, I told myself, some guilty pleasure, knowing that now I could write my history without giving Grandma nightmares, the way I did when she found out I hadn't voted Republican in the last election. ("I dreamed the whole family turned Democrat!" she told my father in horror.) But I didn't feel relief. I felt as though someone had cut through a chain inside me, leaving me unhooked, missing a link to the past. My grandmother had raised me the first two years of my life, when my mother worked full-time to support my father in law school. She had picked raspberries with me. She had attempted to

grace notes

teach me how to knit—and then given up at the sight of my knotted, twisted yarn, threatening to tie a knot in me. She had sung in my presence, a lullaby, an old nursery rhyme, in the beautiful voice no one heard outside the Blue Room where she did her ironing and rocked her grandbabies to sleep. I missed that voice.

I closed my eyes. I imagined other phantom voices passing through me. The voices of the great-grandfathers I'd never met. The one on my father's side, who used to sing whole scenes from Gilbert and Sullivan as he plowed the family fields as a boy; in his later years he made up a song about a grizzly bear—and made his Boy Scout troop sing all thirty-two verses as they hiked. Another, my mother's black-sheep grandfather, used to yodel on the radio. He was the link in the chain that led back through other rebel wanderers, Mormon converts on the frontier, Connecticut Puritans and their forebears, who fled England on the *Arbella*. The family I'd hunted down, as I traced rain-beaten headstones with my fingers in cemeteries all over Stamford and Darien. The taciturn man at the historical society had said, "Those Weeds are buried everywhere." So were their spouses and cousins, the Scofields, and Hoyts, and Seelys . . .

And Catharine. I remembered being mildly interested in her diary, which I'd never bothered to photocopy. After all, she wasn't a direct ancestor, and, glancing through her spiritual musings, I'd thought her too pious. Preoccupied with her health, too. She sounded a little too much like the women in my family. I wanted to connect with a New England ancestor I could look up to, a tough mama who survived childbirth and war and malaria, who hauled stones from the pasture and built a wall with them herself, a woman who braved the mosquito-ridden marshes to graze her cattle, a woman who shattered oysters, Pequot-style, to fertilize her kitchen garden. Not a retiring lady known for her "delicate constitution." Not a ghost in a nightgown. *Catharine. Catharine.* The name moved through my head like the kind of song you'd like to forget but can't, like a breeze breathing in through an open window.

No. It was bad enough, imagining my grandmother transparent, shaking her head at me from the ceiling. I didn't need a nineteenth-century woman in white inside my head. Why couldn't somebody stand up and say something to click me back into the present? The week before, my friend Boris had stood and ruminated about how quickly spring passes, how he wanted to savor each moment. The week before that, soft-spoken Rand had told the parable from *The Brothers Karamazov* about the woman in hell who recalls the one unselfish thing she did in her life, giving an onion to a passing stranger. And then Phil, the urban planning professor, had mused about where the onion came from, the soil, the labor, the tools and the foundry that made the tools, all that went into the miserly woman's field: "Every kindness comes from somewhere." His words had moved me like the logic of a good poem. One day Caroline, who was raised Methodist, had stood to sing a hymn she remembered from childhood. Her voice had spoken to my heart. Didn't anyone have a sick relative they wanted us to hold in the Light? *Please, say something, anything. Distract me from that sickroom in Darien.*

No. Space. Silence. I opened my eyes. I focused on the floor. Several other people were doing the same. Others had their eyes shut. No one showed any intention of standing and breaking into the stillness. *Catharine.* The breeze blew through me. Was it a ghost, or that moment of crisis Quakers call "an unsolicited Leading"? Maybe it was both. Somehow, something was telling me to find bedridden Catharine. To read that diary again. This wind. I'd felt it before.

The first time, I didn't know the Quaker term *Leading*, but my Mormon upbringing had taught me to pay attention to strange inklings. It happened in Carson City, Nevada, when Anders was a year old and I was working comfortably at home as a freelance journalist. One day my editor phoned and offered me a staff writer position. I told him I'd think about it; I already knew the answer was no. How could I leave this child I'd become instantly, shockingly, attached to, and how could I meet more than one deadline a week? Glad that decision was made, I went on with my life. Or tried to. For some reason I couldn't sleep. I couldn't concentrate on my favorite Edith Wharton novel. Sitting on the front porch blowing bubbles with Anders, I kept getting the urge to run around the block. The air seemed to push on me from all directions. "Why don't you at least

104

grace notes

consider saying yes?" Kent suggested one night as I sat up in bed, too edgy to lie down. "Just entertain the thought and see how you feel." I tried it. Peace flooded me like the proverbial river. The next morning I phoned my editor and said yes. He told me I could still do some work at home. I found a reliable, nurturing baby-sitter. I loved my work and, after a year, gained enough confidence to apply to graduate school.

My second "Leading" grabbed me by the hair and wouldn't let go. It happened in Chicago, on a vacation with Kent, Anders, and my sister-in-law. I'd just finished selecting the six graduate programs I wanted to apply to, all of them in the West. I was going to ride the 1990s trend of the "western woman writer." The poets and nature writers I knew had encouraged me. After five years of adjusting to hardscrabble Carson City, I'd vowed loyalty to the desert, to my roots in the Great Basin. Imagine my distress when, looking for a music store inside a Chicago office building, I knew it was time to move east. At first I blamed the music, the strains of "Saturday Night Waltz" from Aaron Copland's *Rodeo* wafting up from the lower lobby, where a youth orchestra was practicing. The music lilted in my blood. The roots of my hair tingled in three-four time. I could have sworn the strings were calling to me. *I'm not used to wandering into a building and hearing music I love, that's all,* I told myself. But if that was all, why did I feel physically arrested, pulled in an invisible, irresistible traction? Why did I get sick to my stomach that night and sob until three in the morning, when my sister-in-law woke and tried to comfort me? "You're just tired," she said. "You need to get back into your routine at home, and you'll be fine." But when I got home, the house felt strange. When I went to work, I felt I'd stepped into the wrong size shoe. I quit my job at the paper the next week. Kent and I started listing cities and graduate programs east of the Mississippi. We wrote "New York," crossed it out and wrote it again, four times. When the brochure from Sarah Lawrence arrived in the mail, I took one look at the tuition costs and threw it away. "Just *consider* applying there," Kent said on the phone. I did. When I closed my eyes and imagined myself there, I did not feel the panic I expected. I felt peace.

Now, sitting in Quaker meeting, I told myself to be cautious. I'd read about a man, offered a job as a college president, who called a Quaker clearness committee (a small group that offers support and insight) to help sort out his feelings and discovered, after some gentle questioning, that what he'd believed was a Leading was really the wish to see his picture in the paper; he turned down the job. I'd read Quaker writer Mary Rose O'Reilly's advice not to take inner directions too literally: "It's when we're too literal that we make regrettable decisions about sailing to Tahiti." Was I being too literal, thinking I'd have to fly to Connecticut to reconnect with a woman dead for a century and a half? Kent and I had already spent all our savings on a trip to Norway, and we hadn't even left yet. Maybe I could stop in Stamford on our way out of New York. Maybe the diary was still there. If not, well, I could find another way. In the depth of my being, I realized, I needed that woman in white in my life. Catharine had some things to tell me.

Early Quakers had another term for "Leading": they called it "an opening." In that speechless meeting, I sat in silence and opened, allowing for space between the sounds and colors that made up my life. The wind blew through that space, pushing me east all over again.

four

diary

My father discovered it in the garage next to the cabin, four months after my grandmother's death. Every Saturday he'd been sorting through boxes with my aunts, all of them hoping Grandma wasn't watching from the ether. They knew that selling the cabin would have broken her heart. My father found the book stuffed in a box of dishes and brought it home. My mother found the heated words, written to no one, at the back. Today, when I bring Kent and the boys to their house for dinner, she hands me the book.

I sit down at the desk in the family room. This isn't an ordinary diary. It says "ROLL BOOK" in faded gold letters on the front. Maybe it was used in someone's school; all the pages before page 43 have been cut out;

there are check marks on the remaining margins. At some point it became a family record book. On the first written page, I find a list of names I know from the genealogy sheets in my Mormon "Book of Remembrance." On page 58, in handwriting much too ornamental to be my grandmother's, are the headings "Birth," "Baptism," and "Death." The names underneath, in what could very well be Grandma's writing, belong to the Fowles family and their spouses, Mormon converts who emigrated from England and Wales in the mid-1800s. Yellowed newspaper clippings fill many of the pages, with headlines like "Buhl Peaches Win Approval," "Man Drops Dead as Home Burns," and "Just Plain Folks." A glimpse of life in Burley, Idaho, where my grandmother and her eight older siblings grew up. Several pages are filled with records of her brothers who fought in World War II: draft numbers, order numbers, serial numbers, and at the bottom of page 52, devoted to Delton, a handwritten addendum: "Died in prison camp from malnutrition, May 28, 1942." I remember my mother telling me that Delton died on the death march in the Philippines. Sheldon, the other enlisted brother, survived; he died recently in Nevada. I turn the page. Another newspaper clipping: Grandma's brother Elwood, dead at forty-six of a cerebral hemorrhage in Billings, Montana. "He was found lying in a pasture."

I don't want to read the words at the back—not yet. I lift page after page, looking for other surprises. Pressed oak leaves, brilliant red and yellow. Blank pages. A dried pink rose. Someone's delicate lace, preserved in a clear paper envelope. More blank pages. I flip backward and find, on page 60, my grandmother's wedding notices, describing the reception at Salt Lake City's Hotel Utah after the temple ceremony. Here's a written image of the bride: "From her head hung a fragile finger-tip veil, about her neck she wore pearls, and a single orchid was her only flower." And another clipping: "Her going-away outfit was a smart black suit, hat and shoes, with a white blouse and a flame colored bag." There stood my grandmother, the farm girl from Burley, marrying into what my husband jokingly calls "the Mormon aristocracy." I know she worried she didn't fit into my grandfather's family of college deans and church authorities. She once told me that when Grandpa came to court her in Idaho and they went to a dance in town, some hired hands were kicking a beer bottle around on the floor. "I was mortified," she whispered. "I didn't know if he'd ever come see me again." Shortly before her death, she told me that someone in her husband's family had understood her: her father-in-law, the respected academic who was a singing farm boy at heart. He took the young couple to the circus after their reception. The newspapers didn't mention this. After the wedding notices, four pages have been torn out.

I turn to the back of the book. Page 142. Yes, it's Grandma's writing, not much different from the no-nonsense cursive on the birthday card she sent my son Evan, a month before her death. She dated the entry Dec. 27, but there's no year. Sometime in her youth, before she went away to Brigham Young University and discovered her talent for drama, before she married my grandfather and became the proper lady I knew, she wrote: "Had a fight with Marvel. Licked the devil out of her. Elwood Locked me in the Bedroom, and Pounded me. Cooked Liver [something illegible] for the Folks and cut it Wrong. Bribed Rose and Alma to wash the dishes and sluffed out of the Mopping. Mama told me to spank Jack and Sheldon for being bad and when I did they Laughed instead of cried as they should." To think that Grandma, who never left a chore undone, who always ate after everyone else had been served, had once "sluffed out of the Mopping." What did she use to bribe her older sisters? Rose, who died last month, can't tell me. And what did poor Marvel do to deserve having the devil licked out of her? She's Grandma's oldest living sister, the only sibling left, in fact. The one I still visit, the one who saves chocolate bars for my boys, the one who came out of Grandma's hospital room last May and said to me with her usual bluntness, "She's not going to make it." She didn't say a word as I drove her home. We sat side by side as trees and cars flashed by, as the world went on with its business, she in her private grief and I in mine.

I run my fingers over Grandma's words. I'm glad she had fire in her. I wish I'd seen more of it. After this hurried explosion of feeling, the rest of the pages in the book have been ripped out, leaving their jagged edges. Did Grandma write on those pages, too? I think of the shredder she kept next to her printer in the assisted-living center, the last year of her life, when she managed to sit at the computer for three hours a day, writing her life story in spite of the shingles pain deep in her back. I think of her words read by my aunt at her funeral, the story about the day the gypsies came to the farm in Burley when she was having a bath in the old washtub. I remember thinking, *Grandma was a writer. Why didn't we know this?* I wonder what else we didn't know, and never will. The words torn out of this book. The words she shredded into spaghetti-thin strips, even after she'd told my uncle, "I want to rewrite my diaries, and this time I'm going to tell the truth."

She said these words from a hospital bed. She'd collapsed after months of caring for my cancer-ridden grandfather. My uncle found her on the floor in their high-rise condo, barely conscious as Grandpa shouted at her from the bedroom, his white hair flying wild. "He was getting senile and didn't know what was going on," my uncle told me recently on the phone. "He was shaking his finger, demanding his pills." And Grandma lay there on the floor of the hall-way, in too much pain to move. I imagine her body screaming what her voice had never been able to: ENOUGH. Finally, in her hospital room, she did find words for the emotions she'd left unspoken for decades. She said she didn't want to go home. She said she wouldn't be her husband's servant anymore. She said she was tired of doing her duty so well. I heard these words through my mother and my uncle. I wish I'd been in the room to hear them myself.

And I wish I could read the written words my grandmother de-stroyed. Not only for the guilty pleasure of it, but because I wonder if I really knew her. Did Grandma speak as freely of physical pain, spiritual epiphany, and friendship as nineteenth-century Catharine did in her diary? To think that a hundred years passed between these women's lives, and it's the twentieth-century writer who couldn't bear to tell the truth.

As a child, I glimpsed Grandma's secret self only rarely. I saw it sometimes when she was outdoors, her body remembering the rhythms of the farm. I loved to watch her picking raspberries, her head scarved to keep the bees out of her ears, or burning the cattails behind the cabin every March, as she tromped through the smoke in her red windbreaker. Traces of her younger self hid in the basement of my grandparents' old house in Salt Lake: my cousins and I used to raid her costume trunks, trying on grass skirts, a red taffeta dress with a Spanish shawl, scratchy pioneer dresses with leg-o'-mutton sleeves, or a silk kimono. Feathered hats abounded. We older girls fought over the sequined flapper dress every Halloween. Sliding my arms into Grandma's dust-creased, too long sleeves, I tried to picture her onstage in a college auditorium, chanting, *Double, double, toil and trouble / Fire burn, and cauldron bubble,* as she told me she had once, in a production of *Macbeth.* Or "playing Hollywood" with her sisters as she said they used to do, walking the road from the farm into town, enormous hats bobbing on their heads.

My grandmother took great, vicarious pleasure in her children's love of stage and song. She perfected a role of her own: the Angel in the House. She raised seven children without help from her husband, who spent most of his time in church meetings, when he wasn't traveling to fossil-fuel conferences all over the world. (Once, my uncle remembers, he ran upstairs looking for his father, and one of his siblings said, "Oh, didn't you know? He's been gone for a week.") While her children were still at home, my grandmother also cared for her in-laws, both debilitated by strokes. When I knew her, her house was immaculate. She wore a spotless white apron. Her kitchen simmered with the smell of roasting beef, baking bread, or boiling peaches. She hosted the perfect dinner party several times a month, crystal punch cups gleaming on the table. She gave an announcement tea (without tea, of course) for each granddaughter's engagement. She had two Christmas trees every December, a flocked one behind the baby grand piano, a green one upstairs on the landing. In the summers, she found time to lead Saturday tours of the Old Home in Huntsville, where her husband's uncle the prophet had grown up; she'd memorized her in-laws' family history, down to the last lace doily. Though she loved the house and its history, they weren't her own. Her job was to be a supporter of Great Men and to preserve the mythology that surrounded them. She knew every line in her part, and every silence. When my grandfather spoke from the pulpit in the Mormon Tabernacle, she sat with the other General Authorities' wives, hidden beneath a sweeping balcony. When I heard her spoken of in church or at dinner parties, people said with great respect, "She never complains."

I ask my mother for a blank piece of paper, so I can copy Grandma's rant from the back of the old roll book. I don't want to forget this moment when she did, Heaven help us, complain. One by one, the words appear in my own handwriting. But as I try to imagine my grandmother young, red-faced and fuming, scratching her pencil across the page, something in me wants the mental film to stop. *Give me back the lady in the white apron. Give me back the refuge of my childhood.* I understand now. My sense of stability as a child depended on my grandmother's playing her part to perfection. I was complicit in her acceptance of traditional gender roles. Whenever I rang her doorbell, I expected to push the door right open and find her inside, canning or dusting or ironing or singing a baby cousin to sleep. Had I walked in and found her hard at work on a novel, or shouting at Grandpa for his chronic silence, I would have run away in horror. Grandma didn't do such things. She didn't get sick or depressed as my mother did, rebelling against her life in the only way she knew. Grandma simply let her house, which had been her husband's parents' house, absorb her. I don't know why she never emulated her mother-in-law, who had graduated from Barnard and served as dean of a women's college in northern Utah. Maybe she could not shake her feeling of inferiority as an Idaho farm girl. Maybe my grandfather expected too much. Unlike his parents, he never hired help for the large family home with its four garden levels. My grandmother spent her days keeping weeds and dust at bay. I couldn't imagine her doing anything else. When I visited, I let the house absorb me, too. I curled up and slept on the tall bed in the Blue Room, the nubby white bedspread over me, a needlepoint of Mozart at the harpsichord above me on the wall, the entry-hall clock ticking its heartbeat through the house. At Grandma's, I knew I was safe, not because Grandma was especially embracing, but because she was there. She would never fall apart or withdraw into her room or drive away for good. She would never complain.

When Grandma wasn't in the house, the air inside it changed. I noticed this when I was twelve and my parents went to Hawaii for two weeks, sending me to Grandma's. In the middle of my stay, she had to fly to California to tend some younger cousins. I was left with Grandpa. Maybe it was no coincidence that I came down with a cold and couldn't go to school. I'd always dreaded being alone with Grandpa in the car. He never spoke. I never knew what to say. Now, he stuck his head into the Blue Room every morning before he left for the university, said a formal "How are you today?" and lumbered down the stairs. When I felt well enough, I made his toast and scrambled his eggs, leaving them as soft as Grandma did. We sat next to each other on the kitchen barstools, on which my cousins and I, as small children, had spun around wildly when no one was looking. Now there were no cousins in the house to distract us: the only sounds came from our forks and Grandpa's throat, which he cleared every few minutes, as though preparing to say something that never came out. Then, to my relief, he was gone. All day I wandered the house with my box of Kleenex, trying to feel the comfort I usually felt there. It wasn't in the kitchen. It wasn't in the dining room, where the afternoon sunlight played on the chandelier. It wasn't in the living room, or the back room, or the bedrooms upstairs. The Angel in the House had vanished. By dinnertime I was ready for any company, even Grandpa's. He sat at the head of the dining room table, which I'd set as meticulously as Grandma did, and ate the casserole I'd heated. He didn't say a word. Maybe I wasn't ready for his company after all. My hands felt clammy as I buttered my bread. Why couldn't this man, who had advised the president on the energy crisis, who stood at the pulpit and tried to connect Creation theory with the second law of thermodynamics, talk to me?

"How were your classes today?" I ventured.

He cleared his throat. "Fine, just fine," he said.

I cleared the table and served the ice cream. We avoided each other's eyes. *Maybe he has important things on his mind,* I thought. *Or maybe he knows I'm not doing well in algebra. Or maybe he thinks I shouldn't have stayed in my nightgown and robe all day.* Our spoons clicked in our bowls. The clock clanged six o'clock. I cleared the dessert dishes. I wanted my grandmother back. It didn't occur to me that maybe she was thrilled not to be here.

"I love being alone," she whispered to me, several months after my grandfather's death. She was standing with effort, still in deep pain from shingles, putting groceries away in her small kitchen in an assisted-living center. I helped her unload the plastic bag. Three cartons of Häagen Dazs. Microwave popcorn.

"I'm glad to see you're enjoying life a little," I said.

She found her walker, and we moved, slowly, into her sitting room. "Sometimes I invite one of the ladies over for ice cream, and do you know what?" She turned to me with a sly grin. "Every night I stay up late and read. I never could before. Grandpa didn't like any lights on." When she said this, I wanted to cry. I wanted to tell her all about the unhappy years in my own marriage, the patriarch husband, the punishing silences. But something stopped me. It was the same fear that had kept my cousins and me from speaking to anyone about our "newlywed hell." Why was I afraid to talk to my grandmother? Even in her newfound widow's freedom, she still represented our family's unspoken code of propriety to me. I could not fall apart in her presence.

Several months later, when I arrived at the assisted-living center, I found her in bed in the room where Grandpa had died. She wore an old black dress. She'd sprayed her hair straight up in spikes. She grinned at me. "I've just been downstairs to the Halloween party," she said. "You should have seen my vampire getup. I just got the blood drops wiped off my mouth."

I sat down on the bed, too stunned to speak. So this was the woman who'd worn the flapper dress, the Spanish shawl, the witch's robe. My happy vampire grandma. I hoped Grandpa was paying attention, wherever he was.

For two years, after Grandma had become too ill to meet his every need and they'd moved from their condo to the assisted-living center, Grandpa lay on his back on this bed, staring at the ceiling. He rarely watched TV. He rarely spoke, even to his wife. She was stuck with the silent treatment for good. When we came to visit, he said his usual, "Hi, how are you?" and looked at the ceiling again. I would have relished any conversation with him, even the speeches he'd given at every family party, when he would stand and clear his throat and begin, "When we meet again in the Celestial Kingdom . . ." Sometimes, when I brought the boys to his sickroom, his eyes would come alive, and he'd open his drawer of M&M's for them. Once I brought Kate, who got him to talk about friends he'd known years before when he was a bishop. I saw him smile and laugh, something that had always seemed to come more easily to him with people outside the family. I was grateful anyway.

My parents said Grandpa had withdrawn more than ever because he was embarrassed about his growing senility. I wondered if there were other reasons. He'd been promised, in a patriarchal blessing in his youth, that he would carry the treasures of the church to the New Jerusalem—in his lifetime. Though he'd spent his life preparing for positions in the highest echelons of the church, he'd been released after five years as a General Authority. Before that, the end of the 1970s energy crisis had made his research superfluous. Without his work and his church service, and with only a tenuous emotional connection to his own family, he must have felt lost in the world. When a freak tornado roared through Salt Lake City and narrowly missed his window in the high-rise condo, did he think for a moment that there was hope, that maybe he'd live to see the Second Coming after all? He never said. His life wound down like a clock. Maybe he'd always imagined it this way, for all his talk of the celestial glories to come. He'd been wrong in his attempt to disprove evolution with the second law of thermodynamics, I discovered as an adult: the law of entropy does not apply to living systems. Maybe that was his problem, I once thought in a moment of bitterness—he got people mixed up with things; he could not imagine changing, learning to speak his feelings, becoming a happier person; all he could do was wait for his system to run down. But then I recalled the way he'd clear his throat when speaking of his grandchildren from the pulpit, forcing down the rising tears, the tenderness he could not express.

The last time I saw Grandpa, when Kent and I brought the boys to say good-bye a few hours before he died, he was barely conscious. "His swallowing mechanism has failed," my aunt whispered to me outside his door; I noticed she didn't say "swallowing reflex" when talking about him, but used the language of machines. She and another aunt had tried putting a sponge to Grandpa's lips, but they knew it wouldn't help. We walked into his room, holding our boys by the hand. He lay on the bed in his temple undershirt and pajama bottoms, no longer the six-foot-five figure who had awed me as a child. "Tell him you love him," Kent said, and I did, for the first time in my life. Eyes shut, breathing hard, he clamped his left hand over his mouth. I stared at that trembling hand. Even at the end of his life, there was something he would not let out. A sob, maybe. Or the words we all longed to hear, though we couldn't have said what they were.

"What was Grandpa like when you married him?" I blurted out as I sat by Grandma on the bed where he had died. For once, my words just spilled out; Grandma the vampire seemed so much more accessible than the lady with perfect white hair.

"He loved everything that was alive," she said. "He used to rescue animals from the lab at the university and bring them home. Even a skunk! And do you remember the story of the blow snake he brought home? It found its way into the heating ducts. When his parents' cleaning lady walked into the entry hall, it stuck its head out of the vent and made this terrible sound. She ran away and never came back. Your grandpa's favorite creature was the praying mantis. He always wanted to know how God had made such a strange-looking thing."

Grandma was not describing the person I'd known. He had loved living creatures? Yes, I'd heard the story of the blow snake. But I'd always thought my great-grandfather had been the one to bring it home. I sat speechless as Grandma went on, "And he was so funny. Everything was a joke to him. We had some fun times."

"I don't remember him that way at all. Except for the nights he pretended to be a giant and scared us. We used to run screaming through the house."

Grandma laughed a deep laugh. "Fee, fie, fo, fum. . . . He made a good giant."

"Why do you think he stopped joking?"

She closed her eyes. She thought hard. Then she said, "He got busy. The first time he was a bishop, he was in his twenties. It never let up after that. He didn't have time for anything else."

Was that all? The next week, my uncle and I talked on the phone until midnight. He's the youngest son, whose subversive sense of humor has given me a glimpse of Grandpa's younger self. In this conversation I could hear the grief in my uncle's voice, not for the father he'd lost, but for the father he felt he'd never had. He told me his theory: "My dad didn't want to do all the things his dad had done. He didn't want to be a super Scout, and never got his Eagle. He didn't go on a mission. For a while he may have rebelled a little against all the family pressure to achieve status in the church, the oldest son stuff." I understood this all too well; my father is Grandpa's oldest son and has worn the family name like an ill-fitting coat. Had I been born a boy, I would have carried on that name—with the Roman numeral *V* attached. "I think my dad did one of two things," my uncle went on. "He either had an epiphany at some point and committed himself completely to the church, or—and I think this is more likely—he gave in to it for ego reasons." *Gave in.* I imagined Grandpa letting the Mormon hierarchy absorb him into its granite walls, as Grandma had let her in-laws' house absorb her.

All I knew of Grandpa's inner self is what I see in my uncle, and what I hear, now, in that noisy throat-clearing, too much emotion to voice. Grandpa left no costume trunks, no voice singing lullabies in the dark, no furious diary entry. All my father found in the cabin boxes that might shed unexpected light was a tiny leather book that looked like the miniature Scriptures people used to take to church. When my father unsnapped it, the shiny-tipped pages were face cards—a Mormon taboo. Who in the family had the nerve to take *this* to church? I hold out some hope that, back in the days when he knew how to have fun, it was Grandpa.

Now there's no one I can ask. Grandma is gone. But I can find out other things. I can talk to my uncle, and the cousin who surprises me when he asks, "Were you ever scared of Grandma?" I can e-mail another cousin this question, and read her answer: "I'd never thought of being scared of Grandma until I realized that what held us together as a family was not love and mutual respect, but authority and fear." I often turn this statement over in my mind. Yes, we've all felt the fear Grandma felt and passed on to us. Or, as one of my aunts puts it, "We loved her too much to rebel and separate the way most kids do. We didn't want to hurt her feelings." Whatever the reasons, we've all suffered from what my uncle calls "emotional constipation." So why, when I think of my grandparents, do I feel a sudden rush of love? And why, when I see my aunts, uncles, and cousins, do I feel connected to them in a sure, wordless way, even if we haven't seen each other in several years? Maybe the answer lies in a dream I had recently, in which Grandpa came back from the dead. I found him in a school gym, surrounded by the extended family. He wasn't wearing his usual white dress shirt but a short-sleeved blue T-shirt. He wasn't the six-foot-five giant he had been in real life; his eyes met mine on the level. He held me close, and we talked. I woke up with a terrible sense of homesickness. There *was* a seed of this spontaneous family affection in all our duty-doing, some instinctive love for the living.

My boys still wave at Grandma's window as we drive by the assisted-living center on our way home from school. "Oh, I forgot Great-Grandma died," Evan said the other day. "Remember when we visited her in the hospital and you were sad?" He reminds me of this often. I'm glad he remembers. He almost didn't get to see her that day. My father had warned me not to take the boys to the hospital. "She looks like something out of a horror movie," he said. Kent and I took them anyway. When my aunt saw us, she wanted to keep us out—until Grandma saw us in the hall and her eyes, the only part of her I recognized, lit up. The four of us stood by her bed, and she touched our hands, feeling out every fold of skin, every knuckle, as she sucked in air through an oxygen mask. She'd gone into heart and kidney failure several days before, as she put on her best blouse for her sister Marvel's ninety-fourth birthday party. She'd planned it herself, down to the napkin rings. That night, after an hour of struggle to get into her clothes, she managed to come downstairs to the social room in the care center. For a while she sat at the table in her wheelchair. She whispered to me, with terrible effort, that the

118   *grace notes*

chicken dish hadn't been her first choice. After dinner my aunt rushed her to the hospital, where, one by one, her organs shut down.

The day we visited, she wouldn't let go of my hand. The nurse told her she had to; it was time for more tests. I unhooked her fingers as gently as I could. We went back into the hall. I leaned against the wall and cried, the boys stroking my arm and my back. My aunt came out and whispered the latest prognosis to Kent. Two days later I brought Great-aunt Marvel to see Grandma, the last time either of us would. We walked into her hospital room together. Soon I would leave the sisters alone together to reminisce in silence about "playing Hollywood" on the farm road in Idaho, kicking up dust as their dress-up hats slipped down over their eyes. But first I took Grandma's hand. Once again, she could not speak, except with her life-lit eyes. We simply looked at each other. I felt, for that moment, that I had always known her.

nine openings

"AND THIS IS FOR YOU AND YOUR MERCEDES AND YOUR MOBILE PHONE!" hollered a voice. Then—I knew it—came the trumpet blast, a tone so hard it cracked, and then another, and another, until the man's breath ran out.

I shut the drapes, upstairs in my grandparents' home. I was eighteen, trying to study for a college exam. This was the house where I'd always felt safe, here in the Blue Room with its mosaic-tiled fireplace and antique dresser. I'd roamed without worry in the backyard with its four levels—lawn, orchard, rose level, decrepit handball court where my cousins and I once pretended to guillotine each other with the fallen basketball standard—and below all this, the gully. In the middle of an affluent Salt Lake City neighborhood, the gully made me forget I lived in the desert. It was a cavern of trees with a creek running through it, acorns all over the broken stone steps, and tulips in the spring weeds. I took my friends down there, and we picked our way down the creek, finding the occasional condom or drug needle. I probably had reason not to feel safe in the gully, but it was my refuge—at least until the horn-blowing intruder appeared.

My father called him "the mad trumpeter." We heard his ranting down in the gully at about the same time every night. My grandparents were living out of the country on a church assignment and couldn't hear the man's insults, sometimes hurled at their neighbors by name. The police had been called, but they always seemed to arrive too late. At least this was a new sound in the neighborhood, something besides the first act of *Tosca*, which someone across the gully played at top volume every Saturday morning.

As I listened to the trumpeter in the gully, shouting and squawking, I wondered what he looked like. His voice didn't sound very old. I wondered how he'd sound in a normal conversation. Maybe his tirade wasn't so different from the baritone's lustful aria at the end of *Tosca*'s first act, a bigger-than-life bellowing, a longing for a woman he can't have. In *Tosca*, church bells swing along to the singer's blasphemy. Our local lunatic seemed to need a trumpet to sing for him, to shout out his rage at the rich.

I didn't think his targets included me. My fairy-tale life was a borrowed one: we lived in this house while our own more modest house was being remodeled. Though, to my father, his parents' house with its leaks and summer beetle infestation and weirdly rigged octopus furnace was more worry than pleasure, I admit it made me feel important. I liked to watch my dates' reactions when they picked me up there ("A Frank Lloyd Wright design? Really?"). I liked to run my fingers over all the books on the walls, and play with the lock on the antique china hutch. My family didn't own a Mercedes (in fact, my father once returned one out of guilt), but we were snobs in our own way.

The trumpeter's noise scared me, but not because it was meant for every snob within earshot, including myself. I was still too protected to realize that. It scared me to hear anybody give voice to primal anger. His demonstration haunted me, even after he'd had given up for the night. Now, when I went to church on Sundays, the soft-spoken pleasantries in the chapel aisles sounded somehow foreign and false.

Several years before, I'd attended a fireside, or informal church meeting, in the home of a neighbor who lived across the gully from my grandparents. The speaker was another neighbor, recently called as a Mormon apostle. We teenagers sat on soft chairs in the living room, a fire in the fireplace, pineapple slush and three kinds of brownies waiting for us on the dining room table. The apostle stood in front of the fire and spoke in the gentle, singsong tones I'd grown accustomed to hearing from General Authorities. I felt safe in that room. As the man spoke of eternal progression and quoted Scripture from memory, I pictured a softly carpeted stairway to Heaven. I wanted to crumple all my doubts about the church and walk those steps. It would be easy. All I had to do was please the people waiting for me at the top.

At the end of his speech, the apostle asked each of us what we wanted most to achieve in our lives. Some said things like "Go on a mission" and "Get married in the temple." I probably wanted to sound especially Christlike when I said, "Never offend anyone." The apostle frowned at me. He said, "You can be a good person and still offend people, even without meaning to. Sometimes you'll step on other people's toes." Though this man is the least likely person I can imagine stepping on toes, his words struck deep. Had I gotten the Gospel all wrong? Was it all right to be mad and say so? Whenever my mother called me into the bathroom to tell me I'd said something "inappropriate," I prickled with shame. I never talked back. I never even quarreled with my parents over my midnight curfew. All my life I'd thought this was what Jesus wanted me to do: be polite.

And I was. People often commented on my "maturity." I had learned to say the right thing at the right moment. When my best friend in eighth grade unceremoniously dropped me for a wisecracking blonde in our class, I was as nice to her as ever. I tried to smile and look interested when the two of them giggled about streaking their hair with lemon juice. My stomach knotted up in pain. I struggled with my algebra problems, bent double over my desk. I thought I was learning to forgive. I was learning to smother myself in layers of niceness, just as my grandmother did, and as she had taught her daughter-in-law, my mother, to do.

four

Several years later, when my college boyfriend turned cold and distant, I sat on the grass in front of the music building, writing a letter. I churned inside. I tore page after page out of my notebook. I wanted it to be perfect. I was going to "kill him with kindness," as my mother had always advised when someone hurt my feelings. "You are so much more noble than I am," I wrote. "You know what really matters in this life." *How could you do this to me?* bellowed a voice in my head. I shut it out and kept writing.

I couldn't shut out the mad trumpeter. He hollered and blasted his brass so loud that we could hear it all over the house. He brought the "inappropriate," the rage never expressed in our family, to our very doorstep. He punctured the safe, proper world I thought of as home. The Blue Room, with its needlepoint of little Mozart, no longer looked benign. As I tapped my pencil on my notebook paper and closed my eyes, trying to remember one significant work by every Italian writer in my notes, I remembered something else: a voice in the street under my window in Siena, where I'd studied over the summer. I woke to the sound of a man's inconsolable shouting. I opened the green shutters. Deep in the still-shadowed street, the man was walking backward, his arms out, his voice calling curses at someone—a relative? a lover? Typical tourist, I had thought the scene as romantic as the bands of young people spinning flags and chanting their way to the Campo Piazza, taunting their rival districts before the famous Palio horse race. Now, as the trumpeter hurled obscenities at the attorney who lived down the street, I shuddered. This was anything but romantic. This was mental illness or terrible pain or both, voiced in my own language, in my own neighborhood, and I didn't want to think about it. I didn't want to think about my own pain, that letter from my boyfriend, now a Mormon missionary, weighing down every bone in my body (*I loved you last week, but I don't love you this week. . . .*).

Maybe the trumpeter's bellowing scared me because, some-where in my body, I longed to bellow, too. At my boyfriend. At my grandfather, whose silence, even when he was thousands of miles away, hung in every room of this house. At my grandmother, the model martyr. At my father for sequestering himself with his books when I wanted to talk. At my mother for teaching me to say and do what was "appropriate," no matter what I happened to feel.

As a very young child, I was normal. I screamed. I scared away any little cousin who happened to touch the meticulously arranged glass dogs on my dresser. My mother must have cured me of this, with exquisite guilt, before I was six. She probably couldn't stand to hear me shriek my rage; her own mother, in excruciating pain from arthritis from the time she was thirty-five, had hollered plenty. She had used words far worse than the *booby* and *pee* my mother forbade me to utter. She had thrown things. She had slapped. When at four I screamed uncontrollably about my cousin's intrusion into my room, my mother said in a voice of terrifying calm, "You got your temper from Grandma." My mother tried so hard to appear perfect, to never contradict anyone or blurt out a painful truth, that she must have suffered terribly when I voiced my rage. She must have heard her mother-in-law's voice in her head: *If you can't say something nice, don't say anything at all.* Now my mother gives herself permission to scream; when she's at wit's end she locks herself in her room and forgets, for a few moments of crazy bellowing, that she's a singer and should protect her vocal cords. "I know people like Thich Nhat Hanh talk about just recognizing you're angry and letting that be enough," she tells me, "but I have to make noise. I just try not to direct it at other people."

I didn't rediscover the screamer in me until I had kids of my own. Children are primal creatures, and mine have brought out the primal in me. "I WANT ABSOLUTE SILENCE!" I ranted, the day Anders toppled a whole jug of orange juice onto the kitchen floor and I watched it spill, wave after wave, down the heat vent. When he offered a timid "I didn't mean to," I yelled from my tangle of paper towels, "DON'T EVEN TALK TO ME!" It was one of those moments where I watch myself from outside my body as I throw the tantrum that's been building in me for decades, over a spill or an hour of whining or the third poop-on-the-bathroom-rug incident in a day. My capacity to use my voice as a weapon frightens me. So does the realization that in my momentary insanity, I'm not so different from the trumpeter in the gully. I promise myself, again and again, not to lose it next time.

"Now don't get stressed, Mommy," Anders advises when he hears my voice start to rise. Though he can work himself into a spectacular rage, he's very adult when I'm not. This pains me. I don't want him to have to take care of my feelings, the way I felt I had to take care of my mother's deep, unspoken sadness. Now that I know my capacity for bellowing, I want to save it for a *real* crisis. And what do I want for my boys? I'm full of good Quaker ideas about restorative justice, talking things out instead of rushing to punish. Sometimes, after the boys and I have completely lost our heads, I dare suggest that we hold hands in a circle. In family meetings we pass around our Talking Rock, a skin-smooth Botswana agate, to keep from interrupting each other. We've even created a Peace Pit in the corner of the master bedroom, with pillows and notebooks for coloring; sometimes one of the boys (or their mother) actually goes in there to cool off. I know, now, the soft, wounded place beneath every angry explosion. Still, I want each of my sons to know his own voice, to know what it sounds like when he get so mad he'd send his brother to Mars if he could. Forever. Too often I hear myself repeating what I heard growing up: "Now let's talk nicely to each other," or "No, we don't hate people." The other day I watched Anders take in the sight of his Lego hospital, wrecked in one sweep by his little brother. He yelped, "I hate him! I never wanted a brother!" This time I said, "Yes, sometimes we do hate people." I thought of a Quaker friend's words: "We all have some of the light, but none of us is spared some of the dark."

The screamer in the gully, in all his pain and craziness, is in me, and in my children. I hear him when Evan chases his brother through the dining room, fists flying, a roar beyond words rising in his throat. I hear him when I holler from the basement, "I CAN'T COME RIGHT NOW! I AM NOT YOUR PERSONAL SLAVE!" There are times when I don't care if I ravage my vocal cords. But my liberation from appropriateness has shown me what lies at the other end of the spectrum: the flash of frightened hurt in my sons' eyes when I whirl around and holler. Maybe I'll get myself a trumpet, haul it into the backyard, and blare at the stars.

grace notes

chant

Lynn Gottlieb, one of the first women ordained as a rabbi, describes a piece of Canaanite pottery that shows two women washing each other's hands, "sitting close to the earth in the old way." In Jewish tradition, the day begins with a ritual washing of hands. This washing consecrates the hands to the service of Shechinah, or divine presence. The seventeenth-century mystic Rabbi Isaac Luria taught that our job as humans is to gather the pieces of Shechinah scattered throughout the earth like broken glass. Some mornings, as I squeeze soap onto my hands, I wonder if they are capable of this.

Several weeks after completing her bat mitzvah as an adult, my friend Jacqueline decided to celebrate water rituals in a new way. She and her husband had rediscovered their Jewish roots in a liberal reconstructionist congregation, a community more about spiritual searching than about orthodox behavior. I looked forward to being part of this event with its echoes of traditional *mikvah,* or ritual bath, ceremonies: I had not yet found the courage to strike out on my own spiritual journey. The week before, Jacqueline had asked her women friends to collect water in small containers and bring them to her house. When I arrived, I saw on the kitchen counter an assortment of flasks, plastic bottles, and Mason jars marked with the names of rivers and cities around the world. I had filled a small bottle at the artesian well where my mother's mother had once collected water.

I felt honored to be part of this gathering of self-proclaimed "Jewish hippie chicks." After laughter and conversation in the living room, Jacqueline uncovered the Torah, salvaged from the Holocaust and now handled with love in her community. I was surprised that she'd been able to take it home. An artist who loves working with textiles, she had designed its cover herself. "I don't know exactly what will happen today, but I want to share with you this week's Torah reading," she said. She unrolled the heavy scroll on a long table. She ran a pen-shaped place marker over the handwritten Hebrew script, possibly more than a century old, pausing to find words to match the foreign, ancestral symbols she was beginning to learn.

Then she asked us to join her in a meditation on the *Sh'ma,* the Jewish confession of faith. As Jacqueline sat on the floor, breathing deeply, eyes closed, I understood that for her the *Sh'ma* was more than a set of repeated words; like the Trappists' chant at the monastery in Huntsville, it was an act of attention. *Sh'ma Yisrael, Adonai Eloheynu, Adonai Ehad.* "Hear, O Israel, the Lord our God, the Lord is One." Jacqueline spoke one word per breath, vowel extended, almost a sung tone. It sounded like water. A definition of God that wouldn't keep still. I thought of theologian Harvey Cox's explanation of the *Sh'ma* as a moment where human beings recognize that they are, like God, "free to change and create."

Was I free to change and create in my spiritual life? As I listened to Jacqueline, I felt, for this moment, that I was. After the recitation of the *Sh'ma,* each of us chose a rhythm instrument from Jacqueline's collection. I picked up an African thumb piano with metal levers that made a soft twang, each on a different pitch on the pentatonic scale, when I plucked them. Karen, the congregation's music specialist, led us in a round. We learned the music not by reading notes but by listening to Karen's voice and singing after her, over and over. Some of us sang in Hebrew, some in English. *The breath of all life blesses you. The breath of all life blesses you.* We sang as we walked in two circles that moved in opposite directions, drumming, shaking, and plucking. Two languages, two rivers of history, flowed together. Our eyes met.

In the church services I had attended every Sunday as a child, I was told to sit quietly with my arms folded. Sometimes I tried to see how long I could hold my body in place, barely breathing, proving my righteousness. In sacrament meeting, I did my best not to squirm during long talks about tithing or repentance or the Second Coming. During the hymns, which often dragged along at a soporific pace, I felt more soothed than filled with religious fervor. One hymn that my body did respond to was a peppy anthem called "Count Your Many Blessings," which I wished we sang more often. As I grew older, I longed for more. Trumpets, drums, dancing—or even better, long, deep-breathing silence. Some physical response to the otherness we so glibly asked to be with us.

Watching Jacqueline reciting the *Sh'ma,* or singing in the moving circle of women, I felt a ripple of fear. *What might happen in this room? What if we really believe in this power we invoke?* I couldn't help but imagine Jacqueline's God as the same wild force I'd wanted to reach, but rarely had, in church. "It is madness to wear ladies' straw hats and velvet hats to church," writes Annie Dillard. "We should all be wearing crash helmets." I believe her. When we sang and drummed together in Jacqueline's living room, leaning into each other's voices, a deep current pulled us. A call from the numinous, from exiled female divinity, the Shechinah scattered at the birth of the world.

After singing and reading poetry aloud, we climbed the steps from Jacqueline's back terrace down to the swimming pool area, where Jacqueline and her husband had recently installed a cistern. This wooded backyard was in the process of becoming a water sanctuary, a private *mikvah.* Jacqueline asked each of us to pour the water we had collected into the cistern's dark, concrete mouth. We could say something if we chose to. I don't remember what I said as I poured my water down. I remember thinking that water, this slight flow from my plastic bottle, has the power to dig a canyon, to freeze cracks in a mountainside, to drown us all. Maybe the words themselves weren't as important as the act of recognizing this power. The water in me. The longings dammed up in my body. I blessed the water, buried for years in an underground reservoir, and poured it back down.

A year later, Jacqueline and her husband, Alan, a voice student of mine, came to my house to practice some chants for their son's wedding. They brought their reconstructionist Passover Haggadah to show me. I liked it so much I ordered one for myself. One night, looking through the words and radiant paintings about the Exodus, I felt a pang. I was supposed to be writing a script for a Mormon children's program titled "Follow the Prophet." I'd put it off for weeks. I couldn't come up with a way to tie the wild, mythic stories of Noah and Moses to the benign reigns of modern Mormon prophets. When the request had come, I'd set my teeth. I'd pictured child after child trotting up to the pulpit and reciting words like

"God chooses righteous men to lead us," or "If we do what the prophet says we will be safe." For someone outside the Mormon faith, the notion of a contemporary prophet entitled to divine revelation may sound presumptuous, if not downright crazy. For those who have grown up inside this culture, the idea is so familiar that it threatens to lull us to sleep. I decided to turn to Alan and Jacqueline's Haggadah for help.

At the beginning of the Passover seder, I read, some Jewish families place a cup filled with springwater on the table. According to the midrash, after the Israelites left Egypt, a well of water sprang up wherever they camped on their desert journey. This miracle has been associated with Miriam, the sister of Moses who watched over him when, as an infant, he floated down the Nile in a basket. Miriam's Cup "reminds us of the redemption occurring daily in our lives," writes Rabbi David Teutsch.

Miriam was more than a conscientious guardian. In Exodus 15:20–21, she's called "the prophetess, Aaron's sister." After the Israelites crossed the Red Sea on dry land and the water closed over Pharaoh's chariot, Miriam led all the women in dancing, and chanted for them: *Sing to the Eternal One, for God has triumphed gloriously.* I shut my eyes and pictured women stomping and twirling, not to be looked at, but from sheer joy at the sensation of freedom. I thought of the concentric circles of women in Jacqueline's living room, drumming and plucking and singing, *The breath of all life blesses you.*

Mormon children sing a song called "Follow the Prophet," a mantra in a minor key that reminds them, over and over, not to go astray. When I heard this song as a Mormon adult, I shuddered. Ever since I was ten years old, I'd felt myself yearning to "go astray." For me, that didn't mean drinking and cavorting with boys; it meant being myself without fear. I longed to blurt out questions about polygamy or Mother in Heaven or why it took so long for the church to give blacks the priesthood. I longed to whirl into a dance in the middle of church, or to plunge my hand into a barrel of fat, shiny coffee beans at the upscale kitchen shop where my mother liked to browse. I didn't do any of these things. I sat quietly with my arms folded. Now, here I was, back in the Primary Room, face-to-face with my past. How could I teach these children without subjecting them to the fear-based righteousness I wore for years like an invisible garment? What would happen if I veered from the approved program outline? Would the dam break? Would all my doubts and questions come flooding out and drive me out of the chapel doors? I thought of Emily Dickinson's agonized query: *Why—do they shut Me out of Heaven? / Did I sing—too loud?*

In Alan and Jacqueline's guide to the seder, I found questions asked by four imaginary children: one who is wise, one who is hostile, one who is passive, and one who is silent. The book points out that we have all been each of these children at different moments in our lives. As I read this, I thought of the real-life children in my Mormon congregation: the eleven-year-old boy genius; the seven-year-old girl who loved to retell her dreams of burglars and murderers; two ten-year-old best girlfriends, by-the-book obedient except for the day they walked the neighborhood in red lipstick and slinky dresses; and the four youngest children, three years old, who sat looking at the ceiling or playing with their shoelaces. How could I expect these children to say the approved words, to speak like perfect little adults? A friend had once told me, "This church treats children like adults, and adults like children." I wanted to respect the childhood of the children in my care. Their curiosity. Their leaps of logic. Their honesty. I hoped this was what Jesus meant when he said only the childlike enter the kingdom of Heaven. I hoped he didn't expect people to be as pathologically obedient as I was as a child. By the time I was six or seven, I'd already learned that I won praise for knowing the right answers in church. I didn't have to ask questions. I found spiritual nourishment in my imaginative life, in my obsessions with outer space and ancient Egypt. As an adult, I didn't want to provide easy answers for the children in our Primary room. I carried the Passover Haggadah to the Story Couch and settled in. I read and reread the four children's questions until after midnight.

"Let me ask you this," Anders piped from the backseat of the car the next day. "Is the world really going to die?"

I told him I thought it would, that it may already be dying from pollution and rain-forest logging and animal extinction.

"So are there going to be wars and earthquakes and then Jesus will come?"

I said there have been prophecies to that effect.

"Do *you* believe the prophecies?" he said.

I had to think hard. Finally I said, "I believe strange things have happened, and I believe more will happen, but I don't know what, or when."

All the way home I worried about my lame answer. Was I depriving my child of the certainty he needed? Would he be free to question this certainty as an adult? *Did* he need it now?

I decided to ask for the children's help in planning the program. My first step was to encourage them to think about what they *didn't* know about prophets. One Sunday I asked several children to come to the front of the room and pretend to be people from scriptural history. The other children could ask each "character" questions. Shivonne, a very articulate seven year old, played Eve. "Does anyone have a question for Eve?" I asked. No one spoke up. The children, who normally raise their hands at any opportunity to show what they know, weren't sure how to respond. Had they turned off their curiosity at the church door, too?

Finally one of the teachers asked, "Did you have children, Eve?"

Shivonne cocked her head and said, "Well, I did. I had one son who was very bad and one son who was very good. They got in a fight."

After a while, the kids caught on. My son Anders asked Moses why his staff had magic power. Another boy asked Adam if he was baptized. I wrote down the children's questions and answers, verbatim. Then I asked the children to brainstorm with me, to tell me their favorite "prophet stories" from the Bible and the church history they'd been taught. Noah and Moses were voted big heroes. So was the current prophet, who, in his nineties, jets around the world at an astonishing pace. Nobody mentioned Miriam the prophetess. I wanted to introduce her, somehow.

The children suggested dressing up like prophets to tell their stories. Maybe Miriam could be the one to narrate the Israelites' exodus from Egypt, I thought. Maybe she could tell the congregation how she led the women in song and dancing, after her people walked on dry land through the Red Sea. Maybe the children could sing with her, shaking rhythm instruments. An ancient, celebratory vision of what a prophet or prophetess could be. After all, a passage in Mormon Scripture reads, "Adam fell that men may be, and men are, that they might have joy." And as Shivonne once pointed out when someone read this passage, "I hope that means girls, too."

Because my Mormon congregation, in a diverse city neighborhood, tended to accept difference more than some others I'd known, I believed this new approach might actually work. I had my worries, though: what if the bishop didn't approve of rhythm instruments in the chapel, or what if someone tried, politely, to coax me back into church-approved formulas? Outspoken women had rarely fared well in authoritarian churches, I knew. The reconstructionist Haggadah didn't mention the rest of Miriam's story: according to the Book of Numbers, she was struck with leprosy for defying Moses in the wilderness.

The day of the program, I sat in front of the congregation in sacrament meeting. To my left, the Primary children stood and sang "Follow the Prophet." That morning when I arrived at church, there had been no sign of the rhythm instruments I'd brought for the children to play. I asked my friend the music leader what happened to them. "They became kind of a distraction," she said. The way our last rehearsal had gone, with five and six year olds wielding their instruments as weapons, I could see why.

A little girl with a giant name tag marked "MIRIAM" walked to the microphone. She told the story of Moses, and the women who danced and sang after the parting of the Red Sea. My son Anders came to the pulpit and asked her, "How come Moses' staff had special power?" She answered, "That was the power of God."

Child after child trotted up to the microphone and spoke a short memorized part. Despite my efforts, this program didn't sound much different from the others I'd witnessed, year after year. Afterward my sister-in-law came up to me and said, "Well, *that* was controversial!" A friend who had left the church, and whose daughter performed that day, phoned me afterward and said, "You can't avoid it. The brainwashing will go on no matter what you do." Over dinner my father said, "What more could you have done? You were just a functionary. The only way to make a difference in this church is to do it from the top, and the only way to the top is through absolute obedience to the system."

I don't want to be a functionary! I wanted to scream. I had hoped I could make a difference. Maybe I couldn't. Maybe I'd have to accept the fact that many people thrive in this church, just the way it is. Maybe I'd have to resign myself and become a churchgoing cynic like my father, who loves the Mormon Scriptures but can't accept the corporate power the church has become. Had I been arrogant, thinking I could change the world?

After dinner I changed out of my dress and drove up into the foothills, to Alan and Jacqueline's house. They'd invited friends and members of their congregation to sit shiva with Alan, whose mother had died suddenly the week before.

I set a tomato-bean salad on the kitchen counter and entered the living room. Alan sat on a cushion on the floor. He looked stunned. So did the people sitting in a circle around him. It had been less than two weeks since the September 11 terrorist attacks.

One by one, we told Alan what was in our hearts at that moment. We told him we loved him. Some spoke about ancient Jewish mourning rituals and what they might mean in this shaken world. Alan asked me to read a poem. After this we stood and sang.

Most of the people in this room knew the Hebrew chants. I hummed along. I joined in when we began the chant I remembered from Jacqueline's water ceremony: *The breath of all life blesses you. The breath of all life blesses you.* I could feel the knots of frustration in my body coming apart. The words flowed in like water. The breath of *all* life . . . I saw all of us in the room, sharing Alan's grief, sharing the grief not only of those who lost loved ones on September 11 but of those who have suffered in senseless tragedy anywhere in the world. Once the breath and the words started flowing, they wouldn't stop. The next chant was one I'd never heard: *Elohay neshamah shenatata bi tehorah hi.* The man beside me translated in my ear: *My God, the soul you gave me is pure.*

These words drummed in my head as I listened to the chant, as we said Kaddish in unison, as the circle loosened and people drifted toward the kitchen. *My soul is pure. My soul has always been pure. I am enough. Can I believe this?*

In the kitchen, I found the man who had translated for me. "You don't know how I needed those words today," I told him.

"I think we all did," he said.

I came home that night to my usual Sunday ritual with Kent: reading the Mormon Scriptures together. We sat at the dining room table. The book lay between us, a marker in the place where we'd left off. "You read," I told him, as usual. Lately I hadn't felt I could speak those words aloud, the stories of war and burning at the stake and miraculous conversion that had colored my childhood.

"I don't think you want to hear this tonight," Kent said.

I breathed. "You're right."

"What are we going to do about this?"

A long silence. Finally I ventured, "Could we try . . . studying the Scriptures separately during the week and then talking about it on Sundays?"

"What do you want to read?"

"I haven't read Isaiah in a while," I said. "And there's a 'Book of Blessings' by a woman rabbi I've been wanting to read."

"Okay, whatever will make you feel you're doing things for the right reasons."

The next Sunday, we talked about what we'd read during the week. Kent suggested looking at the list of goals we'd set as a couple the year before. "I'd like to start a new list," I said.

"What's wrong with this one?"

"There are some areas where we may be different."

"Okay . . ."

I ran into the back room and pulled a big piece of art paper out of Evan's "creative time" stack. I laid it on the dining room table. Then I ran into the kitchen and found a big mixing bowl. I set it on the paper, once, twice, and traced two overlapping circles with my pencil. "This is you and me," I said. "In the middle here, where the circles intersect, we'll write the things we want to work on together.

In the outside parts, let's write the things we want to do on our own."

"Artists!" Kent muttered, trying to be good-natured. We started listing our goals. When we got to the "Spirituality" heading in Kent's half-circle, he wrote some church-related goals. "What are you going to put in yours?" he wanted to know.

"You're going to laugh at me."

"No, I'm not."

"Well, I don't want to read or say things or sing songs just because I've been told to. And I don't want to feel so cut off from my body in my spiritual life," I said. "I want to wash my hands every morning, and pay attention to this washing, to get ready for the day. I want my hands to be involved in the world, finding the good." My face felt hot as I said this. "I feel so inarticulate . . ."

I tried to explain it better the next week, when I suggested an activity for the Mormon "family home evening" we were still trying to have with our children once a week. Instead of acting out a Scripture story or teaching the boys about baptism or tithing, I asked them to wash their hands in the bathroom sink. They splashed. They let the water run into their sleeves. They ran back into the kitchen, trailing wet drops from their fingers. I said, "Now that your hands are all clean, they have something special to do." I showed them a clear glass Kent and I had received as part of a set for our wedding. "I'm going to let you break this," I said. They stared at me. I didn't go into Jewish wedding symbolism; I didn't explain the concept of *Tikkun,* mending the broken shards, from marriages to nations. I simply handed Anders and Evan the glass and put a deep bowl underneath it. They held on with all four of their hands. They dropped the glass. It shattered with a terrible noise. The boys leaped in delight. As we examined the jagged chunks and tiny slivers, I said, "Imagine these broken pieces are all we can see of God in this world. Imagine your job is to find these pieces, no matter how small, and gather them up, and put them back together." The boys couldn't resist reaching into the bowl with their still-wet hands. They knew this touch might hurt, and wanted it anyway.

grace notes

passaggio

They're not monsters, they're just costumes,
Evan sings to himself as he works four pipe cleaners into an intricate
ball. *Don't worry about the dentist, he's so gentle, you won't feel a thing.*
Evan sings as he colors, as he chases the dog, as he wipes excess
toothpaste all over the bathroom towels. Sometimes he sings songs
he's picked up at church or school or music class; most often he
makes them up himself. He doesn't care if anyone hears him or not.
He sings to comfort himself before an impending dental appoint-
ment, or simply to voice the exuberance he can't contain. I wish my
singing were more like this. I've been trained to sing as a performer,
not for the sake of singing.

Many of my voice students share my wish. "I want to let go of
my operatic sound," says Marsha at her first lesson. "I just want to
sing to my kids." Holly gets the itch to improvise: "I was singing my
Puccini aria in the car and I started extending the melody, making
stuff up," she tells me. "Do you think that's weird?" One day Alan
sits down in my music room and says, "I thought I wanted to prepare a solo recital, but now I don't know. I want to use my voice in
a more communal way. I'm not sure how to go about this." The next
thing I know, he's gone to Berkeley and bought a drum. My student
Jeni tells me, "I sang for a friend's baby blessing once, and I had no
idea what I was doing, so I just closed my eyes and told people to be
forgiving. When I opened my eyes, everybody was crying!" Jeni still
closes her eyes or sings with her back turned, but she can't get
enough of the connection she feels to the friends or family who listen. She finds herself singing spontaneously in groups, at a wedding
bonfire or on a women's river trip. For her and for these other students, singing is not about standing on a stage and impressing an audience. They want to sing the way Evan sings, simply to let their
voices out.

I've rarely sung to my boys for the sheer pleasure of singing.
They curl up under the piano bench while I practice and say, "Not
this song again!" or "This one is my favorite," or, as Anders said one
day when I played the introduction to Schubert's "Serenade," "Ooo,

that sounds like a snail approaching its prey." But I don't often sing them to sleep. I don't wake them in the mornings with a perky rendition of "Frère Jacques." Even my repressed grandmother used to sing lullabies. I remember her clear, gently vibrating voice singing "Little Boy Blue" in her favorite rocking chair. When I was very small, my mother used to sing me "Would You Like to Swing on a Star?" and "Too-ra Loo-ra Loo-ra." Why haven't I carried on the tradition? It must be because, for so many years, singing meant the stage—and stage fright—to me.

"I have no desire to perform onstage again," says my friend Bob, a fine pianist whose wedding was the first Quaker meeting I attended. He grins and remembers, "The last time I did a house concert, I came out in my bedroom slippers." When we practice French songs in Bob's living room, we find ourselves marveling at Fauré's delicately shifting harmonies. We're more interested in the music than in what people will think of us when we share it. Still, even a house concert is starting to feel too performance-like to me. Singing French love songs for even the most intimate audience, I can't make eye contact. I'm not telling a story. I'm not singing words of comfort. I am revealing, I am burning, I am practically naked, but I am not "communicating" the way I would to a real lover. I'm playing a part, a secret part of myself I can't show in public without a song to contain it. I am making art and autobiography at the same time. I am singer, performer, "other."

Recently a born-and-raised Quaker woman came up to me after meeting one day and asked about my singing. When I explained what I do, she looked at me hard and said, "So you sing by yourself? Not with other people?" I could have told her I'd sung duet recitals before, but I knew this wasn't what she meant. All the way home I thought about this. Did I *want* to sing with other people, just for the sake of joining voices? *Yes,* said the voice inside me. *Yes, yes, yes.* I want what Alan wants, to use my voice in a more communal way. For me, that means taking a leap off every stage I've stood on in my life, literal or not.

As a child, I performed onstage with my mother in musicals. I could only imagine the people I knew or didn't know in the audience;

it was all black from where I stood, dust motes hovering in the blue-gold stage lights. Often I sang with my mother in front of a piano in the church gym, where she invariably made me sing "Doll on a Music Box" from *Chitty Chitty Bang Bang*. My breath caught in my throat. I didn't want all these people gazing at me, as the song said, and yet I did. My mother looked at me with her downturned public smile, and started to sing the Dick Van Dyke part about Truly Scrumptious. I thought the song was creepy. I'd always hated this part of the movie, with the giggling queen and the lurking child-catcher. When I sang with my mother for church socials or ladies' lunch clubs, I felt trapped in a grownup kingdom, too. But I did it, over and over, for the compliments I accumulated afterward ("What a pretty voice!" "You and your mother look just perfect together!"), and for the access I had, even for a few minutes, to my mother's world.

For my mother, the stage was the only place she could be real. For me, it was the place that took her from me and made her "other." When I was four, I dreamed that I sat in the audience while she sang a program of show tunes. She stood on a stage in front of a grand piano. She wore a suit of armor that reminded me of the Tin Man. In the middle of a song, she took her helmet off. Her head was not inside. She removed one arm and then the breastplate. Nothing but air inside. Piece by piece, her armor clanked to the floor. She had vanished. The piano continued to play. Her voice continued to sing. I looked everywhere for her, under the metal folding chairs and behind the piano. No mother to be found. The stage had taken her from me forever. After I woke, I walked downstairs in a sweat. I found my mother and my grandmother in the kitchen, but I was not comforted.

As I grew older and sang next to my mother, I felt I could claim her, for a moment, as mine. I could keep her from vanishing behind her armor into the imaginary world she loved. I never pictured myself taking her place on the stage. Sometimes, alone in the basement, I mouthed the words to my mother's recordings of *The Music Man* and *The King and I,* but I didn't dare sing those songs aloud. They belonged to her. My private musical life was about listening, not making sound—except for the time I belted out "Rock-a My Soul in the Bosom of Abraham," the first spiritual I'd ever heard, behind the lilac bush in the backyard.

After our year in Germany, I hummed all the time, but not from joy. It was an almost autistic activity, like rocking back and forth on the floor. My only private singing felt almost sinful. First, I walked the house from room to room, to make sure no one was home. Then I sneaked one of my mother's opera anthologies from the cabinet and set it on the piano. There. Puccini. I played the opening chords of the aria Manon Lescaut sings in her luxurious apartment, longing to leave the man she doesn't love. I wailed the aria, not caring that it was far too big for me. For that moment, it was my own. I wanted more of those moments. Once I heard a Poulenc song cycle on the radio and longed to learn it. I ordered it from a local music store and saved my allowances for a month. Seventeen dollars. When the phone call came, I asked my father to drive me to the music store. At last I held the soft yellow score, sent all the way from Paris, in my hands. I took it to school every day, so it wouldn't leave my sight. I practiced it in secret and never told my mother.

My public singing was a different story. In junior high and high school, I did leave the refuge of my room to perform in school productions like *A Midsummer Night's Dream, HMS Pinafore,* or *Seven Brides for Seven Brothers.* Once again, I did it for the compliments. Part of me believed, as my mother had for years, that only the stage could give me a sense of worth. I braved the minefield in my voice, the *passaggio* an octave above middle C, to have a chance at the spotlight. Singing Gilbert and Sullivan in my pretty taffeta dress, the yellow lights warm on my made-up face, at a safe distance from the audience, I felt noticed and appreciated. After the applause and hugs from people I hardly knew, I went home and retreated to my room. I'd accumulated those precious compliments in place of true relationship. Part of me knew this. "I don't want to get my sense of worth from my achievements," I wrote in my journal at fourteen. "I want to feel valuable for who I am."

Sometimes, during high school, I did. When I held hands with my boyfriend in the gully behind my grandparents' house, he said, "Most people don't really know you. I want to know you." I knew

grace notes

he meant it. When my friend Renée and I sat on the floor of her room or my room, we talked easily about whatever came to mind. We looked through art books and talked about our favorite novels. One night she and another friend put on *Ferris Bueller's Day Off* in Renée's basement and tried to get me to dance to "Twist and Shout." They turned the TV up loud. We high-fived each other and waved our arms in the air. This was a new experience for me; I'd never even been to summer camp and learned the goofy songs everyone else my age seemed to know. As the brown-paneled walls tilted around me, my body leaning from one foot to the next, I realized I hadn't danced since my mother and I put on the *Fiddler on the Roof* soundtrack in our basement when I was nine. "This is good for you," Renée said.

Renée was determined to unmask me. More than once during our sophomore year of high school, she said pointedly, "You don't need to wear all that makeup." I winced. I thought of the night my mother had sat me on the toilet seat in our duplex in Germany. I was ten. She taught me to pluck my eyebrows, hair by hair, the tweezers sweaty in my hand. When I gasped in pain, the tears starting, she said, "It won't hurt so much after a while." She taught me to disguise my nose with stick concealer. "Just put a little white on each side, rub it in with your fourth finger so you won't get wrinkles," she said, "and your nose really will look smaller." I could see the worry in her eyes. She must have thought this makeover would cheer me up. All it did was make me think I could never show my face without makeup, the way she couldn't. It made me think if I lived long enough to see the Second Coming and the world was a burning apocalypse and I had no access to my makeup drawer, I might as well curl up and die. When I put on my face in the mornings, taking almost the full hour my mother did, I was preparing to go onstage. It took me until I was a senior in high school—after months of prodding from Renée and my boyfriend—to go without eyeliner to school. That morning I gripped the sink in front of the bathroom mirror. I blinked at myself, my eyes adorned with nothing but eighties-blue mascara. When I came out of the bathroom, my mother gave me her downturned smile. I knew it; she'd noticed. "I really think you look better with more makeup," she said. I didn't know that her mother had said the same thing to her when she was twenty-nine and starting to show the tiniest wrinkles. I didn't know that my mother started wearing heavy makeup not only because she feared aging, but also because she loved the power the bronzy mask gave her. ("When I wore makeup onstage, I didn't feel so invisible," she tells me now. "I realized I could do this in real life, too. If I couldn't have more children, if I couldn't be the perfect Mormon woman, at least I could be beautiful.") At seventeen, I felt my own power when I resisted my mother's words, for once, and threw away the eyeliner. Over the next several years, I did the same with my foundation and blush and eye shadow. Layer by layer, I peeled off the stage makeup I'd worn in real life since our return from Germany. I had not felt more visible behind it; I'd felt trapped in protective armor.

"We play at being who we are," intoned my favorite German professor in college. These words haunted me as I picked up my stack of Kafka and left the classroom, as I walked across the leaf-blown campus where I watched myself, day after day, tossing a perky "How are ya?" to every person I even vaguely recognized. It was true, I thought, trembling as I walked. My whole life, in church, on the stage, in the Mormon sorority my mother thought I'd "just love," was a performance. Even without all that makeup. After high school I'd gone from clammed-up recluse to big-haired coed. Whenever a boy from the Mormon fraternity asked me out, I felt like a fake. *It's only because of my hair,* I told myself. But when Kent came along and told me he liked me because I was "genuine," I stared at him. Was this possible? What had he seen in me? The performer, certainly, but something else, too. What that was would take me years to find out.

After my marriage, I spent my senior year in college preparing for a solo recital. For months I looked forward to standing on the stage in the university recital hall, where I'd watched the woman I called Leska perform years before. Standing there in my red formal felt like an arrival to me. My teacher was pleased. I collected my compliments. Several months later, Kent and I moved to northern Nevada. I lost all motivation to sing, on or off the stage. The performer in me had crumpled into a ball. All I could do was sit behind the organ, letting it sing what I couldn't. Over time, as my confidence grew, I found new stages for my voice: the pulpit stand where I sang for sacrament meeting or funerals; the stage in the local arts center, where I performed a duet recital with my mother; a hastily constructed stage in the Nevada State Capitol, where my mother and I did a benefit concert for a community college.

Once, singing for the funeral of a woman I'd visited as part of my church job, hours before her death, I actually felt something when I sang. The woman's family had requested "Amazing Grace," which I'd never heard sung in a Mormon chapel before. I trusted my instincts and sang with more chest voice than usual. The sound vibrated deep in my body. As I sang I remembered Clarice's cancer-ravaged body, delicate as a bird's skeleton, sucking in air as she lay unconscious on her bed. I breathed. I remembered the spaces between Clarice's breaths, twenty seconds, thirty seconds. I almost spoke the song's words with their gutsy American diphthongs. On the first two pews below me, Clarice's children and grandchildren listened. I sang to them. I meant every word. But this experience was unusual. In most of my performances, the stage kept me safe. I didn't have to mean the words I sang. And if my mother stood next to me, as I usually asked her to, her reputation made me feel I had a right to stand there.

At Sarah Lawrence, my lessons with Thomas reminded me of singing for Clarice's funeral. I spoke those multicolored American vowels over and over. I found deeper resonance in my body. I connected, more than ever before, to the words I sang. One day, as we went through the score of Handel's *Messiah* piece by piece, Thomas paused on the page with the recitative about the shepherds abiding in the field. "You don't have to do anything fancy with this. The meaning, the emotion, is all built into the meter. Think about what's happening here," he said. We looked at the next recitative, one syllable per beat. *And lo, the angel of the Lord came upon them.* Thomas whispered, "Nothing like this has ever happened before." I knew if I ever sang this music in public, I would have to consider the terror of the miraculous. I would have to feel it.

In another lesson, Thomas coached Kate and me on a Poulenc song cycle. With our performance less than a week away, we'd come into the studio with nerves all atremble. "You two are having a conversation," Thomas reminded us. "For a few minutes, your listeners get to overhear it." Kate and I looked at each other and understood. We relaxed. In the year I studied with him, Thomas gave me the courage to stand in front of a piano without my mother, without the imaginary chairs and floor lamps I'd erected to protect myself, and to sing to express, not to impress. "If you do this, expect a response, even a biological response, from your audience," he told me once.

He was right. When Kate and I performed a recital of songs about animals at Sarah Lawrence, he sat in the audience and radiated. I held the piano lid and felt every vibration. Kate touched the keys, breathing with me. As I sang Samuel Barber's song "A Green Lowland of Pianos," I saw fields of beautiful bovine Steinways, I felt their lowing, and I knew the audience did, too. A week later, my friend Jennifer, who had also heard the program, sent Kate and me a poem she'd written. In broken stanzas, she spoke her wish to be the piano, the wood under the hand, the voice inside the voice, that conversation. It *was* something overheard, I realized, not the conversation between singer and audience I'd imagined. It wasn't the same as my talks with Thomas in the studio. I had revealed, I had burned, people had responded. But what had I done? Had I sung *to* them or simply allowed them into these splashing chords, this one wild moment, this mirror of their own wordless experience? Maybe I had, as my mother hopes she does, sung the songs the audience longed to sing.

Whatever I'd done, it happened again. "Your 'Gretchen' was terrifying," my mother said after a Schubert recital at Kate's house a year later. "You're not singing from behind a mask anymore," said my old friend Renée after the same concert. She was right, and she wasn't. I meant every word I sang, but the song itself masked me. I was still "other." At last I could stand on a stage and reach someone, but what if I wanted to take that person's hands in mine and sing, not as Gretchen or huntsman or orphan or the voice of Death, but as myself?

A year after this, when Kate and I had just put on a joyful Easter performance of Bach, we gave up plans for another public recital six months later. It wasn't that we thought we'd failed; we both knew, in some unspoken way, that we wanted to do something different. "I just want to learn music with you," I said on the phone one day. "Me, too," Kate said. I could hear the relief in her voice.

And so I took a step down from the stage. Kate and I started working on Schumann's *Dichterliebe* ("Poet's Love") song cycle, not necessarily to perform but to inhabit this music we'd loved since I'd sung the first song with her in Connecticut. And just for fun, we recorded our Bach and, three months later, ten favorite Schubert songs. In this five-hour recording session, the whole idea of "performance" came apart in my mind. We could eat between takes, for one thing; Kate had, wisely, thought of protein when she loaded her kitchen counter with crackers and hunks of cheese. The project became a community effort. My composer friend Rich, also an experienced studio artist, had offered to lend us his ears. He found an arch in the ceiling for me to stand under, to allow my high notes a little more ring. He moved a rug under my feet. He paced the living room, listening. "I'm hearing some wonderful overtones in this corner of the room!" he gasped to Mike, the aptly named sound engineer, who had turned the kitchen into a high-tech command center. Up went another studio mike. "The soft pedal's creaking again," Mike announced. Kate glared at her elderly Bösendorfer grand. Still, it was a small price to pay for the instrument's melting tone. I wished I didn't have to stand across the room from it. I felt stuck, standing alone in front of the mike. "You have permission to move," Rich said. I shut my eyes and tried to loosen my foot grip on the floor. After the second song, Rich asked Kate for a scarf. Without saying a word, he draped a soft purple one over the mike that loomed in front of me. He fussed it into an elegant swirl. "Now," he said, "it's your friend." Mike swayed to the music in the kitchen, his computer perched on the island counter. Kate met my eyes as we breathed through the long fermata in "Mignon's Song." We started "Litany for the Feast of All Souls" six times; my breath kept failing me. "I have to eat before I do this one," I said, and made a dash for the licorice on the coffee table. Rich grabbed a handful of trail mix. "Wait! I have to turn off the fridge again," came Mike's voice from the command center. Kate heated up some soup. Back to work. I breathed in the middle of a phrase and let that be all right. "I guess I have to let go of my obsession with perfection," I said. Now, take one of "Death and the Maiden." Mike appeared in the living room: "I know this one from the quartet!" Take two. Kate watched me conduct the tempo for her slow, deep-chorded introduction. I sang in the voice of the girl about to die. I sang in the voice of gentle Death. I hit the low D at the end of the song. Kate played the postlude so softly that I didn't want to breathe. She lifted her hands from the keyboard and her feet from the pedals. Rich collapsed on the floor.

The next Sunday, as I walked from my car to Quaker meeting, I met Ann, the woman who had asked me about singing without other people. As I hurried to match her brisk steps, we talked about music again. I told her about the recording session. "So it's different from performance," she said. "It's the difference between singing with people who already know what's going on, and singing for people who may be hearing the music for the very first time." I hadn't thought of it this way. As we walked up the steps and into the Ladies' Literary Club, I wondered what music would sound like in this space. Not the special-occasion music my mother once brought to this building, but community singing. Something to blur the line between "singing with people who already know what's going on" and learning music for the first time.

Recently two Quaker women, also musicians, talked with me about introducing hymn singing in our congregation. One day before meeting I looked through the Friends' hymnal and found songs with wonderfully quirky titles like "Praise to Creation Unfinished." I want to learn that song, to hear it and sing it at the same time, voices all around me in the square. But I want more than anything to sing for the sake of singing, without written music in front of me. I want to sing the way Evan does, the way my student Jeni sang with the women on her river trip, the way I once chanted with Jacqueline and her friends in the living room, the way Caroline stood in meeting and sang a hymn from memory, the way Thomas recited Shakespeare in the studio, the way my husband rocks to the radio in the car.

Several weeks ago, Kate and I sat at her piano, looking for "happy songs" to perform at an elementary school. We'd pooled our Broadway anthologies and my Gershwin and Harold Arlen books, and spent an hour making music for fun. "I Got Rhythm," "Put on a Happy Face," "Get Happy." . . . For the first time, we sang together as she played. "Aren't you tired of all our German songs about death?" I said, laughing. "What a relief to sing in English again!"

Kate started looking through the table of contents in my Harold Arlen book. "Oh, I remember this one from my childhood!" she said. "And this one, and this one, and 'Blues in the Night.' Do you know it?"

I said I didn't. She said it was a shame to let an old song like this fade out of hearing. "Sometime I want to hear it in your voice," she added. "Blues in the Night" was still with her when we went swimming the next day. She sang it in the pool. She sang it in the locker-room shower. I realized that the only time I ever sang in the shower was when I was trying to memorize new repertoire, as anal retentive as ever. I never did it for the sheer joy of resonating in the bathroom. I never sang to the radio the way Kent did, jamming on an imaginary guitar.

I went home and played "Blues in the Night" on the piano, singing along as the boys chased each other, shrieking with delight or fury, I didn't know. I found that I couldn't get the song out of my head. All evening, as I drove Anders and his friend to soccer practice, as Kent and I scavenged in the fridge for dinner food, I found myself belting out the song with as much gusto as Kate had over the rushing shower spray.

The next day, our dog rolled in poop in the backyard. Again. "Bath time," Anders announced, pinning our American Eskimo into a ball to get her collar off. I resigned myself to the chore and got out the towel and Snowy Coat shampoo. We herded the dog into the bathtub. We ran the water and sloshed it over her, ignoring the humiliated look in her eyes. I poured a glob of the bright blue shampoo into my hand. As I started working it into Mitzi's fur, turning it equally blue, I found myself singing again: *My doggie done tol' me, when she was a puppy, that she wanted blue shampoo. . . .* The boys joined in. We belted out the words, fitting them to every phrase in the song. Since that day, we've made up enough dog lyrics for the whole song. Yesterday when Mitzi rolled in more of what Anders calls "stinky leavings" and ended up in the tub again, we sang over the pounding water: *See the water runnin', hear the pipes a-hummin', whoo-ee!* This morning before Anders left for school, I started singing a new line about "bubbles formin'." "What rhymes with 'formin'' that isn't 'Mormon?'" I asked him, stumped. "That's easy," he said. "'Swarmin'.'"

Years ago, when Franco Zeffirelli's film version of *La Traviata* was released, I read a newspaper review that quoted leading tenor Placido Domingo as saying, "When people see this film, they will have to imagine themselves on a planet where everybody sings." We don't, unfortunately, live on such a planet. But sometimes music breaks into everyday life as naturally as rainfall. I want to be ready ground.

conversation

When they were six and three, my sons went through a painful phase. They couldn't walk from the back door to the car without thrashing at each other and screaming, "I wanna be first!" We came up with a system of alternating "leader days," but this spawned bitter arguments about whether today was Wednesday or Thursday. Once I got the boys pinned in their car seats, I'd turn on the radio, hoping for Mozart.

During this dark period, we bought a new car with a CD player. I loaded the storage compartment with Jack Prelutsky CDs from the library, the boys' own *Peter and the Wolf,* and something I thought might work even better than Mozart in the inevitable leader-day crisis. *Sounds and Songs of the Humpback Whales.*

I think these "sounds and songs" helped me more than they did the boys. Underneath all the "He's looking at me!" and "Hey, Anger

Baby!" and "Don't call me a baby!" in the backseat, I heard other, mercifully inhuman noises. The ocean's irregular roar. Low-pitched moans. High-pitched whistles.

Whale researcher Peter Tyack has called listening to humpbacks "a scary experience. Your lungs resonate with the sound. . . . You'll feel it more than hear it."

In a chapter on whales in his book *Arctic Dreams,* Barry Lopez confronts the foreignness of these singing giants: "How different must be 'the world' for such a creature, for whom sight is but a peripheral sense, who occupies, instead, a three-dimensional acoustical space. Perhaps only musicians have some inkling of the formal shape of emotions and motivation that might define such a sensibility." Lopez points out that whales live in a vertical world, defined by depth and surface. I try to think of a time when I've left my world bounded by walls and horizons, and made sound in three-dimensional vertical space. Last year I climbed down a ladder into an ancient kiva in Frijoles Canyon, New Mexico, and called to Anders from the darkness. He said my voice sounded "funny." Singing in a high-ceilinged church, I've sometimes felt I'm at the bottom of a well, trying to reach the top with my voice. Once it happened with poetry.

In 1998 I took part in an all-night reading of Dante's *Inferno* at the Cathedral of St. John the Divine in Manhattan. It was Maundy Thursday, and inside the church, purple draperies covered all the sculpted human forms. I arrived near midnight with a group of Sarah Lawrence students. Most of the well-known readers had spoken their parts earlier in the night, so the crowd was sparse. I sat at the base of a pillar in unearthly cold, and listened to human voices, male and female, speaking English or Italian, as they rose from the belly of the church toward the invisible ceiling.

Here in this cold, deep in the cathedral, deep in Manhattan, I felt desperately small. I thought of my husband and sons at home in Connecticut, warm in their beds. I worried about them. I worried about us. We'd been here six months. Kent had yet to receive his New York and Connecticut bar exam results and was still looking for work. His depression, which could rise like a flood at any time, invaded our house more and more frequently. I feared it so much that I didn't want to name it out loud. Neither did Kent. Sometimes when I came home from classes, I could smell cranberry-orange muffins, one of Kent's projects with the boys. Other times, I came home to a silence so thick I didn't know if I could walk through it. And this wasn't our only problem. We were down to the last of our savings, and my small teaching income didn't go far. One by one, every appliance in our condo had stopped working in the past nine months. The washer had refused to drain. The water heater had flooded the basement. The fridge had leaked all over the kitchen floor. More money gone. I wondered if we'd drown in dirty water and debt. Would we have to pay the exterminator a breathtaking fee to bait the rat that ran around our kitchen at night, banging cupboards like a burglar in a hurry? Would we even *have* beds to sleep in, one, two, or three months from now? Would Kent find himself in an inner ocean so deep he wouldn't be able to pull himself out? For the first time in my life, I looked at people asleep on the street, suffering the effects of mental illness, freezing under cardboard, acquainted with rats, and I shuddered with a very personal fear: *This could be my family.* My sheltered upbringing didn't mean a thing.

At three a.m., my turn came to read Dante. I looked out through my pool of light at the rows of folding chairs, most of them empty. By this time of night, I knew this reading wasn't about impressing people. It was a conversation with the dark. I swallowed hard and stepped closer to the mike. I read John Ciardi's translation of canto 31, in which Dante and Virgil look down into the central pit of Hell. From deep in the well rise shapes that look like towers but are actually the forms of giants. One of them babbles in an unknown tongue. Another writhes in chains. As I stood in front of the podium, between two pillars that reached higher than my vision did, I felt as small as a chained giant in Dante's immense infernal pit. As small as Jonah buried in the whale. As small as that great creature in the ocean's depths. I thought of the words of God to the despairing Job: "Canst thou draw out leviathan with an hook? or his tongue with a cord which thou lettest down?"

I spoke. My words left my body and echoed in the dark, in the pools of artificial light where dust motes floated. Eternal twilight. Inferno. Leviathan. I'd come to this place to find my voice—at a terrible cost to my family. What was I doing here in the beast's belly, speaking poetry to the eight or nine people left in the rows of folding chairs at three a.m.? And if there was a God somewhere up there in the dark, vaulted space, did He or She care? I kept reading. My voice echoed in the cathedral and faded away.

All over the world, in basement rooms, in night-lit offices, under the thinnest bedding, in cars driving nowhere in particular, under trees, under freeways, there are people speaking their longing. I believe their human songs, whether voiced aloud or not, are as wild as whale song. I once heard snatches of these songs in the windowless bowels of a women's jail in New York. One night a week, with a group of other Sarah Lawrence students, I passed through the heavy, buzzing doors, walked through a badly lit corridor, and emerged in the gym. It was a huge space with ceilings so high that I felt like a bug tottering around on the ground. A bug without a shell, clueless white girl that I was. From the cells stacked in the walls above me, women catcalled down to their friends, their lovers, their rivals, and us. Women wandered into the gym and eyed the vast space for a face they trusted—or at least recognized. My team teacher and I handed out lined paper and photocopied poems. Our students heaved themselves into plastic chairs and, when they weren't glaring at each other or getting up to stand in line for medication, they tried to write their longings on paper. *I'm in Love / with that Man Above,* wrote one woman in an exuberant poem that listed her symptoms of desire from head to hips. *Why can't you just set me free?* wrote another woman in her poem "One Question for God." Bugzy, who insisted on being called by her street name and bragged about having been shot six times, leaned over to me one night and said, "Me and God, we kick it, you know?" She wrote a poem that asked, in halting lines that surprised me,

> Please
> can you forgive me
> for what I did

wrong, knowing
I did wrong?

One inmate, the only white woman at our table besides us teachers, chose me to plead to: "Please understand I'm not supposed to be here," she whispered across the table. "Please understand." Voices swirled around the table, interrupting, teasing, chanting in rhyme.

I heard similar sounds in the men's prison outside Salt Lake City where I taught poetry. I didn't ask the men to write about God; the subject simply ruptured onto their paper or into their mouths. *To the Lord aBOVE, just one more TIME, baby, can you show me some LOVE,* rapped a young white prisoner, tattooed everywhere but his face, as far as I could tell. He wouldn't reveal his name. This was the only time he showed up to class. As he spoke, he closed his eyes and rocked back and forth in his chair. Then he got up and left. There was a silence in the room. After class, as I surfaced through the echoing double doors and exited the prison into the spring wind, as I drove to my in-laws' house to pick up my sons, the inmate's words echoed in my body. *To the Lord aBOVE, just one more TIME, baby, can you show me some LOVE.* . . . Would anyone else in this world, let alone God, hear these words? I felt like a whale specialist who's had the privilege of eavesdropping on humpback song fathoms and fathoms down. *Your lungs resonate with the sound.* . . . *You'll feel it more than hear it.*

The whale song I still put on in the car, hoping for peace, is not the real thing. It's soothing. The sound has probably been equalized to fit into the hearing zone most comfortable for human beings. I believe Peter Tyack when he calls the actual experience of listening to whales "scary." The Irish monks who sailed into northern waters centuries ago and thought they heard a chorus singing under the waves—what may well have been whale song—were not comforted by the sound. Job's words in the Bible, and God's words to him, are not comforting. When I read them, I hear a roar. This is what spirituality is for me: not the quiet voices in the halls at church, not the hymns so familiar I could sing them in my sleep, but desire, longing, the cry from the bottom of the well.

grace notes

silence

"Rant." Erica said the word in her soft voice. She said it again, thinking.

"It makes me think of righteous indignation," said Elaine.

"Rant and rave," someone else offered.

"Getting crazy."

"A wild sermon."

"Protest."

"Rage."

We were packed into the kitchen of the Ladies' Literary Club after Quaker meeting, a dozen of us at least, stirring our tea and spreading cream cheese on bagels. It was hot outside and stuffy in here. Someone had introduced the subject of Lady Godiva. "Her famous ride was an act of protest, you know," said Gordon the professional genealogist and walking historical encyclopedia. And then, somehow, we started riffing on the word *rant*. As people tossed words into the close air, I thought of the mad trumpeter who had bellowed in the gully behind my grandparents' house. I thought of "get happy" congregations where ranting and raving could be a form of spiritual ecstasy. I thought of my students in the women's jail, moving their bodies to someone's poem about her deadbeat lawyer. I thought of my own childhood rants, when my little cousin dared to enter my room and touch the glass collie with the chipped foot. Was Lady Godiva's bare-bottom-back ride really a political act, a form of rant? To think she didn't even have to open her mouth!

Several months later, when the United States started lurching toward war with Iraq, Kent said to me, "Are you Quakers planning any protests? I want to go to one. Maybe," he added half in jest, "I could get arrested."

I told him I actually knew someone who'd been arrested for civil disobedience. My criminal-defense-attorney husband looked impressed. Soon we found ourselves folding paper cranes at a September 11 memorial vigil. We took the boys to the winding-down of a peace march in downtown Salt Lake, where they munched on cookies while we listened to Israeli and Palestinian students describe the violence they'd witnessed in their homeland. I kept seeing in my mind the scenes of carnage I'd read under my desk in junior high, until I couldn't read anymore and wrote in red ink in my journal, "WAR IS HELL." Evan finished his cookie and said, "This is boring. Can we go home?" We stayed for a while longer, listening, watching the sign bearers under the trees. We were quiet on the walk back to the car. Finally, in mid-October, I got my chance to rant.

"I get a peace cramp every week," said the girl next to me on the corner of State Street. She was holding her fingers in a permanent V as cars stopped at the red light, some drivers honking for peace, others trying not to make eye contact with us. The girl, fresh-faced in a white bandanna, waved a sign that said "NO BLOOD FOR OIL." The woman on my other side sat still in her wheelchair, holding a sign she told me was the best one of all: it said simply, "PEACE." These demonstrators came to this vigil every Thursday night.

Someone had pulled the sign I wanted from the stack, so I'd made my own: "NO PRE-EMPTIVE STRIKE." I held it high. Then I looked at the polite capital letters I'd made and said to the girl in the bandanna, "I'm going to make this louder." I found my way to the stack of signs and boxes of markers. I thickened my letters and made my "NO" a deep lipstick red. I underlined it three times. The pressure of ink on paper felt better than yelling at people in cars. When I came back to the corner with my sign, the girl with the peace cramp nodded approvingly. I watched her infectious smile. I noticed the drivers who smiled back, and the biker who rang his bell all the way around the corner. I liked this kind of protest.

"We had some Christian Right people here a few weeks ago," the girl said. "They kept shouting and telling us we were going to hell. We tried to talk calmly to them. It was so weird. What would Jesus do, you know?"

More drivers smiled and waved. I waved back. But soon I found myself looking past them to the old theater across the street. Only the familiar yellow front was still standing. The stage and red-carpeted house, complete with balcony, had been demolished the week before to make room for a parking garage. I'd heard the city planned to keep the facade for a quaint storefront, but the rubble behind it unnerved me. For most of my childhood, I'd practically lived in that theater. I'd followed my mother around backstage. I'd overheard dirty jokes in the greenroom. Sometimes I'd appeared under the hot lights myself. I'd watched my mother sink into a stack of pillows, her hoopskirt billowing up behind her, as she ranted about the king of Siam. "Yes, your *majesty*," I could still hear her spit across the orchestra pit in her faux English accent. And I could hear the orchestra pulsing its waltzy rhythm to my mother's "Beautiful Candy" as she twirled around the circus ring in *Carnival* and I waited in the wings in my pink dress, ready to come onstage and hawk balloons— my one moment of glory, the solo the director said I needed to sing "louder, bigger. . . . You *are* the carnival owner's daughter!"

So much for method acting. That stage—my life's mythic stage—had collapsed into a pile of rubble. Here I stood on the street corner, no longer in costume, no longer pretending, waving my sign. I meant the bloodred words I'd formed in marker. A man's voice swore at us through a car window. Two more honks for peace. Next to me, the girl in the bandanna balanced her sign on her hip. "You know what I want?" she said. "One of those old Vietnam protest signs that said 'Girls say yes to boys who say no.'"

I peered around at the words on my sign. Was this what I wanted? I thought of my activist friend who once said, "Some people like to wave signs and sing songs, but I'm for silence myself." I thought of an interview with Thich Nhat Hanh I'd listened to in my car. When asked his opinion of antiwar protest, the Zen master cautioned against protesting in anger against one's own government if one is contributing, even unconsciously, to the causes of war. "The other person is us," he said, and I remembered his words acknowledging that had his upbringing been different, he might have ended up a sea pirate. In this interview, he mused that protesting with this insight is better than ranting one's rage at something "other." I heard in my head Adrienne Rich's question: "What teaches us to convert lethal anger into steady, serious attention to our own lives and those of others?"

I lowered my sign. Maybe I hadn't thought enough about what it meant to come here tonight. I pictured myself curled on the Story

Couch, reading an article about poverty in my tasteful, temperature-controlled house. I pictured the coat I had recently purchased, made under who knew what conditions in the Dominican Republic. I pictured the car I drove whenever I wanted, burning the fuel my country would kill for. Was my sign waving simply a performance, this street corner my stage? Was I more interested in making a point than in actually working for peace? Was I hoping someone I knew would drive by? Yes, I confessed to myself. I longed to flash my very orthodox Mormon uncle, sleepy at the wheel after a long day at the office, my sign and my most exuberant smile.

What would happen if I just sat here on the pavement? What if I sat and thought about what Thich Nhat Hanh called "the unmindful way you live your life"? I would have to consider my summer as an intern in Washington, when I'd written constituent letters in a senator's voice. I was nineteen. I'd taken the job not because politics interested me but because I was running away from the choice that faced me at home: keep writing my missionary boyfriend, or yield to my new feelings for Kent, who was almost seven years older than I and ready for marriage. I commuted every day from Virginia to Capitol Hill. When I wasn't agonizing over my "Dear John" letter, I sat in front of a computer screen, answering constituent mail. In each case, I pulled up a form letter and added a line here or there to make it apply to the individual who had taken the time to speak up. I used the word *I*, as though I were the balding public servant I'd only met once, in a photo-op my first day on the job. When I finished a letter, it went first to a staffer for approval, and then to the signature machine to be passed off as authentic. By the end of the summer, the country was about to enter the Gulf War. I wrote to elderly people concerned about prescription costs, telling them, in soothing bureaucratic tones, that our country's priorities lay with "maintaining a strong national defense." More and more, the words made me sick to my stomach. I wrote them anyway.

Now, twelve years later, I stood on the street corner and waved. At least my actions were consistent with my beliefs, I told myself. But I knew I could do more. People might not understand. If I sat here on the pavement, signless and speechless, examining my own heart,

grace notes

the peace-cramp girl would think me less than valiant. Other protesters might not even notice me. The orthodox uncle would drive on by. I would be an anonymous presence in the crowd. I would sit there and consider. I would breathe. That might take more courage, I understood with a chill, than standing on a stage.

five

diary

"Why didn't you tell me?" I scold my mother on the phone.

"I guess I didn't want to complain," she says. "I just need to have a good cry and go to the chiropractor, and I'll be fine."

"Let me know if I can do anything," I tell her. We say good-bye. For a long time I sit with the phone in my lap. *I'll be fine.* How many times have I heard this phrase from her? I still don't believe it. Especially now, when she's spent a week in Los Angeles caring for her mother, who's had hip surgery and needs twenty-four-hour attention. "My body is feeling all the pain of being a caretaker," my mother has just told me. When I picked her up from the airport this afternoon, she helped me heave her suitcase into my trunk. She didn't

157

say a word about her back pain. Who knows what childhood wounds broke open in her, as she spent her days cooking and fetching and cleaning my grandmother's incision. My mother has lived at such a distance from her family for the past thirty-five years that this sudden intimacy must have done more than throw her back out of alignment. I suspect the pain won't go away anytime soon.

Kent and the boys and I visited my grandparents last summer. My grandfather, dapper as always in his pressed slacks and fedora, greeted us on the porch of their double-wide mobile home. The boys hid behind me; they knew their great-grandmother, whom they had not seen in three years, was waiting for them inside. I wondered what they remembered of her—her wildly crooked fingers, her powdery scent? My aunt, who lives with my grandparents, opened the door. We sat in the living room gleaming with the glass flowers and shepherdesses I'd known since childhood. "Hello there, you kids!" came Grandma's voice. I ran to meet her as she shuffled out of the laundry room with her walker. I started to hug her. She stopped me. "I'm afraid I can't," she said. "Everything hurts in this old body of mine."

I pulled back and watched her steer herself, every step a chore, into the living room. This was the grandmother who had always embraced me. The one who expected nothing, who I knew would love me even if I *did* fail my algebra test. The one who let me stay up late watching TV with her, Hershey's Kisses spilling all over the bed. The one who had once, a great-great-aunt told me, danced into the living room as a teenager and shattered the glass milk jugs she was carrying. Now, as she lowered herself into her wheelchair, I knew this loving, soulful woman was already partly lost to me. I sat across from her on the sofa, the boys nuzzling me, too shy to speak. I asked her about her upcoming hip replacement. "Would you believe I haven't been to a doctor in five years?" she whispered, leaning toward me. "And now this! I find it absolutely humiliating."

I couldn't believe it. But then, Grandma has always been stubborn. I didn't ask who prescribes all those pills she takes every day. "So when are you scheduled for surgery?" I ventured.

"Who knows," she said. "Tests, tests, and more tests." She

waved this thought away with her hand, which, however deformed, has always looked stunningly smooth to me. She used to touch my cheek with it, when I was three or four and perched on the padded purple stool in her bathroom, watching the tub fill with green-salted water. Grandma's bathroom was soft with powders and creams and womanly scents. I could have lived in there. It was nothing like my mother's bathroom at home, which felt more like a doctor's office to me. Cleanser. Ointment. Antiwrinkle cream. Boxes and boxes of tampons, whose printed instructions I read with horror when I was seven. Or was my grandmother's bathroom so different from this? Not long ago my mother said, "Grandma uses powders and perfumes to make herself beautiful, but she also uses them to hide the body that disgusts her. She won't go in public without perfume."

As I sat across from Grandma in her living room, I took in her scent. This was her signature, a smell I'd recognize anywhere. I'd always thought her powders and lotions were a gift to her body, a way of nurturing its ills, the way I treat my tired body to lemon verbena bath gel and lotion at the end of the day. To think that for my grandmother, all those floral scents may also have been as much a mask as my mother's layers of makeup. Grandma resettled her hand in her lap. That hand I loved, worn smooth from decades of lotioning. She didn't want to talk about her hip anymore. She asked about the day we'd spent sailing in San Diego with my parents earlier in the week. We told her about sea lions sunning themselves on the buoys, sunset over the Pacific, and the "green flash" that had eluded us. "I threw up," Anders was brave enough to add. We talked about our treat the next night, hearing Thomas Young in concert with the Three Mo' Tenors. "He's performing here in L.A. tonight," I said. "I wish you could go."

"Oh, I love to watch him on TV!" Grandma beamed. I thought of her day-to-day existence: sleep, the German folk-music hour on the radio, pain pills, laborious meals, a weekly trip to the hair salon—and hours of TV. "I can't abide the soap operas," she told me once. "I can't keep track of everybody's sex lives. But I *love* the music programs." Grandma is not a musician. I've never heard her sing, but she has musical instincts. When I send her a poem, she knows, somehow, to read it aloud. Sometimes she speaks pieces of it back to me over the phone, her voice playing the rhythm I felt in my body when I first put pencil to paper. There is music in her speech.

This is how I know my grandmother, I realized, sitting across from her in the air-conditioned room: even more than her scent, more than her cool, crooked hands, I know her by her voice. The voice that still calls me "you little bit o' doll." The voice that invariably says, when I ask how she's feeling, "Oh, *marvelous*." The voice that carries a spark and a laugh and the possibility of violent cursing. The voice my mother once promised herself never to take as her own. She would be the peacemaker, the one who would never raise her voice in anger, the one who would never complain. She would dam up her own voice, which sang through the house all day when she was a child, and save it for the stage. "My mother's voice was always distressing to me," she told me once. "It came at me in waves. I never knew when it would crash over my head. Living with Grandma was like living with an emotional tornado." As she said these words, I pictured my grandmother the ocean, the maelstrom, trapped in an immovable body. From elementary school until her marriage, my mother fled this tormented life force. As a child she often sought quiet in her room, where my grandfather would bring her quarters, in silence, to make up for his wife's unending noise. As a teen she fled into her social life, arranging to be away from home as often as possible. She resisted the wild life force inside herself, allowing her mother to give her tranquilizers before she went on dates. "I do remember one time when my mother was calm," she remembers. "She'd wait up for me until I came home from my dates. I'd sit by her stocking feet on the footstool, and we'd talk and laugh. I loved the smell of her feet, because they weren't perfumed or powdered, they were just human." I wish I could have heard these late-night conversations. I have to imagine my grandmother's rich laughter and my mother's exuberant talk. After her marriage, my mother continued to tame her voice. She learned from her mother-in-law how to walk into a room without disturbing anyone. "Grandma told me my perfume could be offensive to some people. When I was engaged to Dad, she scolded me for having a noisy pillow fight with her daughters." My mother threw away her perfume. She learned to repress her giggles. No "Oh, marvelous" sarcasm from her. *I'll be fine.*

She didn't tell me about her back pain today. Maybe she's too emotionally exhausted to talk about anything, after spending a week with her mother. I toy with the phone on the Story Couch. I watch out the bay window as a jet cuts a white trail through the sky. Guilt cuts through me. Maybe my mother was afraid to tell me. Several years ago I criticized her for taking a dozen herbal capsules every day, worrying over her diet, going to the iridologist and the reflexologist and performing surreptitious acupressure on herself. "I've always thought of myself as healthy," she said, hurt surfacing in her voice. "Growing up, I thought of you as sickly and depressed," I said. I must have wounded her more deeply than I realized. All those years, she tried to convince everyone, including herself, that she would be fine. Maybe we both needed that lie. Maybe it was easier not to think about the roots, generations deep, of my mother's pain.

Here on the sofa, in the comfort of my healthy body, in the center of this home I love, I have trouble imagining that pain. I no longer suffer from the stomachaches that bent me double in junior high. I haven't had a migraine in months. I've gone half a year without even a cold. What was it like for my mother, spending hours in the bathroom when colitis hit? What was it like growing up with a mother who was never, ever well? I think of my friend Kay, not much older than I am, who has suffered from rheumatoid arthritis like my grandmother's since she was in her teens. I think of what it costs her to work at the computer or, on a bad day, to walk from one end of the house to the other. I think of the silver braces she wears on her fingers, to keep them from twisting into impossible shapes. I have no idea what it means to live with chronic pain. I can't even picture the daily assault of my grandmother's ranting. And what about Grandma's own childhood? There was her terror at having been abandoned by her father at age nine. In the generation before that, there was my great-grandmother's public shame after her divorce in the 1930s. Her debilitating bite from the brown recluse spider. Before that? A family legend of multiple wives beaten sick by their husband, secretary to prophet Brigham Young. Pioneer women giving birth on the prairie. Stillbirth, typhus, diphtheria. Young mothers asked to share their husbands with a ripe young virgin or two? I wouldn't be surprised. And, on a not-so-distant branch of the family tree, Catharine in her sickbed.

No wonder I didn't want to copy the diary when I first discovered it. Catharine's complaints were the words under my mother's words, what she really meant when she said, "I'll be fine." I still remember the line that made me shut the book, shaking my head: "My constitution is so extremely delicate." I didn't want to claim this fainting flower as my relative. I wasn't yet a Quaker; I didn't have regular reminders to look beyond a person's off-putting words to the roots of her suffering. I didn't read far enough to meet Catharine's grief over the loss of her mother, or her account of having to lie down in the street, exhausted, on her way to teach school. I closed the book before I could meet her astonishingly quiet mind, her capacity for love, the "deep plunging" of her spiritual life. What will happen if I don't close the book on my mother's life? What if I read beyond my assumptions and listen to the words under the words she speaks? I close my eyes and try to hear them.

"Oh, I just want this one bite," she said when I was eight years old. She stood over the kitchen sink, a piece of chocolate in her hand. She opened her mouth and set the chocolate on her tongue. I watched her chew, the tendons straining in her neck, as though this piece of chocolate tasted so good that it hurt. Then she bent over and spit it out. "Are you worried about gaining weight?" I teased her, my ninety-five-pound mother who worried if the scale's needle teetered toward one hundred. I must have sensed this fear under her "I just want this one bite." She wanted more, and I knew it. She could have eaten every sugary morsel in the house, if she'd let herself. But pleasure meant poison to her. Even at eight years old, I heard these words under her words: *Disgusting. You ugly, you evil, you dangerous body.* There was my grandmother's voice, those crashing waves, throttled inside my mother.

"I just need to stay in bed until the thermometer tells me my temperature," she said when I was nine. I knew what was up. That chart on the nightstand? I'd looked up *ovulation* in the dictionary. My mother was trying to have another child, desperate to fill her emptiness. She thought I didn't see her pain as she prayed for twenty minutes at a time, kneeling by her bed in the dark. She thought I knew nothing about sex. She didn't know that when I was seven, my older cousin had told me, in sticky detail, exactly where babies come from. She thought I didn't see her hurt when someone at church asked the inevitable question: "Now, why haven't you had more children?" She thought I didn't see the words she wrote in her spiral notebook as she sat watching my swimming lesson: *I am an empty vessel.* I read the words as I stripped down to my swimsuit, standing next to her chaise longue on the hot pavement. I plunged through the sun glints into the water, letting it circle my body with the most delicate touch. I pictured my mother floating on the surface, the shape of a woman, arms pressed to her sides, all taut white skin. Nothing but air inside.

"I'll be fine." My mother spoke from the tall bed in the Blue Room in my grandparents' house. She'd had her most severe colitis attack yet, and her in-laws had taken her in. For weeks I came home from school to an empty house. My father and I ate dinner in silence. He went to see her in the evenings. Sometimes I went with him. My mother lay back on the pillows, so pale without makeup that she looked like a stranger. She'd collapsed after attending a dozen extra church meetings she'd been assigned as a leader in the children's program. "I'll be fine," she said, and I didn't believe her. I feared these endless meetings might kill her one day.

When I was a child, my mother's body was a diary of shame and fear. The makeup she wore told me that she did not feel acceptable without it. Her bone-thin frame told me of her guilt over food that would make her fat or make her sick. Her eruptions of colitis told me how she'd kept rage wound in her belly like a parasite. Her chilly touch made me wonder if she was really alive in her body. On some level I've been reading this subtext all my life. But what if I refuse to close the book there? Who is my mother now?

"You are so present right now," said our therapist in our first mother-daughter session. She wasn't talking to me. I sat on the sofa, my face turned toward my mother, my body turned away. And here I'd thought I was the one prepared to do this. My mother faced me in a chair, her hands on her knees, tears in her eyes. She *was* present in that room. I was not. When she came over to hug me, all I could do was pat her back and say, "It's okay," playing mother, as usual, to the frail child she was in my mind. "Can you imagine letting your mom hug you?" asked the therapist in her quiet voice. I couldn't. The story of my mother's life that I had carried for years said nothing about this. Could I turn the page? What would I find?

"I can't, I can't, not yet," I whispered to myself as I drove home. But I left the book in my mind open, a little.

nine openings

Late again. And no poem to show for it. I slid into the lamp-lit office, hoping Tom Lux wouldn't notice me. Of course he did. There were only four of us in this poetry workshop, four who had been chosen to study with the head of the graduate writing program at Sarah Lawrence, and I felt like a delinquent. I sat down in the armchair left empty for me. I tried not to make a sound. Judith was reading her week's work: a poem about starlings breaking from the sky, a metaphorical annunciation. Tom glanced at me. He flung back his shoulder-length hair. "Now, I'm not as well versed in the Bible as some people . . ."

Part of me heard his words. Here were these birds taking off in a cluster, here was the logic of the poem. . . . Most of me could hardly sit straight in the chair. Late again, and no poem! I'd been the perfect student all my life. I could blame motherhood, weaning Evan, potty training Anders, missing Kent since he'd taken a job in Manhattan and could no longer help me. But I knew none of this was the problem. I could not write, I could not eat, I'd lost fourteen pounds in a month, and I could not manage to get to class on time. All I'd brought to my one-on-one conferences this semester were a few halting lines, my attempt to back-talk Theodore Roethke's woman-as-object love poems. Tom had been kind. He'd even said, after some suggestions for expanding the poem, the words we all wanted to hear from him: "This one's a keeper." But to me it was not. I was shutting down, and I didn't know why.

"I'm sorry," I said when my turn came to read.

"Everybody gets blocked sometimes," Tom said, looking at me over his glasses. He moved on to Vince, who read a new draft of a poem I loved about two guys sitting on a roof talking about God, or maybe one of them *was* God, I could hardly tell at the moment. I tried to pay attention. I tried to think of something intelligent to say.

After class I walked down the wooded road to my car. I didn't think about the darkness, or who might be lurking behind the almost-bare oaks and maples. I hardly heard the dead leaves rattling on the beech trees. I was thinking of my walk down this road the semester before, when a girl, maybe ten years old, appeared out of nowhere and asked me to touch her dogs. I hardly heard her at first. I'd just come from a reading by a teacher of mine who wrote unflinchingly about the body—varicose veins, lover's touch, whip bruise, arthritis, abortion, and all. I was still trembling from her words. "Do you want to touch my dogs?" the girl said again. I looked down. In the streetlight's arc, I saw two runty poodles straining at their leashes. "No, no," I muttered, looking at the gloves on my hands, and hurried away. I came to workshop the next week with a new poem that began, *"Do you want to touch my dogs?"* Suzanne Gardinier, a favorite instructor known for her aura of calm, burst into joyful laughter. "I love the music in this!" she said. But nothing came of that poem. I still didn't know what it meant.

Now, as I unlocked my car in the dark and felt the cold steering wheel under my hands, I wondered what in the world I was doing here. I'd thought I was making progress. Suzanne had helped me slough off the pretty language I'd let distract me from the core of the poem. I'd filled a notebook with new work. I'd spent the summer teaching in the women's jail, where the students at my table sang praises to God and to their bodies. What was it they'd written? Random lines surfaced in my head as I drove under the Cross County Parkway and stopped at a red light. *My body is my JEWEL. . . . Legs legs legs. My legs has a mind of their own. . . . Hello Stomach, I am writing to you because you stand out.* I remembered the ending of a poem by

Freshie, who'd lost most of her hair from the unrelenting stress of life on the street, but dazzled me every week with her smile. In one session she wrote a letter to her body—and forgot the comma after the word *Love* at the end. *Love your body.* I drove up the on-ramp. *Love your body.* I hardly existed in mine. What did I think I was doing, praising myself for going another day without food? Trying to disappear?

I didn't *want* to get to the core of the poem. Suzanne had loved the language I was learning to speak, the fragments of poems I brought to our biweekly conference, the ruptures of anger, the hints of sensuality. But that was all I had written. Fragments. First drafts. I'd seen what was in there, and I wanted to run away. Yes, to disappear. Now, when I undressed at night, Kent noticed my shrunken breasts and the ribs edging through my skin. My father-in-law, who was visiting, had offered to give me a priesthood blessing.

I decided to let him. On Saturday, when Kent was home, we all gathered in our living room. My mother-in-law shut the front curtains. "For privacy, you know," she said. She settled into the sofa with the boys. Kent pulled a chair into the middle of the room. I sat down. I felt him dab some consecrated olive oil in my hair and place his hands on my head. I closed my eyes. He spoke the anointing prayer to prepare me for the blessing on the sick. Then his father, legendary for his gentle service as a Mormon bishop years before, placed his hands on my head and spoke of God's love for me, and of my family's love for me. I heard his voice as though it called to me through water. I felt my body relax. Someone had touched me. Someone had anointed my head with oil. Here in this room, I knew I was loved. In his blessing my father-in-law told me that my appetite would return. That I would have peace in my heart. *Amen.* I opened my eyes and surfaced into the room. "We're going to get you better," said my mother-in-law with her usual certainty. "All we have to do is pray."

That afternoon I felt strong enough to visit Kate, who was recovering from pneumonia. "I don't have any new poems for you," I said. We talked instead, as darkness fell over the house. Kate coughed her deep cough. "Do you want to sing?" she said, knowing neither of us had been near a piano in weeks. I nodded. I didn't have to tell her what I wanted to sing. As she started to play the first song in Schumann's *Dichterliebe,* I had to grip the piano. She looked so pale. She had smelled death, and I knew it. I'd been more afraid of losing her than I'd been willing to admit, even to myself. No wonder I hadn't been able to come up with a new poem. How to write about *this?* I started to sing. I noticed Kate's copy of the song was in a lower key than mine. The sound of my voice surprised me. It seemed to have risen out of deep water, a warm, live thing. I sang the words of the poet who remembers how, in the blooming month of May, he broke his silence and spoke of his love. Kate finished the song, which ends on an unresolved seventh chord, ready to circle back to the beginning and repeat itself forever. The chord hung in the yellow-lit room. I sat down next to Kate on the piano bench. We were both still alive, and the music between us would not stop.

That night I met Kent and the boys and my in-laws at a Chinese restaurant. I put a spoonful of egg drop soup on my tongue. I ate almost half of my rice. We brought the boys home and put them to bed. My parents-in-law retired to the basement family room to sleep. Kent went to bed upstairs. I sat down at the kitchen table. I knew what was about to happen.

I started to write.

> "Do you want to touch my dogs?" asks
> a girl I've never met, whose poodles sniff
> my ankles as I try to cross the street. . . .

The lines pounded in my body in iambic meter, the rhythm of the heartbeat. *I'm not afraid of touch,* I wrote, allowing the lie to stand transparent on the page. I wrote about the time I almost drowned when I was four, how my body surrendered to the chlorinated depth, until my mother's hand reached me, almost too late. I wrote about the silence between us during her last visit. Her cold touch. Fourteen lines. Day after day, words pulsed in my head. I scribbled them on scraps of paper until, the house quiet with breathing sleepers, I could sit down at the kitchen table. I wrote about my body in the mirror, thin as the jingle shells I kept in a white bowl. I wrote about my breasts, empty of milk. Fourteen lines. I wrote about the Carson City woman whose body I'd helped dress in Mormon temple clothes after her death. Her pallor and my unfelt touch. Fourteen lines. Internal rhyme webbed words together. The meter wouldn't let up. This insistent music surprised me. I'd never intended to write a crown of sonnets, first and last lines interlocking, rhythm echoing my pulse. But here they were, one after the other, seven "Body Sonnets." I didn't know if they were any good, but I did know they were the most necessary words I'd ever written.

Why the sonnet? I thought of Adrienne Rich in the 1950s, back when she was a housewife attempting to tell the truth on paper, using traditional form as her "asbestos gloves." I remembered what Suzanne had said about metered verse: "Every meter has its own voice. Every sonnet will hold echoes of its ancestors." I was writing in the form Shakespeare and Petrarch had used to objectify women and their bodies. I was writing in the form other twentieth-century women had reclaimed before me, choosing to write as the poem's subject, not its object with eyes more or less like the sun. My sonnets' ancestors included Marilyn Hacker's blood-and-broken-glass "Eight Days in April"; Rita Dove's mother-daughter sonnets based on the Persephone myth; Adrienne Rich's "Twenty-one Love Poems," which break open the fourteen-line form to speak of lesbian experience; and Joan Larkin's "Blackout Sonnets," which record a rape. I couldn't hope to make the radical statements these poets had made; so many words had shaken the earth before me. But I could "word" my way back to my body. I could try to see from inside my own skin, not as I'd viewed it from outside since I was ten, as a bleeding burden or as church property or as my husband's private treasure. I could risk falling back under the water, the pool I'd almost drowned in. I longed to enter the mythic deep Adrienne Rich had explored in her poem "Diving into the Wreck." I remembered the words of Eavan Boland, writing of the woman poet's journey: "The object she returns to rescue, with her newly made Orphic power and intelligence, would be herself."

Three days later, my sonnet crown had almost doubled. The seven-sonnet form was not going to be enough. Though I'd never wanted to be a "confessional poet," here came my body's history, flooding my kitchen. I'd have fourteen poems before I knew it. And then, one morning when Anders was in preschool, I came to the poem I knew I had to write. *Revisit the moment of your most passive silence,* came a whisper inside me. *Give the girl you were a voice.* No. I couldn't. I slammed my notebook shut and bundled Evan into his stroller. Anything to keep this one inside.

We walked down the tree-lined street toward the Point. I didn't turn down Sea Beach Drive, my usual scenic route. I wasn't even looking at the haze that clung to the old colonial houses, or the leaf litter sticking to the stroller's wheels. I was seeing acoustic tile on a ceiling above me. Fluorescent light. The puffed dark hair of a nurse, who turned from me when I screamed. The doctor's gloved hand, bright with my blood. His paternal voice: *Be glad it's me and not your future husband.* He'd given me a useless local anesthetic. He had not given me a choice. *We're going to perform some surgery, to make things easier on your wedding night.* He made an incision, but that wasn't enough. He pulled a plastic dilator from its paper sheath. It looked like a miniature nuclear warhead. He worked it into my body. Pain seared me, clear to my teeth. He pushed harder. I said nothing. My insides would not give. I remembered the scene in Faulkner's *Sanctuary* where the girl is raped with a corncob. I imagined the whites of her eyes showing. Her hand slipping on planks full of nails in the barn loft. Was it a loft? Was there light coming in? I shut my eyes against the fluorescent tubes above me, against this doctor my mother had recommended, against the nurse standing there with her face turned away. I writhed. I screamed. I could not form words. The nurse said nothing. The doctor pushed harder. No one had warned me about this. I was just another nineteen-year-old Mormon virgin going to her prenuptial exam. My recently married friends had told me it was no big deal. They had not been torn open in the examining room; this was not an established part of Mormon culture. One friend said she'd been given the option of taking a dilator home. The option. Imagine that. I'd thought I'd get my pap smear and my birth control prescription and my little talk about intercourse, maybe the take-home sex toy, and that would be that. No one had told me I'd lose my virginity in a paper hospital gown. I said nothing. I wanted to be lifted out of my skin.

Present time. An idling engine. Leaves blowing toward the Sound. My hands gripped Evan's stroller so hard, I had to stop and release the plastic-coated bar. Evan was asleep. I closed my eyes. Now, as the doctor's office flashed in front of me again, I got my wish. I was lifted out of my skin. I saw my body broken open under fluorescent light. I saw the whites of my own eyes. And this, I understood, was how I'd seen myself that day. I'd hovered somewhere near the ceiling tiles, watching, speechless. My body not my own. Just now, as I'd walked toward the water, I'd experienced that moment from the inside. And now I could go there again, with unnerving ease.

The doctor pulled out of me, the plastic dilator bloodied to its base. I swallowed my tears and still said nothing. The nurse handed me a fat maxi pad. "You'll bleed for a week to ten days," the doctor said. "And you'll need some Tylenol when you get home." I said nothing. The doctor washed his hands. "Come next door into my office when you're ready. I'll call in your fiancé." I was left alone to dress. I could hardly lift my feet out of the stirrups. At last I waddled into the hallway. Inside the doctor's private office, I eased myself into the chair next to Kent. He looked at me. I looked at the floor. I hardly heard the doctor's words about sex. Something about swinging from the chandeliers. I said nothing. The doctor handed me a plastic dilator to practice with. I cried all the way home in the car. I tried to tell Kent what had happened, but the words came out in pieces.

My parents were out of town. Kent and I walked into the darkened house in silence. He heated tomato soup in the kitchen while I had a hot bath. The Tylenol wasn't helping. I sank deeper into the water, biting my lip in pain. Could I tell my mother?

When she was home again, I tried. I found her folding laundry in the basement, five pairs of shoulder-to-knee undergarments like the ones I would wear after my first visit to the temple. "I was just wondering about something," I attempted. "I wondered if it's normal to be cut open on your first visit to the gynecologist."

She put down the soft white garments. "I was afraid this would happen," she said.

"What?"

"Do you remember when you were very little, and the doctor told me to stretch you every week? He could see, even when you were born, that your hymen was impenetrable." She wasn't looking at me. "I've had so much guilt over that."

I said nothing. The memory surfaced: my five-year-old body spread on a towel in the hallway, my mother bent over me, her cold fingers pulling and pulling, her voice murmuring, *I'm sorry, I'm sorry, the doctor said to do this, does it hurt?* It did. I stared at the frosted-glass light fixture. I said nothing. When I was sixteen, my mother told me I couldn't wear tampons. Now I knew why.

I stumbled out of the laundry room. I wandered into my father's study, where the bill for my hymenotomy had sat on his desk for a week. Who knew what he thought about this. He never talked about such things. I retreated to my room. There on my dresser sat the practice dilator the doctor had given me, still in its paper sheath. I had no desire to get to work, to reopen that wound. So I'd been born a "stone maiden." I wish I'd known. I might have been proud of it.

Can I write about my violently ruptured virginity? The question swirled inside me. I'd reached the Point before I knew it. I lifted Evan out of his stroller and stood him up on the concrete wall overlooking Long Island Sound. He struggled to free himself from sleep. I held him tight against my shoulder, breathing in the baby scent that still hung around his hair and skin. The water looked almost white in the haze. On a clear day I could see Manhattan from here. No sign of it now. I didn't mind. I let the sound of the water wash through me. It spoke of the bride who had drowned in her own silence. I scanned the unbroken surface. Evan breathed evenly against me. His warmth and rhythm pulled me back to this moment. I breathed with him. I was no longer that silent bride. I was no longer the disembodied self who watched her from the ceiling. I did not have to grow so thin I could disappear in this white light.

We started back up the peninsula. I would write when I got

home. I would say the words, and this time, they would come out whole.

Be glad it's me, and not your future husband. . . . I sat at the kitchen table and spoke the words aloud. Who knew the doctor had made his patronizing speech in iambic meter. But as my words fell out, leaving their staccato music on the page, I felt split between two bodies. There was my body lying on the examining bed, bare feet in stirrups, mouth open in pain. The object. There was the body inside that body, my conscious self. That self spoke in the poem. She longed to be a child again, to soak in Grandma's yellow bathtub, lathering Dove soap—or was it Ivory?—deliciously over her arms and legs until it melted to nothing. She longed to lie under the nubby bedspread in the Blue Room, the needlepoint of little Mozart on the wall. The body on the table flashed in front of me again. The perspective wouldn't stay still. I thought of Eavan Boland's words: "The woman poet is in that poignant place . . . where the subject cannot forget her previous existence as an object." I could write this poem for a year and never get it right. I leaned back in the kitchen chair, my whole body aching.

A week later, I had my first voice lesson with Thomas. He asked me to breathe. He stood behind me with his hands on my shoulders. I wondered if his enormous masculine energy would take me over. I felt as permeable as eggshell. I hadn't even begun to gain back those fourteen pounds. I thought I might fall over. "I think you need to lie down," Thomas said. He asked me to notice the place where the small of my back touched the floor and to breathe, as my mother had asked her students to do, as I asked my own students to do. I did. The air in the room fell through me. Thomas stood, rooted to the floor, at my feet. He counted my breaths. I was afraid, and I was not. He helped me to my feet. I sat across from him as he straddled the piano bench, his hands on his knees. "You have not yet claimed your body," he said.

"I know."

"No one else can do that for you."

I knew I could trust him not to try.

I left the studio shaking. That afternoon I drove to Sea Beach. I

grace notes

needed a refuge, a quiet place to be in my body. I parked the car and looked back at Evan and the toddler I was baby-sitting, both of them asleep, sweaty-headed in their car seats. I got out of the car and walked several feet to the hurricane wall.

High tide. Sunlight broke all over the water. A tanned, white-haired woman sat below me on the rocks, watching the waves rise almost to her feet. At first I thought she looked like Kate sitting there, the healthy Kate I knew, who loved to swim in the ocean and feel the sun on her face. The woman turned toward me. I didn't know her, but then, as we smiled at each other, somehow I did. We'd both come here for this quiet, this light, the water pulse that washed through our bones. The woman turned away again. We both looked out across the Sound. In this water lived sea star and shark and horseshoe crab, moon jelly and mussel and skate. The waves dragged sea lettuce and Irish moss onto the sand. The cycle of living and eating and dying went on, and the woman below me was part of it, and so was I. We looked across the water. In this light we could see the power-plant smokestacks on the north shore of Long Island, where, in the last Ice Age, a glacier had reached equilibrium and begun to melt. I sat down on the wall. I felt my body softening, my ribs retreating back into my skin.

Another car pulled up and stopped. A couple with two dogs got out. Before the man and woman could restrain them, the black labs thundered toward me along the hurricane wall. They brushed me, warm and bristling, as they passed. *Do you want to touch my dogs?* Yes. Yes. New words whispered in my head: *tail-lash, dog-touch.* I hurried back to the car. I would write this down. I would note the woman on the wall and the look that had passed between us. I would note the water, heavy with life.

chant

Highway 53, New Mexico. "There's the river!" I call out. Kent, whose turn it is to drive, slows down. We're traveling with Anders and my father. My first time in Zuni country since I was eleven years old. We're looking for the last houses of a farming community on the edge of the Pescado River. My thumb is stuck in Dennis Tedlock's book on Zuni storytelling, marking the page where I first read the tale of the woman who vanishes into a flute. The location of the story, a ruin called Striped House, is said to exist somewhere nearby, weathered almost to the ground. Dotted with pinyon and juniper, the desert floor looks alternately blue and gold as clouds pile up and pass over. The same dance of light and shade that struck me twenty years ago. It's early November, almost the same time of year. Willows and cottonwoods, almost bare, crowd the river's autumn-thin body. Whatever is left of Striped House could be anywhere.

We turn right on an unmarked road and head toward the water. Some years ago, Tedlock's Zuni guide took him to the place where Nepayatamu and his companion are said to have stopped to rest. Tedlock says he could never have found it on his own. I can see why: in this changing light, I can hardly tell stump from stone. I picture the flute player examining the cottonwood limbs, peeling back the calloused bark in search of a branch to test with his breath. I imagine the silent woman sitting on a rock. I've been reading more about her. In the tales Tedlock collected, Zuni storytellers recalled a mythic gender war. A virgin, one of a group of women who lived independently of men, once argued with Nepayatamu about the time of the sun's rising. He raped her to teach her a lesson. She cut off his head in revenge. A medicine man sealed it back to his body. After this, the woman had to walk with Nepayatamu as far east as they could go, to see the sun's rising for themselves. Here, in this mesa-shadowed river valley, they stopped to rest. Here he sucked her into his flute, and, when he breathed out music, she flew away in the form of white moths.

I scan the valley for any sign of ancient rubble. Who knows what I'm looking for. The story is just a story, after all. But it troubles me. Sometimes it keeps me up at night. It's one reason, besides the pleasure of bringing my father back to Zuni, I had to take this trip. What does the story mean? The independent woman is put in her place—somebody's phallic flute. She has changed from spitfire virgin to silent companion. She has been raped. She has lost her voice. I find this story disheartening. I know it too well. At least the woman breaks free of her husk and flies away, transformed into music and wings.

"Let's go on," I tell Kent. "Thanks for trying." We turn around and head back toward the highway. "How long till we get to Zuni?" Anders wants to know. My father guesses twenty minutes, after the bend in the road. I strain to see Corn Mountain mesa or any landmark that looks familiar. Nothing yet. No houses, no waffle-style farmland, just a turquoise-shop billboard looming overhead. That's right. I'll have to look for a ring when we get to town. I lost one once, the simple inlaid ring my father brought from Zuni when I was eight. It slipped off when I was playing with a friend in the front yard. The bare place on my finger made me sick. My friend and I spent hours on our knees, feeling out the grass blades for cool silver, squinting to see the turquoise triangle set in the ring. We even tried a kitchen magnet to draw the missing treasure. But a ring is just one of the things I've come here to find. I've come for my father's memories of the tribal land he worked for years to win back, and did, at least in dollars, for the Zuni. I've come for my eleven-year-old self, the one who disappeared inside her skin.

Clouds sweep the sun away again, the ground sweeps out from under us, now gold, now deepest gray. No wonder this place is full of transformation tales. The Zuni have traditionally viewed themselves as "daylight" or "cooked" beings. To enter the "daylight," or human community, one must undergo a series of initiations—natural experiences like menstruation and childbirth for women, ceremonial acceptance into the kiva for men. "Raw" beings include newborn babies, prey animals, gods with animal traits, and the dead. At least in story, the line between "cooked" and "raw" seems as easy to overstep as the line between sun and shade. I've read of web-footed people who emerged from the earth at the beginning of time. A boy raised by deer at the edge of a river. Priests who play flutes made by the gods, singing the songs of birds. In ceremonial dances, kachinas intercede between these states of being. Is this the reason, when I stood watching the kachinas fling corn and Twinkies to the crowd, years ago in the sunlit plaza, my dead self seemed to wake? I remember the heartbeat drumming. I remember voices chanting, a sound from deep in the belly. The rhythm moved inside me. It shook the invisible casing from my body. I was as quiet as the moths that swarmed from Nepayatamu's flute, but in that moment, I could feel.

There is another Zuni story about women transforming themselves. One day the Corn Maidens, when they dance for the gods in the Cave of the Rainbow, notice that the gods are eyeing them with lust. They pass their hands over their bodies and disappear, leaving their skin husks behind. Later the Dew God finds them and persuades them to return to the tribal planting grounds for half of each year—a seasonal cycle similar to the one the Greeks associated with Demeter and her daughter Persephone. In the Greek story, after the girl is dragged to the Underworld and raped by Hades, she's allowed to reunite with her mother for half the year, ensuring an abundant harvest. Where do the Corn Maidens go when they're not blessing the corn? Sacred Lake, the Zuni equivalent of the Underworld? I don't think so. I imagine them free to wander this jagged earth at will.

The car trembles under me. We've rounded the mountains. There. Clay-colored tract houses on our right, Corn Mountain on our left. Minute by minute, the sun bakes and retreats from the mesa. So this is what the Zuni call the Middle Place, the navel of the world. Or is it "middle" meaning liminal, a threshold where one state of being meets another? Where cultures collide? Here the Spanish forced their crosses on the Zuni. Here the U.S. government fenced off the sacred waters. Here we drive our well-appointed rental car, strangers with only our memories to connect us to this place. I want to recognize the buildings we pass—a museum, two trading posts, the tribal offices where my father says he used to sit in meetings until three in the morning—but I don't. The girl I once was took all of this in, but I no longer see through her eyes. "I wonder if Pat's Chili Parlor is still in business," my father says.

At last I see something I know: the pueblo's squat adobe houses, their rooftops littered with TV antennas. And the rounded spires of Our Lady of Guadalupe Church. We park in front of the Turquoise Village. Even before I open the car door, the smell of pinyon smoke assails me. Someone is baking piki bread in a clay oven, though most of the *hornos* in town are covered with black plastic today. As I step out of the car, I shut my eyes and inhale the scent I remember. I think I could follow it all the way to the warm, heavy loaves.

"Remind me to go in the store and find a ring," I tell Kent. For now, we walk in silence toward the church. A pickup truck backs down the road; there's no other sign of human activity. A placard tells us the plaza is closed to visitors. "I can't even remember how to get there," I say to my father. He points to a narrow space in the adobe compound. I can't see inside. It's nothing but a crack, like the place where the Zuni believe their web-footed ancestors emerged from the earth. I imagine the plaza empty of people, and probably smaller than I remember. No heartbeat drumming today. No pounding feet. No voices chanting in the sunlit square. A girl stands on the edge of the shade. She is still half child and so pale that she looks only half alive. She's been standing there for twenty years. I walk toward her. She doesn't see me. I start to hear a sound, the rhythm of feet on the soft ground. I circle the girl. The sound is coming from her body. I circle closer. I hear her heart. I hear her breath as delicate as moth wings.

"Look, it's all overgrown," comes my father's voice.

The sound of gravel under my feet. Yes. I am here, alive, now. There's the church, all its plaster peeling, with the cemetery in front. Dad's right; I can hardly make out the headstones in the waist-high weeds. They wave in the light wind, like the bodies of trees. They make a breathing sound. We walk around the churchyard wall, past a bundle of pinyon limbs. The church door is locked.

We walk back to the Turquoise Village. My father heads to the tribal offices to see if anyone can unlock the church. Kent, Anders, and I walk into the trading post. Inside, the air is soft with rock dust. Anders yelps with pleasure when he sees the bins of rough semiprecious stones. I walk past displays of animal fetishes; pottery painted in clean, sweeping lines; and non-Zuni dream catchers. Kent helps Anders choose a souvenir. I plant myself in front of the jewelry counter. A woman lifts out ring after ring, and I try them on. This one's silver slides too easily off my finger. That one sticks. "Here, I have some lotion you can try," the woman says. She dabs it on my fingers, and I rub it under the too tight ring, easing it off. I try another one, a simple row of turquoise, malachite, obsidian, and shell. It fits my finger perfectly. I won't lose this one.

"Do you know when the church is open?" Kent asks the woman as she takes my credit card.

"Oh, Ken should be over there painting today," she says. "I'll call him and see if he can open it."

An hour later, the new ring on my finger, Anders pressing a hand-sized dream catcher to his heart, I walk with my family back to the church. The side door is wide open. I grip Anders's free hand as we enter. Inside, a crooked spiral staircase leads to the balcony. Rows of wooden pews stand empty. I wonder if anyone actually worships in here. Then I see it: color sweeping across the walls on either side of me. Kachina figures tower over framed pictures of Christ bent under the cross. These figures are life-size and so brilliant, they still look wet. Did I take in these lucent blues and yellows twenty years ago, or was my vision as dim as my body was numb?

A huge white canvas is propped in front of the altar. Silvery lines make a picture of Zuni Pueblo as it must have looked ages ago: stacked adobe houses, ladders leading to rooftop doorways, a vertical world. In the center of the picture is this church. Jesus stands suspended in the air above the two blunt spires. I recognize the bent head, the longish hair, the nail prints in the hands and feet. But this Jesus isn't wearing the neatly tucked white robes I've come to expect. He's dressed in the ceremonial robes of a Zuni rain priest.

I'm so taken with the picture that I don't notice the artist at first. He's sitting at the bottom of the canvas. When he hears us, he turns, puts his brush away, and walks toward us with open hands. "Hi, I'm Ken Seowtewa," he says.

"I remember your father," my father says. When he explains what brought him to the pueblo years ago, Ken brightens. Then he bends down to Anders and says, "Did you know, when I was a little boy about your age, I used to play in this church?" He shuffles some papers and finds a photocopied picture of the church as it looked before its reconstruction in the 1960s. A ruin. "This was my fort," he whispers. "See these beams?" He points to the rafters. "My brother and I, we used them for our high-wire act."

For the next hour, we listen. Anders stands with eyes bright and mouth wide open. Ken bends and points to a place on the wall, at the level of the pews. "My grandfather used to say, there were once kachinas painted on that wall, after the church was built in the 1600s. The other elders said so, too. You know the bogeyman? Well, these kachinas were like the bogeyman, to scare the people, to remind them to go to church. Years later, when an archaeologist came and found traces of the old painted kachinas, the elders were proved right."

Ken's father was the first artist to paint new kachinas on the walls of the church. Instead of painting disciplinarian figures, he wanted to show Zuni seasonal traditions and their similarities to Christianity. "See the Sha'La/Ko' bird way over there?" Ken says. We turn to the towering feathered figure. "Six of them come at the winter solstice festival. It's like Lent in the Catholic Church, or Passover, because we have a ritual fast, and the men selected as Sha'La/Ko' take a vow not to hurt anyone physically or emotionally. Now. See the Little Fire God's wand? Like a priest's censer. Our kachinas are like the saints, or guardian angels." At one point, Ken even compares the kiva initiation to a bar mitzvah.

The last time I was here, the walls behind the oil kachinas were bare. Now, the wall on my left is a storm of color. Ken and his father have created a habitat for these half-human, half-animal creatures. "Summer clouds over here, autumn clouds there," Ken says, as if we're as aware of the difference as he is. On the opposite wall, he tells us, he plans to paint a winter blizzard. Ken has brought weather into the church. Another transformation. The thought blows through me, fresh and cold. This church is nothing but a husk of Spanish power. It won't survive the Zuni. Already the kachina paintings overwhelm the stations of the cross with the force of life. Outside, the roots of weeds embrace the buried dead. I imagine a long crack running through the ceiling of the church. I see it splitting open, as kachinas whirl from the walls and into the air.

I can't take my eyes off the summer rain dancers painted on the wall. Both are portrayed by men, though one wears female dress. Their faces masked and veiled, they hold pinyon fronds and something that looks like a white maraca. They are standing still. They seem to hold their breath, ready to erupt into movement. I can almost hear the heartbeat drums. I can almost hear the chant rumbling in the two men's chests and rising into their throats. They seem poised to shake off their feathers and slit-eyed wooden masks. As I watch them, hoping I don't blink in case one of them leaps to life, I remember something I read not long ago. In pueblo culture, there is a moment in the kiva initiation in which the kachina dancers unmask themselves. Hopi writer Emory Sekaquaptewa calls this moment a change not from belief to skepticism, but from unconscious belief to conscious participation in "the make-believe world, the world of ideas and images." A leap from one world to another.

One kachina on the south wall wears no mask. He's an old man, his back bent, his eyes clear. "He's the one figure my father and I modeled from life," Ken says. "He was an elder who testified in the land claims case. Now that he's died, his grandchildren and great-grandchildren will know what he looked like."

"Do you recognize him?" I ask my father.

"I do," he says, smiling, amazed.

As Ken tells us about his current project, the pueblo with rain-priest Jesus suspended in the air, I hardly hear his words. I'm looking at the barefaced man. Though he's only a painting, though the man whose portrait this is has died, there's life in his eyes. His fine, wrinkled skin seems lit from inside. He belongs to the past and the present. He belongs to the living and the dead. He lives in that liminal place where the half-child I was still stands on the edge of the plaza.

Clouds sweep across the church's high square windows. Daylight and darkness at once. Rain starts to beat on the roof of the church. The painted kachinas pound their boots and yellow-painted feet on the ground Ken has brought to life with cactus and wild grass. Jesus floats over the silver-painted church, his wounded hands open. Through the open church door, I can hear voices outside in the street. People are coming out of their houses. The kachinas dance down more rain. It drips through a crack in the ceiling. The web-footed ones crowd out of the earth. The dead elder swims in

Sacred Lake. The Corn Maidens shake off their skins. Out fly the moths. After twenty years, the girl in the plaza is dancing.

passaggio

It hurts to sit still. I want to dance. My hips start to swivel, right to left, against the padded theater seat. My knee starts to bounce. My foot steps in rhythm on the floor. My mother sits next to me, her body locked in place. Onstage, amplified, stomping her boots, Lila Downs sings. A mordant border-crossing song. A love song to Death. A gentle anthem to working women. A polyrhythmic celebration of African immigrants to Mexico. A song, in Mayan dialect, about a woman who smells like an armadillo. The cries of the legendary Llorona, a native Mexican woman abandoned by her Spanish lover; she's said to roam the earth as a ghost, ever since she killed her children in her grief. Behind Downs, a woman squats over her drum, her shoulders loose, the heels of her hands digging into the instrument. There's a saxophone, an electric bass, and a metallic-sounding harp played by a young man who stepped in at the last minute; without looking the least bit interested in what he's doing, he plays to break my heart. Downs strokes the furrows of a pre-Columbian rhythm instrument with a stick. Sometimes she slings an acoustic guitar over her shoulder and strums it. Her mother, once a cantina singer in Oaxaca, Mexico, so bewitched Downs's father, a married American cinematographer, that he fell in love at first sight. "I can see why, if she sang like her daughter does," my mother said after she read this in the program notes.

My student Holly sits on my other side, holding her daughter on her lap, both of them swaying to the music. "Listen to all those voices coming from her!" Holly whispers in my ear. Evan has noticed the same thing when we listen to Lila Downs in the car: "Mom, she's playing with her voice again." It's true: this singer can sound like a child, a man, an old woman, a high-pitched pulsing flute, or a ghost. And every sound she makes is her own. My mother puts it this way: "She's singing without any filters. She's not imitating other singers. It's all authentic." As I listen to Downs pump out her chest voice and then switch to a high straight tone, or confide in a breathy mur-mur and then sing with full vibrato, I understand. Lila Downs is not afraid of her *passaggio*. Those transitions classical singers spend their lives trying to smooth over are this artist's richest ground. Trained in classical singing, Downs knows the rules well enough to break them. *Hear the very limits of my chest voice,* she seems to say. *Hear what hap-pens when I cross the line.* Her album *Border* is all about in-between territory, whether patrolled by armed immigration officers or not. She switches from English to Spanish and back again. She moves from speech to song. She flips from chesty shout to gentle entreaty. She does what I've tried to communicate to my voice students: *Love your "passaggio."*

"So these are the places where my voice is asleep," said my stu-dent Jeni in her first lesson. We'd moved up the scale from her duski-est chest voice to her whistling stratosphere. She'd thrown her hands over her face when I told her she'd hit a high C. She had noted, with a little shock, each place where her voice broke. "It's just kind of . . . *dead* right there."

"Don't be afraid of those notes," I'd said. "They're transitions, that's all. You have a three-octave range. A lot is going to happen be-tween your low voice and your high voice."

Jeni sank into the chair by the piano, trying to comprehend this new information about the dancer's body she knows so well. "I had no idea this went on inside me! For years I've just sung to the radio or my favorite CDs, and I always thought when I hit a note that cracked or didn't sound, that meant I couldn't go any higher."

"That was a signpost," I said. "You were leaving the speech range that's so comfortable for you. That's the place where your voice can start waking up."

A few weeks later, Jeni came to the studio with a question. "Okay, I've been getting aware of my transitions, especially the low-est one between chest voice and head voice. I'm not so scared. Can we spend more time singing higher? I want to see what happens when I get beyond the break."

Thrilled to hear a student take charge of her own learning, I played a five-tone scale on the piano. I asked Jeni to follow it higher and higher, half-step by half-step, into her middle range. She sang on an "Ah," the vowel most likely to expose her transitions. On middle C, her voice flipped from gutsy chest tone to little-girl breathiness. Another transition on G: the voice seemed to retreat and reappear on the next pitch. We moved higher, until Jeni's breathy sound became clear and ringing.

"Your middle will get less breathy as we work on technique," I said. "It takes a balance of air pressure and muscle relaxation, openness and focus. That rich core of your voice is just going to expand. But all of these sounds are part of you. Sometimes you may *want* a breathy voice." As I said this, I realized that to many traditional voice teachers, I would sound like a heretic. Only a sweet, ringing head voice was acceptable to the teacher who molded my mother's voice for years. Chest voice, says an article in a voice teachers' journal, is for those lesser singers who—Heaven forbid—"belt." A *New York Times* review of a young singer's American debut calls her use of chest voice, somewhat condescendingly, an "Eastern European" thing to do. Another review notes that singer Ewa Podleś's husky middle voice "would be anathema to many conventional voice teachers."

As I work with my students on their transitions, I think of how much voice they'd never know they had if I tried to keep them locked in head resonance. I think of Lila Downs. I think of my black-sheep great-grandfather who yodeled on the radio. Before he left his family, when my grandmother was small, he embarrassed her every time he broke free from a written tune to yodel his heart out. He wasn't a trained singer; he discovered what wild sounds his voice could make, and he let them out. He cultivated the breaks in his voice, from deep chest to fluting falsetto. Recently my mother told me, "A cousin who knew him said that when he drifted into Ferron, Utah, he'd sit on the fence and yodel. The neighbors gathered around him, spellbound." As she said this, I thought of what another cousin once said about the men in my mother's family: "They're so sensitive, they hardly speak." This one sang. Somehow, it's easy for me to picture that freckled cowboy swinging one boot from the fence. I can almost hear his voice—no, the many voices my great-grandfather knew he had. If I'm a black-sheep singing teacher, I like to think I owe some of this to him.

"You can keep your voices separate, you can mix them, you can smooth them over," I told Jeni in my studio. "It's all about choice." I searched my brain for ways to illustrate the last two options. First, we played with a Broadway-belt exercise that uses a nasal vowel to mix chest and head voice, naturally changing the ratio as the singer moves up the scale. "Okay, I like this," Jeni said. "This feels like what I do when I sing to the radio." Then, to take the classical smoothing-over approach, I asked Jeni to sing the five-tone scale again, lowering her larynx and lifting her soft palate into an "inner smile," to create more room to ease through the *passaggio*. "Think of the inner smile in yoga," I said. She understood and sang the scale again. "That felt like it was all resonating in my head," she said. I nodded. She sank into the chair again. "This is all so new to me. I think *all* of my voice has been asleep!"

I wish Jeni were here at this moment, listening to Lila Downs. One of the few students I've had with zero formal training, she's shown me the human voice in its raw state. This is the voice Downs has rediscovered and made public. It's a courageous act. Over and over, when I hear her recordings in the car or in my living room, I hear a voice waking up, a song sung for the very first time.

Downs speaks into the microphone. Her voice is husky and confiding. "'La Martiniana' is based on a Zapotec Indian song," she says. "The words go like this: 'Girl, when I am dead, do not weep over my grave. If you cry, I will haunt you. But if you sing for me, I will never die.'" She stands with her feet planted on the stage. She starts to sing. I close my eyes. She sounds breathy and stark all at once. This voice could be male or female. It vibrates in my rib cage. It holds the final note on the word *vivo*, without a trace of vibrato, for what feels like a whole minute. This is no "pretty voice": this is one soul singing to another, raising the dead.

After the concert, my mother excuses herself and finds a rest room. She says she's not feeling well. Holly and I crowd close to Lila Downs, who has just emerged in a bloodred bolero jacket, even more striking in person than she is onstage. Holly whispers to the

grace notes

Hispanic man next to her, "How do I say, 'You sing really well' in Spanish?" He tells her, and she murmurs the words over and over, not wanting to forget. When our turn comes to meet the singer, Holly presses Downs's hand and speaks her new words. I ask Downs to sign a CD for my boys. She's glad they love her music. I could kick myself for not bringing them tonight.

My mother emerges from the rest room. We walk to my car, as Holly and her daughter dance all the way to theirs. I start the engine and pull into the dark street; my mother is quiet. "Did you like that?" I ask, wishing I had the words to talk about what I've just heard.

She says, "Oh, it was amazing. But listening to her and watching her move and hearing those rhythms, I felt a terrible pain in my lower body. It feels like something in me has been asleep for a long, long time, and it doesn't want to wake up."

conversation

I haven't been to dance class in weeks. Tonight I braved the cold and drove downtown. The darkness whipped through my thin sarong as I crossed the street. Now, warm inside the theater rehearsal room, I write a check for my drop-in fee and take off my socks and sweater. I hike the front of my sarong into my bike shorts, for more freedom of movement. Two Chinese women stretch in front of the mirror, their conversation halted only by long, deep breaths. I haven't seen them here before. I sit on the soft, scuffed floor and listen as I lean from knee to knee. I can get no purchase on the women's rapid tonal speech; I'm not even well enough informed to distinguish Mandarin from Cantonese. Still, these voices and their breathing rests make music in the room.

My student Jeni, who teaches this African-based dance class, swings into the room with her bag and her big smile. Our eyes meet; I smile back. She hugs one of the drummers, who hasn't been here in a while, either. I keep stretching. I find, to my surprise, that I can touch my nose to my knee. Yoga must be doing me some good.

The seven drummers start to play. Some use sticks on drums

suspended in wooden frames, to keep the floor from stopping their resonance. Others, straddling freestanding drums, pound with their hands. They move from the worn goatskin surface to the edge of the drum, palm, hand heel, palm. My body remembers this rhythm. It can't wait to move.

We form a circle in the room. Jeni stands in front of the drummers, her feet bouncing slightly on the floor. "Start with the feet," I remember her saying in my first class. "Find the ground before you get the rest of your body moving." I lift my toes and rest them back down on the floor. Jeni starts the warm-up. She doesn't use her voice to give instructions, since she couldn't be heard over the drum thunder. She speaks with her hands. She points to her parallel feet. She holds up one, two, three, or four fingers to signal how many shoulder rolls or hip thrusts to do. She demonstrates a flat-back stretch, then shows the "wrong" way to do it and shakes her head, her dark curls flying.

From where I stand, directly across from Jeni in the circle of swaying bodies, I mirror her. Her left means my right. I've never been good at this. But once we start moving in an isolation pattern I've done before, I stop fretting about directions. Chest out. Chest in. Chest side to side. Jeni points to her heart. This, I know by now, is where all upper-body movement starts. "Don't shimmy with your shoulders," she told us once. "Start with the heart. The shoulders will take care of themselves." I let my chest cave in and then inhale, pressing it out into the room. I hear Jeni's words, though she isn't speaking: *Lead with your heart.* I close my eyes and see my student Holly singing with her hand over her heart, a trick she learned from a New York voice coach. "Feel those vibrations in the chest," he told her in a master class. "Give an 'ah' of pleasure like an infant would. Find the most basic human sound you can make."

I've read that the ancient Greeks believed the human voice originated in the heart. How I wish it did. Tonight, hearing these complex African rhythms that dance with my own pulse, I wonder if the meters I've learned on paper have ever really entered me. Is it possible to feel a Mozart aria the way I feel this throbbing in the floor? I remember the day Thomas marked up the twelve-eight version of

"Rejoice Greatly" in my *Messiah* score and said, "This is the rhythm of an Irish jig." I remember when I realized that the opening of Bach's *St. Matthew Passion* is a dance, and that his Cantata no. 82, which sings good-night to the dying soul, is full of bourrée rhythms, rocking the body to sleep. A folk singer friend has told me, "The way to expose kids to classical music is to turn the volume high enough for them to feel the rhythm in their bodies." I can see why. As the drums call to me from across this cavernous room, I can't help but answer.

Jeni flips her hands back to front and side to side, to show us which way to move. Pelvis to the front, to the right, to the back, to the left. Right, left, right, right. Left, right, left, left. Shoulders, torso, hips. Now they move all at once in an intricate rhythm, without a thought from me. How do I know how to do this? The movement came easily, even my first time in class, once I let the drums talk to my bones. My body answered. This is nothing like ballet, which I tried more than once and renounced forever when I was eighteen. This is not an attempt to coax the body into the shape of a porcelain figurine. This is movement embedded in human DNA. This is the wild, sacred dancing my mother used to do in the basement.

At the end of the warm-up, Jeni leads us around the room. We walk in snaking circles, tipping our heads side to side and front to back as the drums pulse a heartbeat rhythm. Even walking is a dance, as natural as breathing. Now Jeni teaches us a foot pattern that will move us from one end of the room to the other. The drumming changes. *One-TWO-three, one-TWO-three.* By now I know better than to learn the pattern solely by watching Jeni and imitating her movement. When she leads us across the room in a line, my feet follow the drums. *One-TWO-three, one-TWO-three.* Now Jeni adds a sweeping arm motion. She leads us across the floor again. My brain is thinking, "Up, down, forward," my arms are flailing, my feet have lost the beat. Jeni waves the drums to a stop. "Start with the feet," she reminds us. "If the arms throw you off, forget about them." Good. We try again. Just when I think I could dance this rhythm in my sleep, the drums thunder to a halt, everyone applauds, and it's time for a break.

When I come back from the drinking fountain, I notice one of the "real" dancers in the class demonstrating that last step to a young man from England who's here for the first time. "I can't seem to master it," he tells her, distressed. She does the pattern slowly, her long, loose body moving to an inaudible drumbeat. Standing beside her, he locks his eyes on her feet and follows her movement. He stumbles and tries again. Like me, he's afraid to turn off his brain and let his body move. I walk to the dancer's other side and follow her as well. We do the pattern again and again. We add the arms. This time, my shoulders start to move before I tell them to. The Chinese women join us. Jeni watches and claps in time. More dance students wander back into the room and form lines near the wall opposite the mirror. Time to learn an actual African dance.

"I thought we'd do *Yankade* tonight," Jeni says, facing us. "It's from Guinea. This is the dance of lovers, when you sneak out of the house at night and find a whole bunch of people, and when you see a person you have a crush on, you dance up to them or even wrap them in a scarf, pulling them close to you. It's a slow, mellow dance." She starts the foot pattern. We mirror her. "Now imagine you're dancing with the one you love—past, present, future, or whatever. Boy, will *that* make a difference!"

The drums start pounding. ONE-two-ONE-two-three, ONE-two-ONE-two-three. My feet answer, slapping across the floor. I reach the mirror and circle back to the opposite wall. We start the pattern again, this time flinging up our arms and bringing them in to touch our hearts. We circle back again. Now we do the same foot pattern with an outward-reaching motion to the left. "Open up your heart!" comes Jeni's voice from somewhere. Back we come. We add the next pattern to the dance, a walking step with one arm, then the other, reaching up like a flamenco flourish. The left hand comes across the torso, palm lifting the breasts for all the world to see. We circle back. Now an exuberant jump, and back to the beginning we go. Again. And again. The drumming accelerates, calling to us. We line up facing the drummers and start the dance from a new direction. Crushed close to the others, I hear thirty bodies breathing as we dance faster and faster until we reach the drummers. We sink to the floor with our arms outstretched and fall to the floor at their feet. The drumbeats crash like a wave and fall silent. We holler and applaud.

Jeni turns to face the class. "Our culture doesn't encourage us to be this free with our bodies," she says. She swings her hips and rolls her shoulders. "We get comments, or we get scared of ending up in a dangerous situation. But these dances come from a place where you *have* to swing your hips when you've got sixty pounds of water on your head, or the jug won't stay still." She demonstrates, keeping her head in perfect alignment while she saunters across the room. "And you have to be able to *move,* to sling a baby on your back and pick things up off the ground." She plants her feet and sweeps her upper body to the floor.

"It's so graceful!" one of the drummers blurts out.

Jeni bends over in a laugh. "I guess it is." She sounds surprised. She hasn't been thinking about whether she looks graceful. All evening, as she's rocked her hips or flung her arms or jumped into the air, she's done it for joy.

silence

Sheila takes a crystal bell down from the mantel. I half expected a gong. I've come with my mother to learn a Tibetan Buddhist practice called *tonglen.* Sheila, who has done this practice for years, has opened her century-old house to us. She sits in an armchair to my right. My mother sits, feet planted, spine erect, on the sofa to my left. "I have a hard time staying in my body," she has just told Sheila. "I keep leaving. I think this practice will help me stay. I'm just not very good at it yet."

"Over time this practice gives you spiritual confidence," Sheila says. "I've done it for quite a little while, and I'm starting to get glimmers of what the Tibetan teachers say will happen when you do *tonglen* for other people. I'm starting to receive in return. It's something I have trouble putting into words."

Sheila turns the bell in her hand. "What do you think about starting with five minutes of meditation?" she asks in her soft voice. We nod. "Then I'll ring the bell, and give us another five minutes.

I'll ring the bell again, to start *tonglen*. Does twenty minutes sound all right?" We nod again. I get the sense that Sheila doesn't plan to give us more specific instructions. She's not the guru I expected, full of wise, paradoxical sayings. She's made room for us tonight; she's not here to tell us what to do.

"Do you mind if I sit cross-legged here on the sofa?" my mother asks.

"Oh, not at all," Sheila says. "I'll just go turn off a few lights."

I slide off the love seat and sit on the pale-blue carpet. The room softens into semidarkness. I watch my mother close her eyes. I notice we're not sitting side by side. We no longer twin each other the way we did for years, singing duets or perfecting our makeup in front of the bathroom mirror. The connection we forced for so long has ruptured. We don't sing together anymore. The last time, less than a year ago, my voice shut down in my mother's presence. We were singing with a community choir in a university recital hall. I stood up in the audience and walked to the front of the room, to sing a folk song arrangement with my mother. I had to enter the song in my *passaggio* zone, on the "ah" vowel that had once troubled me. I'd thought I was over this. As I sang next to my mother, my tongue fled into my throat. My voice wavered, hardly more than a whisper. The time before that, we'd sung together in the Mormon Assembly Hall. After our dress rehearsal my mother said, "This isn't fun for me at all. It feels like work." When we performed, I felt I was singing next to a wall. I'd erected it myself, to prove to my mother—what? That I didn't need to ride her reputation anymore? That I wasn't the hollow-voiced daughter she'd felt ashamed of, or so I imagined? In a recent therapy session, my mother admitted her jealousy. I admitted my fear of her disapproval. She told me she thought I'd finally found my voice.

Sheila sits down again and rings the crystal bell. I close my eyes. I think of "centering down" the Quaker way. I think of moving my awareness throughout my body, as Buddhists do. These methods are not so different from each other. I'm taking the radical step of stepping nowhere. Being, not doing. Here, in this high-ceilinged, soft-curtained room, I realize how rarely I sit still. Even now, after nearly a year of Quaker meetings, I spend my days flying from phone to fridge, from computer to piano, so many songs to sing and words to write and friends to call, so many afternoon snacks to make for my boys, never enough time, never enough time. No wonder I look forward to Sunday mornings. I came tonight to do what I do in meeting, but with greater attention. To practice stillness.

Nyingje the calico cat romps into my lap. Her name is a Tibetan word meaning "liberation through compassion." I open my eyes long enough to see her nuzzle my arm and leap away to sit next to my mother. Now I'm the jealous one. Does the cat prefer her because she's more still, more aware than I am? Will she prove the better Buddhist? How I'd love to be liberated through compassion. How I'd love to shed the psychic armor that has kept my mother and me in competition, fearing each other, unable to touch. I think of Buddhist nun Pema Chödrön's advice to be compassionate to oneself, to see one's weakness with precision and gentleness at the same time. So I get jealous when a cat prefers my mother to me. So we no longer feel comfortable singing together. I am still a wounded child.

Sheila rings the bell again. Five minutes already. I wiggle my toes. I've been sick and haven't done yoga for two weeks. Will I be able to sit cross-legged for thirty minutes? Why am I even trying? I could sit comfortably on the sofa, the way I sit in Quaker meeting. Sheila stays in her armchair; she doesn't even try to look the Buddhist part. Am I showing off for my mother, matching her straight-backed centeredness? Am I trying to prove myself again, to show what I can endure? I admit I am. I tell myself, *Precision, gentleness.* I focus on my breathing. I realize I'm cold. The furnace in this house must be so old that it blows lukewarm. I listen. It sounds like a giant breathing through the floor. It lurches off. The refrigerator hums. A click and it's silent, too. The clock above the fireplace ticks the seconds, gently. A car drives by outside. There is no silence in this world. Layers and layers of sound. A joint creaks in my neck.

And Sheila rings the bell. I wait to hear if she'll say anything, to guide us through this practice we're only beginning to learn. No. I glance up. She sits in her chair, her hands relaxed, her mouth slightly open. She told us earlier that she's doing *tonglen* for her sister, who is seriously ill with diabetes but too in love with life to spend it fretting over her blindness or bad heart. "*Tonglen* is good for the dying, and the people who care for them," she said. "I've worked in hospice care for fourteen years. I've seen what a comfort it can be." My mother wants to do *tonglen* for her mother, and, she told Sheila, "for my two daughters." I guess that means me. I'm not sure I want someone breathing on my behalf. I had no suffering person in mind when I came here tonight. I came to practice sitting still. To breathe, selfishly, for me. No one in my life is dying. There's Kent, of course, fighting the depression that tugs harder at him during the holidays. I've told him he may want to learn this practice, too. "I don't want to get sucked down in negative thoughts," he told me this morning. "Medication can only do so much." Well. He may never get around to trying this. I'll do *tonglen* for him.

Pema Chödrön recommends thinking of a family member when you begin *tonglen* practice. She suggests taking in that person's suffering, or the suffering you feel when you're around him or her, each time you breathe in. Then, on the out-breath, release whatever painful sensation you've allowed yourself to feel. As I sit here, cold on the carpet, I picture my husband. I see the places I associate with suffering and peace, images I brought home from Norway last summer. Chödrön likes to think of a hot, claustrophobic space when she breathes in during *tonglen* practice; I think of a Norwegian fjord, walled by cliffs and clouds. The place where I once felt what Kent feels, after one of his depressive episodes, worsened by jet lag, made me think our marriage would never heal. I leaned against the window of a cliff-climbing train, too pained to form words as I hung on the edge of the abyss. I return there as I breathe in. The intake of air hurts my throat. Clouds tug at my feet. The cliffs close in. On my out-breath, I see the clear, fresh light I watched for hours from the deck of our ship as we sailed over the Arctic Circle. Gold on the water, the ocean crazed with light. Wind sang in my throat. I wanted to drink that light. I didn't know if I could bear to be so full of it, so open, so willing to love.

I breathe in. Fjord, stone tunnel, train, bodies crushed together in artificial light. I breathe out. Sunlight on the water.

I breathe in. Despair. I breathe out. Hope.

I breathe in. Others feel this despair. I breathe out. May others feel hope, too.

I breathe in. Will Kent be willing to try this? I breathe out. Sunlight on the water.

I breathe in. Sheila says her sister doesn't know she's doing this for her. I breathe out. Does a prayer in a monastery make a difference in the world?

I breathe in. A girl tells Pema Chödrön she feels like a caged bird. I breathe out. The girl exhales for all the caged birds in the world.

I breathe in. Is my mother really doing this for me? I breathe out. I don't know if I want that gift.

I breathe in. What would happen if my mother and I did *tonglen* for each other? I breathe out. Could we do this at exactly the same time? Are we doing it, now?

I breathe in. My mother breathes out. I breathe out. My mother breathes in.

I breathe in. I see my mother and my teenage self, side by side in front of the mirror, gripping our mascara for dear life. I don't want to share this mirror. I think I'll have to share it for the rest of my life. I say nothing. I swipe the black liquid over my lashes, my knuckles white on the brush. I breathe out. My mother and I turn from the mirror and look at each other.

I breathe in. We're singing a duet. Brahms. The piano rocks in three-four time. We stand side by side, on opposite sides of a wall the audience can't see. I breathe out. We turn lightly on our heels, face-to-face, breath-to-breath. We sing to each other.

I breathe in. Do I *want* to sing to my mother? The question aches in my chest. I breathe out. Good thing this practice keeps me from staying too long in pain.

I breathe in. There is pain I'm not ready to feel. I breathe out.

I breathe in. This time, not images but words. I breathe out. I don't want to hear them. I breathe in. Here they come. I breathe out.

I breathe in. *Hurt Abandonment Fear*

I breathe out. These are the big abstract words no poet should use.

I breathe in. *Shame Abandonment Guilt*

I breathe out.

I breathe in. I am the story under the story, the wound beneath the anger.

I breathe out. And so I write.

I breathe in. My mother shares my story. She feels what I feel. I breathe out.

I breathe in. I feel what my mother feels. She wants to prove herself to me, too. She is abandoned and afraid.

I breathe out.

I breathe in. Kent sits next to me on the train in the fjord. I press my forehead to the window. Fog closes us in.

I breathe out. Sunlight on the water.

I breathe in. My mother breathes across the room from me.

I breathe out. My breath meets her breath. I breathe in. I breathe out. I breathe in. I breathe out.

Sheila rings the bell. I blink and surface into the dim, yellow-walled room. I stretch out my legs. Liberation Through Compassion lifts her head. She's been sitting with my mother this whole time. I realize I don't mind. We sit in silence for a minute. "So how did each of you become interested in *tonglen*?" Sheila asks.

My mother describes the reading she's done. I describe the places where Quakerism and Buddhism intersect. My mother names the therapist who suggested she try *tonglen*. I tell Sheila about my student Jeni, who recently had the idea to think of *tonglen* when she sings. "This had never occurred to me," I say, "but it makes sense. When you sing, you let your voice out as you exhale. It's a gift to the people who listen. And maybe to the singer in return."

"We're both singers," my mother tells Sheila. "I don't know if it would be appropriate to use *tonglen* in singing, but it sounds wonderful."

"Of course it's appropriate!" Sheila says. "That would be a greater gift than I could imagine."

We get up and move into the entry hall. An image rises in my head: my mother and I stand together in front of a piano; we inhale in that silence before the song breaks through; we breathe out, opening to each other. I almost laugh out loud. It could happen.

Sheila holds my coat open for me. I want to thank her for giving my mother one more key to her freedom from "appropriateness." For not guiding us through those twenty minutes. For giving me the silence I needed to feel, for a moment, what my mother feels. For reminding me why I sing. As we open the door to the snow that flies over the wide brick porch, I hug Sheila and say, "Thank you." To say more would be too much, and not enough.

six

diary

February 8. Rain thrums on the windows. I sit at my dining room table with two Quaker women, singing. Caroline stirs her tea. Hymnals and scattered papers surround us. We've been listing songs to introduce in our new singing time before meeting. We've talked about the hymns we grew up with, the spirituals we love, the people who haven't attended Quaker meeting in years because they long for music. We're sight-reading an arrangement of "Brother James' Air" Kate found in Connecticut. Across the table my folk-singer friend, also named Kate, hums her melody. I'm the only one who's sung this song before, but with no piano and no audience, it feels new in my mouth. Three women's voices pulse in rhythm with the rain.

We sing in unison. We break into harmony. *The Lord's my shepherd, I'll not want. . . .*

"Most unprogrammed Quakers have not been comfortable with organized group singing," the Friends hymnal, a twentieth-century innovation, tells us. "Friends waiting on the Lord have felt that planning might interfere with the direction God would take them in worship. Some friends have also been afraid of the emotional power that music can create." Sitting here at the table, with a hymnal open to these words, we sing anyway. We let the music do its work. We let it carry us. *Goodness and mercy all my days will surely follow me. . . .* The song takes me back to Connecticut, where I sang it with a group of Mormon women, our voices rocking together like a net on the water. Where Catharine once lay in the silence of her room.

In September 1835, Catharine recorded in her diary a visit from an unnamed friend. She wrote that after "we opened our hearts freely, we settled into silence." No one preached. No one read from the Bible. In the decade before her death, Catharine's religious experience became less and less formal. The meditative silence of the "little meetings" held in her sickroom twice a week seems to have spilled into her ordinary visits. I wonder what the "emotional power" of music might have done to her, had she and her visitors united in singing, as the three of us do today.

Catharine joined the Quakers in 1818, at a time when freethinking, socially active members in the United States were breaking away from the more evangelical, Bible-based Orthodox Friends meetings. An entry from her diary about this time notes that "many have departed from the true and living faith which they profess." I admit I read these words with dismay, since I feel at home in the more liberal, Hicksite tradition of Quakerism, which has no hierarchy, no strict reliance on the Bible, and no programmed meetings. In the 1800s, Hicksites claimed to be closer to the original spirit of Quakerism, which involved sitting around someone's dining room table with no minister and no agenda but to "wait on the Lord." They included such social visionaries as Lucretia Mott and Susan B. Anthony, though even their Hicksite communities, in the nineteenth-century period of Quaker quietism, thought them too outspoken.

According to an 1828 census among New York–affiliated Friends, Catharine and her cousin Deborah counted themselves as Orthodox. My friend Gordon, a Quaker genealogist, has pointed out that in this context the word means more "Orthodox Christian" than "Orthodox Quaker." No wonder Catharine's diary, especially in its early years, often sounds more pious-Protestant than clear-eyed Quaker to me. Lately I've been reading Catharine's words with a deeper understanding of our differences—and more awareness that as she grew older, she let go of her "one right way" idea of religion.

At the end of 1825, Catharine wrote of her growing silence on doctrinal points. She mentioned the ongoing controversy among Friends and concluded, "All are brothers and sisters, equally entitled to the Divine favor." As her health deteriorated, she relied less on the religion of "empty, formal professors" and asked herself, in 1831, "Where is to be our meeting? Is it not in the secret of our own hearts?"

The longer I meet with Friends, the more I believe there's no one right way to approach the divine. During spontaneous vocal ministry, some people quote the Gospels freely. Others do not. Some can't believe in a fatherly God in the sky but believe with their whole souls in the power of human love. Some never stand to speak. Others feel moved to do so several times a month. Some, including me on a few occasions, break into song or read a poem. The group is open enough to take in all these differences, and, recently, to allow for our group singing, with all its power to rouse or bring tears.

The discussion started in the Ladies' Literary Club kitchen, after I'd attended meeting for several months. Over lasagna and crusty bread, the word *music* kept surfacing in our postsilence talk. Caroline pulled me into the conversation. "We've tried several times to introduce singing," she told me, "but it's never worked. Now that you're here, that makes one more person who can help bring this about." It took some time for the subject to come up in the monthly meeting for business, but when it did, Friends came to consensus, and I found myself on the newly formed Music Committee. I didn't feel the familiar "Oh, no, they're asking me to be chorister again" dread that had followed me through my years in the Mormon

Church. I grabbed Kate the folk singer by the arm after meeting and said, "Do you think we could try 'Praise to Creation Unfinished'?"

So on this rainy afternoon, the three of us sit at my dining room table, singing. Soon we drift into the music room, where I sit at the piano and play "Simple Gifts," "For the Beauty of the Earth," and "How Can I Keep from Singing." We sing together. I do my best to transpose songs we think might be uncomfortably high. The rain splashes on the ivy and milk-jug bird feeders outside the window. We sing in unison. We sing in harmony. We have no audience, no one to impress. Before my Music Committee friends arrived at my house, I imagined us singing our "Brother James' Air" trio for our community, standing in front of them at the piano. Now I don't care if this ever happens. Our singing is not about performance. Weaving our song together across the dining room table was an unexpected gift, as joyful as singing with my boys as we give the dog a bath. We'll let the music happens as it happens, no "one right way."

Weeks go by. Ann, the Quaker woman who once asked me why I didn't sing with other people, has died of cancer after a trek to Tasmania with her family. Ann's family, colleagues, neighbors, and friends join with us for a Quaker memorial service. We sit in a circle at the Ladies' Literary Club. We look into the empty space in the center of our circle, no casket, no sickly sweet bouquets, just our voices speaking of the woman who knew she wanted to be a doctor at the age of eight and became an expert on children's immune disorders, the Friend who cut to the quick in a conversation, and would always look us in the eye. I wish I could tell her I'm singing with other people now. I wish I could thank her for making me think beyond my performer's role.

If Ann were still here, I believe she would join us on Sunday mornings around the piano in the literary ladies' parlor. Though she came from a Quaker family in Pennsylvania and was sometimes surprised at western Friends' novel ways of doing things, I believe she would find joy in the music her ancestors may have feared. I believe she would pick up her stapled sheet music and plunge right into singing "All God's Critters Got a Place in the Choir." I wish she were with us as we sing "Simple Gifts" with all the pep we possess, as we stumble through a round, or tap our feet to "Ev'ry Time I Feel the Spirit" with guitar and Autoharp. I wish she could see her friends wipe their eyes after singing Sibelius's "Finlandia" set to words of peace. Maybe she knows all this. Maybe she's glad we couldn't keep from singing.

nine openings

"I don't know how I know," I said to Kent, as maple blossoms blew toward the house and stuck to the kitchen screens, carrying in the Connecticut spring I loved. Kent looked up from his plate. Evan dumped his on the floor. For once, I didn't rush to clean up the mess. What I had to say held me to my chair. "I can't even describe it in words," I went on. "I don't want to leave the East, we feel so at home here, you know how we wanted to look for a new house, but even if you *do* keep your job, I know it's time." I sat back and breathed.

Kent didn't stare at me. He just nodded. "I'm too numb to feel anything right now," he said. "I'll have to trust you."

Earlier in the day, I'd gone for a walk, alone, while the boys played at a friend's house. On the news the night before, I'd heard about a weird weather pattern passing over the East Coast. The jet stream had reversed. Sometimes this just happened, the weather reporter had explained. How informative. As I walked down toward the Point and turned left toward Sea Beach, I felt the inexplicable change. Blossoms blew into my eyes. A wind chime hammered on a wide front porch. And then, as I neared the hurricane wall, I saw the water. The waves seemed to pull away from the shore, over and over, instead of lapping against it as they should. Their rhythm had changed. The sky had turned white. So had the hazy length of Long Island Sound. I gathered oyster shells washed up between the rocks, their chitin broken through to jeweled inner lining. I stared at the pale water splashing the wrong way.

My family's life had turned the wrong way, too. We'd been living in Connecticut for almost two years. I was finishing my graduate course work, while Kent commuted to work in Manhattan. One day he phoned to say his boss had called him in and suggested he look for another job. I laughed; I thought this was one of his jokes. "I'm not kidding," he said. Silence. "Well, what do we do now?" I said. Silence. My knees shook.

That night I taught a writing class for foreign students in Greenwich. I stood in front of the blackboard, hardly able to speak. I listed vocabulary about houses, to help with the week's assignment, "Describe your dream home." My students, from Japan and France and Germany and Hungary, blinked at me. I couldn't tell them I might lose the roof over my head. I swallowed and turned the chalk in my hand, praying I could stay on my feet for the next forty minutes. I spent the next day with Kate; we waited by the phone until Kent called from work to say his boss had rethought her decision and given him a six-week probation period. "I guess I haven't fit into the New York caste system," he said. "I didn't realize my opinions weren't welcome. I'll try to do exactly what they want."

These words sounded again in my head as I watched the waves from the hurricane wall. Every day for the past month, Kent had left the house before dawn and the office after dark, trying to write the briefs his superiors wanted, trying to speak in their voices instead of his own, trying to fight his downward-spiraling moods. I worried about him coming home tonight on the subway and the train and the bus, trying to focus on his *New York Times,* the reading he loved to do on his hour-and-a-half commute each way. I hoped he'd still be folding that paper into quarters a year from now. They might let him stay. And even if they didn't, he could find another job. It would be hard, maybe impossible for a while; there were few opportunities in his specialized field, and he still had to take the required ethics exam to be admitted to the Connecticut Bar. We had no savings left. My teaching paid too little to live on. But maybe, eventually, Kent would find something closer to home.

Home. Tears pushed into my eyes. I couldn't stop them. I sat on the hurricane wall and sobbed. The wind was blowing east to west, entering my body, speaking to me without words. I knew it was time to leave. The week before, I'd seen an ad for a job in Kent's field in Salt Lake City. He'd dismissed it, but the thought followed me everywhere. I kept his bar journal open on the kitchen table. "Criminal Appeals." Every time Kent walked by that ad, he shook his head. "It's a long shot," he'd say. "Just entertain the thought," I'd tell him, the same words he'd said to me when Reno's weekly paper offered me a staff position.

I knew what this meant. We'd move back to our families, back to my grandparents and the duty-bound life they represented, back to the silence between my mother and me, back to religiously divided Salt Lake City. No, thank you. Besides, what would I do without this saltwater refuge and the woods where I went walking with the boys? I felt rooted here. I cried all the way home, and when I phoned Kate, she cried, too. Her own circumstances were pushing her back to Salt Lake; we had tried not to think about being separated in the first bloom of our friendship. Now this strange wind was blowing, and who knew what might happen. I told Kate about the apple blossoms and the white waves and the oyster shells in my hand. "Is it wrong to want to live somewhere because it's beautiful?" she said. But as we talked we understood, with something between grief and tentative excitement, that the wind was after us both.

Now, as Kent sat across from me at the table, taking in my words, he was quiet for a long time. "I'm trying so hard at work," he said, "but I feel this inertia in every page I write. It will never be exactly what they want."

"Oh, I think it will," I said. I believed this. "But do *you* want it to be exactly what they want?"

He sat thinking. I sensed he was giving up more than his professional voice; he was giving up his will. I told him about my walk to Sea Beach earlier in the day. "I couldn't stop crying," I said. "I felt I was saying good-bye to this place."

"Do you know what it would cost to move across the country again?" Kent said, his eyes fixed on Evan's spilled peas. "You and your epiphanies."

"It's either that or be unemployed again, and this time we don't have a cushion," I said. I tried to sound cheerful. "My last epiphany turned out pretty well, bringing us here, don't you think? And not just because of graduate school. Look at the adventures we've had.

Look at the friends we've made." I told him about my conversation with Kate. I told him that maybe we could take some of our friendships with us.

Kent wasn't looking at me. He said, almost to himself, "And so God picks us up and takes us away."

"I don't know if it's God. It might be the wind that made me cry. Or that ad in the bar journal."

"God moves in mysterious ways."

A month later, Kent lost his job. We gave ourselves three weeks to pack up and move. I walked through our condo without speaking, filling boxes it seemed we'd just emptied. I watched Kent, who still went to work every day until his time was up, his eyes showing through to an open wound. I drove Anders to preschool and Evan to the baby-sitter's. I drove to school. I sat with Kate in her wooded backyard, sharing a carton of yogurt and staring speechless into the trees. Kent and I went to dinner with friends. Over and over, I watched my husband tell the truth about his job. "I've cost you so much," I said to him one night on the way home. "Do you ever wish you'd married a nice contented girl who didn't ask you to move three thousand miles so she could find her voice?"

"I came here for me, too," he said. It was true; he'd been raised on the Yankees and loved New York like nobody I knew.

We drove the rest of the way home in silence. The boys slept in their car seats. We hauled them into the house, stepping over boxes and stacks of books. In another week I'd board a plane with Anders and Evan and fly to Utah. Kent and his brother, who had offered without complaint to help us move again, would drive west with the rented truck. We would stay with my parents until we found a house. As I lay in bed that night, I toyed with that word in my mind. *House. Home.* I thought of the dream houses my students had imagined. One, a Frenchwoman, had reentered her childhood home in the country, down to the tasseled draperies. A German au pair had pictured a house with slides instead of stairs from floor to floor. A Japanese woman had described a house with more windows than walls, rooms with air blowing through them day and night. I turned toward my own bedroom window. Our renegade Tree of Heaven was shooting its way to the roof again; soon its leaves would stroke our screens all night. The window was open a crack; I could hear something shuffling in the grass, a skunk or opossum, most likely. I remembered the thunderstorms that had kept me pinned to the window, amazed at the force of the rain. The rasping of crows in the branches, the night before a snowstorm. The roar of a snowplow, lifting the night's accumulation into thick, bright piles. I loved this place the way I'd loved my own backyard as a child. I was returning to the city that held that portion of my memory. Maybe the child in me still loved it.

The next day, I went to my last lesson with Thomas. He straddled the piano bench. I sat on the sofa and cried. "You're autonomous," he said. "You could stay here. But if you choose not to, you'll be all right. Your geographical location won't matter, because of the person you are and what you carry." Wind blew in through the open window. I wanted to believe him.

Thomas's words stayed with me as I wandered Manhattan for the last time with Kate, as we chewed our bagels on the subway, rain pounding the streets overhead. *Your geographical location won't matter.* The words stayed with me as I boarded the plane with my sons, not wanting to let go of Kent's hand. They stayed with me as my mother drove us to her house from the Salt Lake airport, the desert light stinging my eyes. I knew that I was home, and that it did matter. My mother and I would learn to speak freely with each other, or we would not. Kent would, I hoped, find a more supportive workplace and heal from his hurt, surrounded by the family that loved him. I would have to face my doubts about the Mormon Church. And I would find out if, carrying whatever it was Thomas believed I did, I could make a life here. He was right about one thing: I'd had a choice. God or a wordless wind had not pushed me home. I'd listened, that was all.

Four years later, I sit in the Ladies' Literary Club, remembering that wind. Quaker meeting has ended; a small group of us has returned to the square after our bagels and fruit. Jerry Knutson, a guest speaker from Pendle Hill, has come to talk about discernment. It's both a skill and a gift, he believes. It requires patience, creativity, and sometimes a clearness committee to help a person through a difficult life change. I scan Jerry's photocopied outline, which includes a list of questions to help distinguish a Leading from personal whim. Some stop my eyes: "Does it feel right to my Higher, Authentic self?" "How does this decision feel in my body?" "Is this uniting or dividing people?" Jerry adds another question, which early Quakers asked themselves: "If I don't act on this Leading, will I feel diminished?" He quotes Peggy Senger Parsons, who describes the experience of deep intuition this way: "Divine messages have a feel and a smell to me." He cautions that some tests, like "Is it persistent?" are more reliable than, say, "Is it my passion?"

I close my eyes. Jerry is trying to fit something beyond language into words. It's not an easy job. When I write, I attempt the same thing. How do I describe what happened to me that day in Chicago, when the sound of Copland's "Saturday Night Waltz" pulled me under, or what I felt the day I knew I needed to find Catharine's diary, or what happened as I sat on the hurricane wall at Sea Beach? I can mention the waves sucked from under the rocks again and again. I can ask questions: A change in the weather? A Leading? I can try to answer: Yes, the strange wind persisted. Yes, it entered me with a scent I recognized, and it rocked my bones. I can look at the results in time and space: Three weeks after our arrival in Salt Lake, Kent was offered the job I'd seen in his bar journal. My sons were able to know their great-grandparents before they died. My mother and I have gone into therapy together. Kent and I have embarked on an interfaith marriage, joining hands across our differences. With Kate beside me at the piano, I've continued to find music to sing and people who want to hear it. And had I not moved back home, I might never have begun, with many fearful pauses, to find words for my own history.

"In the end we need to remember that there is only one commandment, to become love," Jerry is saying. "It may not matter if we move to Key West or to Fairbanks." My eyes fly open. Does it matter? I might not be here if I hadn't listened to the wrong-turned wind. But now I grasp it: commandment or not, I moved for love. Because Kent was too beaten down to apply for that job on his own. Because

Kate was going my way. Because I knew, with a sense beyond words, that it was time to cross the divides in my family and in the city I'd avoided for seven years. I did what Quakers have advised each other for centuries, though I didn't know this saying at the time: "Proceed as Way opens." It opened, and I have not been diminished.

chant

Mount Benedict Monastery, Ogden, Utah.

I fumbled through the prayer book, in search of Marian Antiphon no. 3. Sister Vergine leaned toward me and found the page. We were singing a contemporary version of the *Salve Regina*, set by a woman composer, with English words. A hymn to Mary, "gentle, loving" intercessor.

I could hear Kate's clear alto in the choir stall behind me. We hadn't expected to be part of the vespers service. We thought we were here for a weekend retreat, outsiders, observers. Before the service, Sister Mary, the prioress, strode into our sitting room with two prayer books. "Now," she said, "I want to explain a little of our service, so you'll have a sense of it before you sing with us."

She assigned me to Sister Vergine, who pressed my hand in both of hers when I slid into the stall and introduced myself. I liked singing with her. Despite her years, her voice rang true. She knew the old Gregorian melodies by heart. I followed partly by listening to her, partly by reading the shape-note pitches marked above the text of each chant. One of the chants I knew by memory, after years of visiting the Trappist monastery in Huntsville. For the first time in my life, I was singing it myself.

After vespers, we joined the sisters for a buffet-style dinner. Hot dogs, hamburgers, and leftover vegetables lined the enormous kitchen island. At our table, decorated with mid-November chrysanthemums from the garden, we met Bonnie, a resident oblate from an old Utah Mormon family. She said she was a widow. She wore a silver cross. Though she hadn't taken formal vows, she lived by Benedictine principles, volunteered in the community, prayed with the sisters, and made sure visitors like us had enough towels. She told us that when the sisters had moved into this new building two years before, the Mormon neighbors had pitched in with casseroles and cookies. "Shame on us if we don't take the time to learn about each other," she said. "We're not so different. We all want to believe in God, don't we?"

I liked Bonnie. I liked the anomalous place she occupied here in the convent, and in the local, mostly Mormon community. She had found room for her unique spiritual voice. I'd been back in Utah for more than a year, and I was losing mine. I sang hymns whose words I didn't mean. Often, when I taught lessons to the teenage girls assigned to me, I spoke words I didn't believe. I wondered if I'd ever find my place in this community, if I could speak my truth and still be friends with my Mormon neighbors.

The bell outside chimed six o'clock. At six-thirty, we found ourselves back in the chapel, this time for vigils. The huge north-and-east windows had gone dark: I couldn't see the mountains, or the road my family used to take to our cabin before the new highway was built. This was familiar territory to me, but, at the same time, strange.

Facing us across the chapel, Sister Luke, the cantor, struck a bronze bowl three times with a mallet. The sound was a more resonant version of the mallet tapping in the Mormon temple, at the moment before symbolic passage into Heaven.

We sang a chant called "Homesickness in Exile." The title said all I felt, only I was in exile in my own hometown. I felt almost as foreign as I had when my family had moved back here from Germany. Over and over, Sister Luke intoned a short declaration, and we responded with the words, *God is lasting love!* I wanted to believe this. I wanted to believe the words Hildegard von Bingen wrote for her own Benedictine sisters in the twelfth century, addressing wisdom, or divine presence, in the form of a woman:

> Sophia!
> You of the circling wings,
> circling encompassing
> energy of God
> you quicken the world in your clasp.

At least for now, in this monastery, removed from my family history and my church assignment, I felt circled and encompassed. The Mount Benedict building, completed in 1999, is the brainchild of two architects, male and female. "You'll notice we have a lot of curved walls," Sister Luke told us when she took us on a tour. As Sister Mary put it later, "We're women. We told the architects we didn't want to feel boxed in." A circle. A clasp.

After vigils, Kate and I found our way down the rounded hallway to the guest quarters. We changed and settled into the sitting room with books and a bunch of red grapes. But before we could adjust our reading glasses, Sister Mary strode in again. "I want to show you something in the library," she said to me.

I followed her down the hall, barefoot in my pajamas. She wore a denim dress. This was a casual convent, I'd discovered: some sisters even come to prayers in jeans. How would it feel, I wondered, to worship without having to put on a dress? To worship in the same building where you ate and slept? I liked imagining a life with no dividing line between the spiritual and the everyday.

Sister Mary opened the glass door to the library and turned on the light. "Now. You are interested in Hildegard von Bingen. Let me show you everything we have." Before long we were sitting on the floor, looking at Hildegard's brilliantly colored mandalas, several novels based on her life, and postcards from her native Germany. We talked about Vatican II, and Sister Mary told me how Benedictine nuns shed their habits in the 1960s. She showed me an old prayer book with chants written in shape notes, Latin and English texts side by side. I'd noticed that Hildegard's compositions are not sung in contemporary Benedictine prayer services, though early-music specialists who record them have found a popular niche in the music industry. I wondered if her music was too difficult. Was she simply viewed as an eccentric patron saint? An anomaly?

The next morning, after the sisters had gone to mass at the local parish (they had no priest to officiate communion, after all), Kate and I sat reading in the library. She read Anne Lamotte, sometimes speaking a passage aloud to me, laughing until her glasses fogged over. I pulled all the Hildegard books from their shelf. Kate opened one. "Listen to this," she said. "Hildegard saw every human being as a stone, a piece of the city of worshippers." Kate knew I'd been working on a long poem about stones.

"I wonder if she thought of herself as the rock that didn't fit," I said. "Did you know she didn't start writing poetry and music until she was in her forties? Maybe she felt she couldn't until then. Maybe she thought she wouldn't meet the church's approval." We read silently for a while. Then I found a quote from the mystic and poet Mechtild of Magdeburg, who lived a century after Hildegard. I read it aloud: "I am forced to write these words regarding which I would gladly have kept silent, because I fear greatly the power of vainglory. But I have learned to fear more the judgment of God should I, God's small creature, keep silent."

After this, I sat thinking. How many creative women, in the history of this world, had kept silent? I thought of those who had the means, the opportunity, and the courage not to. I thought of Ruth Crawford Seeger, whose dissonant choruses for women's voices reminded me of Hildegard's sweeping polyphony. I shut my eyes. In the car on the way to the monastery, I'd played my Crawford recording for Kate. We'd listened to her third chant for women's voices, which she originally titled "To a Kind God." The voices sang twelve pitches at once. Crawford once called this a "complex veil of sound." Out of the tangle rose a single voice, singing phonemes that didn't belong to any known language, a voice so low it could have been male or female. The voice rose to an almost animal cry: was it the same voice, or a soprano, taking over the melodic line? We couldn't tell.

Musicologist Charles Seeger, who would become Crawford's husband, suggested to her this image when thinking about Chant no. 3: a group of worshipers in a monastery, singing the syllable OM "at the pitch most suited to the individual voice regardless of any harmonic relation with the other pitches of other voices sounding at the same time." Maybe he had in mind what German composer Peter Michael Hamel did several decades later, when he wrote that every person has his or her "own note, that inner sound which is most intimately bound up with our very body and soul."

grace notes

Singing with the sisters at Mount Benedict, we matched each other's pitches. We sang according to the rules. But what would happen if each of us found an individual pitch and held it? Chaos? A new kind of beauty, of community?

Later that Sunday morning, I sat on my bed in the monastery. The clock told me it was time for sacrament meeting, and I wasn't there. It was my first time missing church, except for the occasional cold, since our return to Utah. Kent had taken the boys on his own today, an act of faith for him. I thought of the members of our Mormon congregation, some who struggled with doubts like me, many who tried their best to live good lives, just as the sisters at Mount Benedict did. My absence didn't make me love them any less. How would my life intersect with theirs, and with my husband's? What would we teach our boys about God? Who knew what my Sundays would be like from now on.

I sat on the bed reading Emily Dickinson. Like Hildegard von Bingen, like Mechtild of Magdeburg, like Ruth Crawford, she found her "own note." I read a poem Dickinson wrote around 1862, when she was my age. She wrote about choosing her spiritual life, rather than following the religious culture she'd been baptized into as a child, "a half unconscious Queen."

Kate sat down beside me on the bed. I didn't have to tell her what troubled me. She picked up my book and read the first line of the poem aloud: *I'm ceded—I've stopped being Theirs—*

passaggio

A heavy summer storm has scoured the Salt Lake Valley. I stand on a hill at the mouth of Emigration Canyon, where prophet Brigham Young, seriously ill after leading his persecuted people across the plains, told his wagon train to stop. The city's tree-lined grid looks strangely still. I can see the valley floor, broken free from the clouds, clear to the open-pit copper mine that used to be a mountain. I can see the gleaming edge of the Great Salt Lake. I step over thick mud and climb a gravel road into a reconstructed pioneer village, silent except for cottonwood trees roaring in the wind. The lights are on in the basement of the little white church. Good.

Inside the basement room, eighteen people sit on benches, facing each other in a square the way we Quakers do. I can't see the woman who invited me, but these people seem used to unexpected visitors. "Pick up a loan book," says a woman with complicated earrings. "You can sit in the middle if you want," says a man who looks like he's come straight from the office. "It sounds even better that way." I sit down on one of the benches and look around.

Teenagers to senior citizens, Mormon to Episcopalian to not particularly religious, these people meet every other week. Most of them are not trained musicians. They come not to perform but to sing together, and to preserve a little-known tradition. The "loan book" I thumb through as the group prepares to sing is a hymnal, compiled by B. F. White and called *Sacred Harp,* an old term for the human voice. The singers learn their parts by shape note, an archaic system of pitch notation developed in Philadelphia around 1800. These shape notes look something like the ones, based on medieval notation, that the sisters at Mount Benedict read in their hymnals. The *Sacred Harp* songs are written on a conventional staff, but instead of the usual black or white circles, each note has a different shape, triangle for *fa,* oval for *sol,* rectangle for *la,* and diamond for *mi.* These shapes are repeated up the scale, because four syllables were once thought easier to learn than seven.

As I look through the *Sacred Harp* songbook, I find hymn titles I know from the contemporary Mormon hymnal, and some I've never seen in any church. They range from revival songs like "Heavenly Armor" and "Weeping Sinners" to oddities like "The Dying Californian" and "Ode on Science." According to the singer who invited me, many of these songs have survived in Utah's remote polygamist communities.

The singers take turns choosing and leading songs. Tonight they begin with a 1707 tune by Isaac Watts, but before they sing the words, they sing the shape names of each note. I'm not prepared for the sound.

SOL. The voices land on an open fifth and stay there. I feel the voices in my rib cage, the way Peter Tyack describes hearing whale song. Then the hymn begins, full volume, no vibrato, as the singers pound the floor with their feet, four-four time, a heartbeat in the ground. The shape-note names do not sound like a foreign language, as I expected they would. They are pure sound. Then, without a pause, the singers plunge into the hymn's English words: *Salvation, O the joyful sound! / 'Tis pleasure to our ears.* If this is what salvation sounds like, let us pray.

Though the tenors carry the melody in shape-note singing, the altos in front of me threaten to overpower them. I notice one alto who belts out her part, full chest voice, no apologies. After a half hour she pops in a throat lozenge and keeps on singing. From what I've read, she's part of a little-known tradition herself. In *The Chicago Sacred Harp Singers' Free Beginners' Guide,* Lisa Grayson (a self-described "amateur with no pretense, musical knowledge, skill, or even taste") warns the newcomer alto to "leave your Marlene Dietrich impersonation at home." She continues, "Sacred Harp altos do not go for thrilling, sultry, rounded low tones. It's more like grinding, wailing, ear-shattering low tones." Mary Rose O'Reilly, a Sacred Harp alto in her spare time, lists the six elements of her type: "rage, darkness, motherhood, earth, malice, and sex."

Here I am with my loan book in my lap, trying to sing along with the sopranos. My heart doesn't want to. These high notes feel wrong to my body, the way those coloratura runs always felt wrong, no matter how easily they came to me. Deep down, I want to be an alto. This has been coming on for several years. It started in Thomas's studio, when he asked me to sing in the core of my voice, the lower register I didn't know I had. One day I came to him and said, "I think my dominant *passaggio* is moving. It used to be exactly an octave above middle C. Now when I first warm up, I get all cracky on D."

"Don't worry about it," he said. "Your voice is changing and growing, that's all."

After I moved with my family back to Salt Lake, my *passaggio* moved up again, this time to D-sharp. Was I committing the classical singer's sin of carrying chest resonance, or "heavy mechanism," too high? I wasn't sure. "Listen to this," I said to Larry Gee, my teacher at the time. I opened my binder to Schubert's "Gretchen at the Spinning Wheel." "I'm going to sing this phrase two different ways. Tell me what you think."

The first time, I shifted into light head voice on the higher notes. The second time, I let my core voice continue up the scale. The sound resonated in my whole body. "I don't know what you just did," Larry said, "but you're not fighting yourself anymore." He was right: as a singer moves up the scale, the *vocalis* muscles, active during chest-voice singing, fight the muscles that lengthen the vocal ligaments, which vibrate in head voice. Balancing these muscles' action takes patience and attention to the body's own wisdom. I don't know, any more than Larry did, how I made peace between my warring muscles. I suspect that until my late twenties, I didn't know how it felt to resonate in the chest. I had never, in the most literal sense, sung from the heart—until Thomas pointed out the resonance in my low speaking voice.

"Do you know what?" I mused that day in Larry's studio. "I've been stuck all my life in a French poodle voice. I'm really a chow."

A year later, my voice came apart. I had sensed, studying with Larry, that it was time for me to take more responsibility for my vocal learning. Knowing I had not yet fully absorbed the soul-level voice practice Thomas has asked of me, I stopped taking lessons and started experimenting with my voice in the bathroom, in the car, or at the piano. In Larry's studio, the muscles in my throat had made a temporary truce; now the battle raged again. I was singing Bach every day, preparing for my recording with Kate. When I reached my upper-middle register, my voice would not bend to the notes. It creaked and groaned. At first I cried. I threw my music on the floor. I felt like a twelve-year-old choirboy who's just been told he'll never be a soprano again. I kept practicing; I kept cracking. I let my voice fall apart. In the privacy of my music room, it became less of an embarrassment and more of a curiosity. Then, one day when I warmed up in the shower, something felt different. I was singing an "ah," my nemesis vowel, the one Larry had said scared my tongue back into my throat. I sang an octave arpeggio, feeling my body expand as I met the high note. I felt no shift from chest to head. The labels fell away. I was simply singing in my own voice, no words at all, an "ah" of joy. The change was complete, at least for the moment. My most troublesome aria from the *St. Matthew Passion,* full of soft, sustained E's, was no longer troublesome. My dominant *passaggio* had moved to a high F or F-sharp, depending on which vowel I sang on that pitch. This was a "normal" *secondo passaggio* for a high soprano, or so I'd believed. But why didn't I feel like one anymore? And why did I no longer dread the "ah" vowel? All I knew was that my lower-middle notes were home to me; my low voice no longer cut out, exhausted, after a long practice session; the "ah" no longer scared my tongue. For the first time, I sang the "ah" in *mama,* the *Aaaah* of physical pleasure. Now, after a year of singing with new ease and heart, I understand: until I accepted the natural cracks and breaks, my voice refused to heal. The broken places will always be part of me. But they no longer stop my sound, and I wonder what they'll ask of me in another year, or ten, or twenty. I now tell my students, "Don't be alarmed if your voice keeps changing your whole life."

A changing voice can mean changing repertoire, or at least changing keys. "The soprano edition isn't right for me," I said to Kate when we started to work on Schumann's *Dichterliebe* song cycle. "It makes me fight myself again. Remember when I sang this first song at your house, when you were getting over pneumonia, and it was in the lower key? Even then it felt just right." We ordered the mezzo-soprano edition. I felt slightly wicked, and brave.

Yes, deep down, I want to be an alto. I envy a singer friend who sticks to chest resonance because that's home to her; her sound is as wild as it is caressing. But even deeper down, I want to be a voice. The old labels feel suffocating now. If I want to wail on a high B-flat, though it's not as easy for me as it used to be, I can shake the windows. If I want to plunge to a low D at the end of "Death and the Maiden," just watch me. And if I want to shut my mouth and listen, as I do tonight in the little white church, I will.

Before the Sacred Harp singers begin the tune named "Schenectady," I get up my courage and accept their invitation to "sit in the middle." I take off my shoes and sit cross-legged on the floor, right in the center of the square. I close my eyes. I hear familiar words

(From all that dwell below the skies / Let the Creator's praise arise)
sung in a strange new melody. Thirty-six feet pound their rhythm
into the floor. It jolts my spine. Soon the melody breaks into a fugue.
This is better than playing the stops on a big organ. I'm inside a
human singing organism. The voices move through me until I can't
tell them apart. One voice. Praise be.

conversation

"I could smash the piano," wrote Robert
Schumann in 1839. "It constricts my thinking." The composer never
did give up writing for the piano, but during this period he found a
way to approach the unspeakable on paper. In his *Romanze* in F-sharp
major, opus 28 no. 2, he heard a melody buried in the right hand's
broken chords. He added a third stave between the usual treble and
bass lines, and wrote the melody there. The same thing happens in his
Humoreske, opus 20, where the hidden melody sings long, slow half
notes. He called it the *innere Stimme,* or "inner voice."

Last week I heard another form of the "inner voice" as I practiced Schumann's *Dichterliebe* with Kate. In one song, the poet walks
through a summer garden, mourning his lost love. The words of the
song, by Heinrich Heine, touch the language of romanticism with
irony: *The flowers whisper and speak, but I wander in silence.* At the
end of the song, a melody rises out of the piano's descending arpeggios. The almost inaudible speech of flowers. As her fingers discovered this secret voice, Kate jumped a little and leaned closer to the
keyboard, not wanting to miss a single note. I closed my eyes and listened to the sound, beyond words, that has hummed between us
ever since we heard this music together in a cramped theater in New
Canaan, Connecticut. I held my breath. I sat down next to Kate on
the piano bench, as mute as the poet in the song. Her fingers barely
touched the keys. She released the melody into silence.

Carsten Schmidt, a teacher in graduate school, taught me to listen for hidden voices in music. "Sometimes you can think of a song's
piano accompaniment as the singer's subconscious," he said. "Or
what the singer feels but can't utter aloud." One of the *Dichterliebe*

songs is an apt example: the singer insists that *"Ich grolle nicht"* ("I don't complain"), while the piano rages with pounding chords. Throughout the song cycle, the poet comments on his or her inability to speak or to remember the all-important word heard in a dream. Traditional romantic sounds—the song of a nightingale, the voices of flowers—speak instead. In the last song of the cycle, the poet vows to bury these "old wicked songs" in a coffin, so heavy it must be lifted onto a barge by twelve giants. The whole cycle, as I hear it, is a mordant and sometimes mocking farewell to romanticism. The old songs of lilies and roses will be heaved into the Rhine. And so, the poet adds in a sudden adagio, will the old tormenting love. In this final song, the piano shifts from minor to major, from heavy chords to delicate arpeggios, and repeats the hidden melody spoken by flowers in the earlier song. The music ends with a sweetly ornamented coda, a breath from a bygone time. "I do this whole ending by myself!" Kate noticed, staring at the voiceless page, the first time we practiced this song.

"Well, I certainly can't do it," I teased her. "My words are buried in the Rhine."

Thank Heaven for songs without words. Often I feel like the poet in Schumann's song cycle, unable to speak or write exactly what I mean. Music, with its direct line to human emotion, can be the "inner voice" that sings through one's life. I once heard a piano coach give this advice to a student playing Chopin: "Imagine this phrase is the secret you tell your best friend." The music Kate and I learn together hums through our daily spoken conversations, our own inner voices. And one day, as I read music with another friend, the notes said what neither of us could.

Renée and I have known each other since high school. She's the one who tried to get me to dance and to shed my layers of makeup. Our first year in college, we took ballet and Asian religions together. We shared an apartment as interns in Washington, D.C. Then I got married, and she moved away to another university. We lived in different states until last year. And though we'd written each other faithfully and visited often in the past decade, when we found ourselves in the same neighborhood, we discovered how little we knew of each other. "You haven't been around to see how *I* see now," she told me, shortly after her move back to Salt Lake.

Last month Renée asked me to come play Bach with her. She'd bought a cello and started taking lessons over the summer. I'd watched her talk about her instrument, a secret smile under her smile, the way people talk about a new love. I'd never thought of her as a musician. I had been wrong.

I sat down at Renée's digital keyboard while she put the toddler she was baby-sitting down for a nap. A book of Bach pieces arranged for cello and piano accompaniment sat open in front of me. I started to sight-read, my fingers adjusting to the keys. "His mom said to let him cry," Renée whispered as she shut the bedroom door behind her. Sure enough, the child started to wail. Renée opened her cello case.

"It's beautiful," I said.

"Well, it's student quality. I fantasize about getting a really good instrument someday." She settled the cello between her knees. She shut her eyes as she tuned it. "When I first got this, I'd sit and play an open C for fifteen minutes," she said, "like this." She drew her bow across the cello's bridge without stopping the string farther up. "I love the cello because it vibrates in the chest. Its range reaches from the lower male voice to the higher female voice. It's a very human in-strument." She leaned against the cello's neck and continued to play an open C. The deep, raw sound made me forget everything I'd ever learned about vibrations and overtones and partials. This was horse-hair and resin and wood. It might as well have been alive.

"One, two, three," I counted, and we began a minuet. I wished I could see Renée, who sat behind me. I heard not only the notes she played, still learning where to press her fingers, but the sound of the bow itself, as its tiny horsehair hooks clung to each string and let go. I could hear Renée's concentrated breaths. She wanted to play this music more than she wanted anything in the world, and I hadn't seen it coming. In this moment, we understood each other.

"Let's try it more slowly this time," I said. Renée breathed against the fingerboard, relieved. This time, as her bow hesitated over the strings, I heard what sounded, almost, like human speech. I stopped playing. "You're right, it *is* a human instrument," I said. "It doesn't just sing, it *talks*."

Renée grinned. She'd known this all along. We started the minuet again. In my peripheral vision I could see Renée's courage rising. She leaned into the cello, giving more weight to each attack. We ended the piece and breathed. "Hey, I don't hear any crying in the bedroom," I said. "We've put him to sleep."

"That could be good or bad," Renée said.

We moved on to a gavotte, gave up on "Jesu, Joy of Man's Desiring," and attempted "Sheep May Safely Graze." "Let's go *really* slow on this one," Renée said. She began her delicate melody. She stopped. "Even slower." I counted, we breathed, we started over. The melody sang between us, in spite of the notes we both missed. It said what we didn't have words to express. It sang of impossible distance, and of grace. It sang our old wicked words, years of "I am this and you are that," to sleep.

silence

In the forest full of wandering people, the mossy earth soundless under our feet, I look up into the leafy sky. I am dreaming, and half know it, but I keep walking. Soon a granite building blocks my view. It looms taller and taller in front of me, a giant block with tinted windows. I'm swept in through an automatic door.

In my waking life, I sit under a tree. A late-May heat wave has driven me to this shady bench on the playground at my sons' school, where I wait for the bell to ring so I can take them out for the ice cream I promised. I'm reading a book I haven't picked up since I was twenty-two: Elaine Pagels's *Gnostic Gospels*. The last time I read it, waiting to get pregnant in our Nevada apartment, I thought, "*I* want to be a Gnostic!" but didn't see this as an option. I felt as powerless as I did in last night's dream, whisked into a granite building that had appeared out of nowhere. Now, I see my own experience in the book. Some passages I underline ferociously; some I whisper until they're fixed in my memory. I'm preparing for my Quaker clearness committee, the circle of gentle questioning that precedes admittance into full Friendship. I feel I'm not just joining a sect dreamed up by seventeenth-century visionary George Fox; I'm entering what Pagels calls "a river driven underground" for centuries, from the time the early Catholic Church stamped out the Gnostic tradition until its sense of spiritual intimacy resurfaced in such medieval mystics as Meister Eckhart, and later, in the Society of Friends.

I don't know where this current will take me. I trust it. In the letter I submitted to our community, requesting consideration for membership, I said I'd felt like a Quaker all my life—I just hadn't known enough to use that name. Much of what I responded to in Pagels's book, years ago, might as well have described Quakerism: a nonhierarchical community marked "not [by] its relationship to the clergy, but [by] the level of understanding of its members, and the quality of their relationship with one another"; a tradition that honors both the male and the female aspects of the sacred and believes in the equality of the sexes; a place where "gnostics, like many artists, search for interior self-knowledge as the key to understanding universal truths." As I read these words ten years later, sitting here in the heat, I feel them as wind blowing through me—a memory of the gale that rattled the windows as I paced our apartment in Nevada, longing to escape the life I'd been initiated into without thinking. Words buried in the desert, waiting for rediscovery.

The building is cold inside. People in suits come and go. Someone takes me by the elbow and leads me into a small room, where I see a soft white rabbit and pick it up. I stroke its fur, overcome with tenderness. Someone takes the rabbit away. I cry like a child.

I hold Kent's hand. Five Quakers sit around us in Phil and Elaine's living room, a loose human circle that changes whenever someone gets up for sparkling lemonade or a second helping of potato chips. Turbo the cat jumps up on the coffee table and tries to take a bite from my sandwich. I stroke him between the ears with my free hand.

Diana, a former Mormon herself, leans toward us and speaks softly. She knows what Kent and I have in common in our marriage, and what we don't. She says to me, "Our biggest concern is for you and for your family." She says to Kent, "This isn't easy, and your support of your wife is a great testament to you." There are tears in her eyes. I squeeze Kent's fingers. I remember the day he squeezed mine, as he left me to enter the temple dressing room. I remember the women who touched my hair with oil. I think of a Gnostic text in which a female divinity speaks: *I am the real Voice. I cry out in everyone, and they know that a seed dwells within.*

I am led into a wide corridor. A woman in white greets me at the door to a room with glass walls. The woman is thin and efficient, like my grandmother who is dead. "Now you enter the Chamber of Silence," she tells me, and opens the glass door. Inside, a white tile floor. Fluorescent lights. Nausea floods me. "Can I get out of this story?" I ask.

Rand, Diana's husband, asks how I feel about the Christian tradition, and how it informs my spiritual seeking. I think of my dream, and my first experience of Christianity as an institution that kept me from speaking my truth. Then I ask Kent to pull *The Gnostic Gospels* out of my bag. Everyone lets out a little gasp of recognition. "No wonder you're here!" says Elaine.

Phil asks Kent and me if we feel the journey will get harder, or easier, from here. We take time to think. "It was so hard to get out of the church I felt was suffocating me, I feel great freedom and ease now," I say. "But I'm sure this will challenge me in new ways, and make me look at things in myself and in the world that are hard to face."

Kent is thinking about our sons. "It will be painful," he says, "if they decide to go through the temple before they go on missions or get married, and their mom can't be there." I have to agree. I tell the group all I can do is hope my boys will grow up knowing they have a choice in how their life stories will play out.

Phil tells Kent, "Over time, as people in traditional faiths get older, they often start to see through the rituals and obligations to the mythology behind them. You may find yourself mellowing. The journey may be easier than you think."

"We've been on this journey for eleven—maybe even twelve or thirteen years," Kent says. He tells the group how he used to obsess about obeying every rule, how he did his duty without joy. I tell them what a following he's gained as an unconventional Sunday-school teacher. "I think I've already let go of a lot," Kent says.

The woman in white will not let me out of the story. I realize I'll have to escape on my own. She's following me down the corridor. My feet drag on the floor. I reach for the "down" button on the elevator, but nothing happens.

Gordon asks what has surprised or even disturbed me about Quakerism as I've experienced it in our community so far. "The diversity of belief," I tell him. "It was kind of disorienting at first, to hear some people talk about Jesus in traditional terms, and other people say they couldn't believe in God but they did believe in human love. But this has been liberating, too, to start to ask if God is outside or inside, and to learn to say, 'I don't know.'" As I speak, I hear in my head the music of Jesus' words in the Gospel of Thomas, a riddle I memorized, reading Pagels's book on the edge of the playground as I waited for the boys: *The Kingdom is inside of you, and it is outside of you. . . . When you make the two one, and when you make the inside like the outside and the outside like the inside, and the above like the below, and when you make the male and the female one and the same . . . then you will enter.* Last night I spoke these words to Kent on the Story Couch. "You're right, Jesus said some cool things that aren't in the Bible," he said.

I'm a stranger in this building. No one comes to help me get out. The woman in white comes closer. At last the elevator opens. I turn and see her coming toward me, with my grandmother's lively eyes. I realize I want to take her with me, but too late: the door has closed, and I go down.

Jesus said: *If you bring forth what is within you, what you bring forth will save you. If you do not bring forth what is within you, what you do not bring forth will destroy you.*

The shadows lengthen outside Phil and Elaine's living room window. We've been discussing the Quaker testimonies of simplicity, peace, integrity, community, and equality. Phil asks, "Do you think you can imagine these ideas, not as discrete notions floating around, but in relationship to each other? How would that kind of perspective change you as a person?"

"I don't even know yet," I tell him. "I feel there's so much I've found in myself, and so much that's been given to me, that I've longed for all my life, and I'm just holding it all in my hands, not sure what to do with it." I cup my hands in front of me. Inside them, music, touch, the sound of my voice when I tell the truth. What would have happened had I stayed in my Chamber of Silence? Would my locked-up voice have destroyed me? I look into my hands. They're ready for anything.

"It's all right not to know what you'll do, or what will happen next," Elaine says. "Do you feel you can live in a community where things don't always go smoothly, where people disagree and discuss, and changes happen? Can you feel at home being in the process?" I tell her it sounds like a great relief to me.

Elaine Pagels on the Gnostics: "They celebrated every form of creative invention as evidence that a person has become spiritually alive. On this theory, the structure of authority can never be fixed into an institutional framework: it must remain spontaneous, charismatic, and open."

Outside at last. I'm no longer panting from fear. The mossy ground meets my feet. Overhead, the leafy sky I love. I find my way through the forest as others pass me, traveling their own paths. Soon I come to an enormous tree with a door carved in the side. I enter. Inside, darkness and daylight at once. A circular stairway leads into the crowns of the trees, and deep into their roots. I take a step onto the stairway. I don't know where it will lead.

"Remember, it's all right to just plant flowers," Diana is saying.

"Remember to find joy, amid the world's suffering that Quakers pay so much attention to," Elaine tells me. "You don't have to take on every problem. Save your energy. You need to be there for your family, and for yourself. If God created this world we try so hard to keep alive, we can't forget to walk in the woods and enjoy its beauty."

Gordon notes that two hours have gone by. Elaine says this feels like a good stopping place. After some discussion about what to do next (after all, no one's in charge here), Diana asks if anyone has a problem with my becoming a full member. Gordon says, "Why don't we say, 'Are we in unity?'" We are—even Kent. Diana looks at him and says, gently joking, not knowing the truth she strikes, "So you feel good enough about this not to go home and torture your wife, or get passive aggressive?" He laughs and tells her those days are over.

Our decision will "season" for a month before final acceptance is given, again by consensus, in business meeting. The only ritual in store for me is a group hug in the next meeting for worship. For now, we stand in a circle and hold hands. No one lights candles; no one pronounces a blessing or drapes me in ceremonial robes; I don't have to speak from a script. We stand in silence. I welcome it, not a glass room but a circle of human breathing. Here, if I learn to listen, I may hear the woman's voice that speaks in the Gnostic poem "Thunder, Perfect Mind": *I am the silence that is incomprehensible. . . . I am the utterance of my name.*

acknowledgments

Without others' gifts, the journey that is this book would never have begun. Deepest thanks to Thomas Young, the teacher who knew better than to give me scales to sing; to JoAnn Ottley and Lawrence Gee for their keen ears and expertise; to Carsten Schmidt for his wisdom about words and music; and to Sharla Hales, for the organ lessons that saved me from despair. My gratitude to poets Suzanne Gardinier, Joan Larkin and Thomas Lux, for teaching me to trust my ear and to ask the most difficult questions.

I would like to thank the following for opening new experiences of sound and authentic living to me: Alan and Jacqueline Fogel, for including me in their rhythms and rituals; Ken Seowtewa, for sharing his work on the kachina murals at Our Lady of Guadalupe Church; the Sisters at Mount Benedict Monastery, for opening their doors to me; Jerry Knutson, for his talk on discernment; the Salt Lake Sacred Harp Singers, for inviting me to "sit in the center"; Jennifer Wallace and Rich Smith, for a collaboration that taught me to voice my hidden longings; Lila Downs, for the singing that has taught me to love my *passaggio*; Jeni Indresano, for her joyful dance instruction and her courage in learning to sing; Sheila Despain, for the gift of *tonglen* meditation; Teri Holleran, for her gentle guidance in my moments of anxiety; my voice students, for all they teach me; my poetry students at Westchester County Correctional Facility and Promontory Correctional Facility, for sharing the words I've included in this book, though I haven't been able to locate the gifted poets who wrote them. Special thanks to the Salt Lake Monthly Meeting of the Society of Friends, for silence and room to speak the truth, for help in researching Quaker history, for the opportunity to sing together, and for true Friendship.

I gratefully acknowledge the Connecticut State Library for access to the diaries of Catharine Seely and Deborah Roberts; their words have helped me find vocabulary for my own journey. My appreciation to the many readers who have nurtured this book with their insight, honesty, and encouragement: Guy Lebeda, Teresa Jordan, Phyllis Barber, Ken Handley, George Handley, Kay Fahey, Renée Buchanan, Jennifer Wallace, Anita Hallman, and Marilee Swirczek. To my editor Dawn Marano, who read my manuscript like a musical score and helped unlock the stories I'd been afraid to tell, thanks beyond words. Loving gratitude to Kate, my first reader, brave friend, and companion in song. Finally, I am indebted to my family for their help in the writing of this book: the Harts, for their kindness to me despite our differences, and for hours and hours of child care; my maternal grandmother, who died shortly before this book went to press, for the stories she shared in long phone conversations and for the musical voice I can't forget; my newfound cousin Heather, for the wild Emery County tales that have informed my book but really belong in her own; my sister Kiri and the aunts, uncle, and cousins who have given me the gift of honest discussion about our family; Anders and Evan for their understanding of my hours at the computer and for their unique voices, always in my mind as I work; Kent, for his unfaltering love, for his good-humored support of this project, and for his courage in letting our story onto the page; and most of all my parents, for their support in the sometimes painful process of writing this book, for the healing they have allowed it to bring to our family, and for the love of music and language that they passed on to me.

Quakers often discuss the tension between integrity and peacemaking; in the words of a wise Friend, "Unless you speak the truth there never will be love." I hope this book speaks both.

credits

Grateful acknowledgment is made to the following for permission to reprint previously published or unpublished material:

Excerpt from "Night Crow," poem by Theodore Roethke, from *The Complete Poems of Theodore Roethke*. By permission of Doubleday, a division of Random House, Inc., Anchor Books Edition, 1975.

Excerpt from "The Breath of All Life Blesses You," self-published song by Rabbi Shefa Gold. By permission of the author.

Excerpts from three of Emily Dickinson's letters to Susan Dickinson, c.a. mid-1860s, September 1871. By permission of The Houghton Library, Harvard University (MS Am 1118.5 B56; MS Am 1118.5 B163b; MS Am 1118.5 B184). © The President and Fellows of Harvard College.

Excerpt from "God Is the Tall Man," unpublished poem by Jennifer Wallace. By permission of the author.

James Ricks

about the author

Heidi Hart is a poet, singer, and voice teacher who lives in Salt Lake City with her husband and two sons.